JOURNEY TO FREEDOM

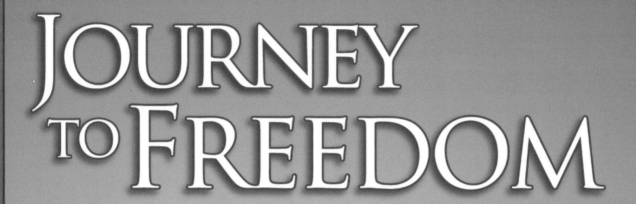

A 40-Day

Encounter

with the

Heart of God

Daily Devotional Guide

VISION run

Published by Vision Run
305 Portsmouth Rd.
Knoxville, TN 37909

www.visionrun.com

Scripture Quotations

Cover design by Mike Taylor, Taylor Graphix
          mtaylor2521@knology.net
          Knoxville, Tennessee

Printed in the United States

Dedication

We offer this book to the One whose journey to the cross made possible our journey to freedom. Our desire and prayer is that the Lord Jesus Christ would be immeasurably honored and pleased by this work and that His Spirit of truth and liberty would so fill these pages that many hearts would be released to receive the grace of our Abba Father.

Table of Contents

Introduction

Welcome to this 40-day *Journey to Freedom!*

You are poised to launch out on a six-week spiritual journey that could change the course of your life – bringing refreshment, hope and freedom in ways you might not have thought possible.

Maybe this is the first time you've taken concentrated time to work on your spiritual life. As humans we have a physical body and we also have a personality (soul). But we are more than that. We are spiritual beings as well, designed to relate to God. Chances are you've gone through intensive times of improving your physical health – through nutrition, exercise, etc. Chances are, too, that there have been times when you have tried to bulk up your brain power, maybe by taking a class or pursuing a course of study.

Many times, however, we neglect our spirit. When that happens, we end up spiritually out of shape, flabby and lethargic. Since our spirit is at the core of our being, if we are spiritually "out of it," our personalities and bodies are negatively affected as well.

This journey will unfold in manageable pieces, with daily bite-sized chunks. Most of the 40 days will open with a *Warming Up* story that will invite your heart into that day's topic. We'll follow that with the meat of the day's teaching, called *Walking On.* At the end of each day we'll conclude by *Winding Down* (a summary) and *Wrapping Up* (some practical application of that day's journey). You'll find it all very easy to follow.

Who knows? By the end of the 40 days, by God's grace, you could be in much better spiritual shape than when you began. As you may know, you can make significant progress during six weeks of intense physical training, but it takes consistent work to keep those gains. In the same way, *Journey to Freedom* is a 40-day program of intensive training for your spirit. You'll learn to exercise your spirit in new ways while beginning to develop routines and habits that you can use your whole life. These next 40 days are not an end, but a very powerful beginning!

We sincerely hope that you are embarking on this journey as part of a church-wide *40 Days of Freedom* campaign. It's not that you can't take this journey on your own, but it's just a whole lot more fun… and fruitful… to be part of a group! Eugene Peterson puts it this way in *The Message* (**Hebrews 10:22-25**):

So let's do it – full of belief, confident that we're presentable inside and out. Let's keep a firm grip on the promises that keep us going. He always keeps his word. Let's see how inventive we can be in encouraging love and helping out, not avoiding worshiping together as some do but spurring each other on, especially as we see the big Day approaching.

So whether your church is part of the whole *40 Days of Freedom* campaign or not, find a trusted friend to serve as a traveling partner with you on this journey. Let this "freedom partner" speak loving truth into your life and vice versa. Be honest with one another and pray for each other. A covenant for you and your freedom partner to sign is provided on page 12.

Destination: Freedom

Important Preparation for the Journey

What is freedom anyway?

In America, freedom and liberty are certainly among our most cherished possessions. We consider freedom of speech, freedom of the press, freedom of religion, freedom of assembly, and so forth to be basic human rights. Many men and women have died preserving these freedoms, and yet we often take them for granted because we can't even imagine life without them. When Patrick Henry proclaimed, "I know not what course others may take, but as for me, give me liberty or give me death!" he captured the American spirit. Now think about it for a moment. What do you think would come to mind if you asked the "average American" what he or she thinks freedom is?

Freedom means different things to different people.

- A teenager might define it as car keys and no curfew or as a credit card and a mall!

- To a college student it means the last paper turned in and the last final over.

- To a homeowner it's the tearing up of the paid off mortgage loan.

- To a young adult it might mean blue skies, open roads and a Harley-Davidson.

- To a young mother it means an empty house and a bathtub!

- To a married couple, freedom might be "when the last child moves out and the last dog dies!"

When pushed for a definition of "freedom" many would probably say something like, "Freedom is being able to do whatever you want!" Sounds heavenly, doesn't it?

But what if everyone just did what he or she wanted? Seems pretty selfish if you ask us, and we're sure it would actually make planet earth more like hell than heaven!

Believe it or not, the Bible talks a lot about freedom. Now we can hear the skeptics out there laughing. After all, there are many churches that are so filled with rules and regulations that people attending them experience everything *but* freedom. True enough.

But despite that unfortunate reality, God is really into freedom. *2 Corinthians 3:17 (NIV)* says:

Now the Lord is the Spirit, and where the Spirit of the Lord is, there is freedom.

From that verse we can conclude that a) God wants us to be free and b) somehow his presence (the presence of the Holy Spirit) ushers in freedom.

Jesus was speaking to a group of Jewish leaders who claimed to have put their faith in him.

His words will form an important framework for our 40-day Journey to Freedom:

You are truly my disciples if you keep obeying my teachings.

And you will know the truth, and the truth will set you free.

John 8:31-32 (NLT)

Anyone familiar with the academic world will recognize at least part of those words of Jesus. "Know the truth and the truth will set you free" is a phrase engraved over the hallowed halls of many universities. The source of the quote, unfortunately, is all but forgotten. Jesus wasn't talking about the mere accumulation of information or knowledge as being the source of freedom. He was talking about life lived in accordance with the word of God.

At the time Jesus spoke, the reaction from the crowd was less than enthusiastic. They reacted the same way a lot of us in America would respond. "What do you mean free? We're already free. We're not exactly slaves here! Here in America, this IS the land of the free and the home of the brave… isn't it?"

But Jesus wasn't talking about political or even economic freedom. He was talking about freedom of the spirit and soul, freedom of the heart. His reply cascades over the centuries and presents itself to each of us, face-to-face:

Truly, truly, I say to you, everyone who commits sin is a slave to sin. If therefore the Son shall make you free, you shall be free indeed.

John 8:34,36 (NASB)

There it is… from the mouth of the Son of God himself. You can be the citizen of the freest nation on earth and be very much a slave… in your heart. A slave to sin.

What did Jesus say would set us free? Knowing the truth. If it is the truth that sets us free, then what is it that keeps us enslaved to sin? Believing lies.

"Lies?" You might say, "I haven't believed any lies!"

How do you know? What we mean is, how do you really know? You see… that's the problem with being deceived. You don't realize it… until you are trapped.

For example, have you ever been caught up in any of the following beliefs or behaviors?

- Being driven to work harder and harder in order to live better and better.

- Trying to please certain people more and more because you thought you needed their approval to be happy.

- Being driven to do everything with perfection.

- Thinking that God loves the world but that he isn't particularly thrilled with you.

- Trying to break a habit or get out of an addiction and finding it was stronger than you, no matter how many times you tried to convince yourself you could stop.

- Feeling locked inside a cage of fear, anxiety or depression.

- Boiling over with anger or being aware of simmering anger just below the surface.

- Trying hard to get over what someone did to you – even years ago – but finding yourself haunted by that incident day and night.

- Longing to know, really know, that you are forgiven and accepted by God but running face first into religious teaching that only fills you with guilt and shame.

- Telling everyone around you that things are "Just fine!" when you know deep down you just lied.

- Seeing your relationship with God exist at a "comfortable" intellectual level but missing out on anything that looks like real relationship.

- Reading the Bible or going to church and battling distracting thoughts… or worse.

- Hearing a tape playing over and over in your head with messages like, "I can't do anything right", "I'm stupid", "Nobody loves me", "I'm dirty and evil".

If you have ever found yourself in any of these predicaments, welcome to the human race, the human race that has been trapped in deception… the human race that Jesus Christ came to save and set free! Nearly 700 years prior to Jesus' earthly ministry, the prophet Isaiah predicted the mission of Messiah Jesus:

> *The Spirit of the Lord GOD is upon me, because the LORD has anointed me to bring good news to the afflicted; He has sent me to bind up the brokenhearted, to proclaim liberty to captives, and freedom to prisoners; to proclaim the favorable year of the LORD, and the day of vengeance of our God; to comfort all who mourn, to grant those who mourn in Zion, giving them a garland instead of ashes, the oil of gladness instead of mourning, the mantle of praise instead of a spirit of fainting. So they will be called oaks of righteousness, the planting of the LORD, that He may be glorified.*
>
> *Isaiah 61:1-3 (NASB)*

Based on the Scriptures we've looked at in this Introduction, here's our working definition of "freedom":

Freedom is being released by Jesus from the control of all damaging and destructive influences so that you can enthusiastically worship God and be all he wants you to be and do all he wants you to do.

The following chart will give you a picture of what freedom looks like compared to bondage. Let it encourage you as you see what God can do in your life.

Bondage vs. Freedom

Living independently from God	Dependence upon God
Leaning on your own understanding	Guidance from God
Misplaced priorities	Worship of God
Conformity to the world	Transformation by the Spirit
Deception	Truth
Denying or merely managing pain	Facing and being healed from pain
Fear/Anxiety/Worry	Trust and security in Christ
Resentment/Bitterness	Forgiveness
Revenge	Mercy
Shame/Guilt	No condemnation
Negative words	Encouraging words
Rebellion	Submission
Pride	Humility
Control	Surrender
Being driven by the flesh	Resting in Christ/Led by the Spirit
Prejudice/Favoritism	Unconditional love
Controlling habits	Freedom in the Spirit
Giving into temptation	Victory over temptation thru self control
Curses	Blessings
Damage in relationships	Restored relationships
Laziness/Apathy	Passion
Critical attitudes	Significance and confidence in Christ
Rejection	Acceptance in Christ
Immaturity	Maturity in Christ

So what's a *journey to freedom?*

To "journey" means to travel from one place to another and has (at its root) the concept of a daily walk. Inherent in the word "journey" is an element of mystery or adventure, something that makes it more than just a "trip." A journey is more like a *quest.*

This is a journey, an adventure with God, a daily walk that can begin during these 40 days and last a lifetime! You might be wondering ... *what can I expect out of this?*

The purpose of these 40 days will be to help you get to know or get to know better the God who invented freedom… the God who came to set people free… the God of freedom! And in coming to know this God of freedom, you will catch a glimpse of the life he has for you, a life that we trust will create a yearning, a longing and a thirst to live free.

Prior to writing this book we wondered…

- What if tired, discouraged, defeated believers had a refreshing, hope-filled encounter with the living God?

- What if godly, spiritual men and women could take hold of truth that would set them free on an even deeper level?

- What if people who are weighed down by life or tied down by sins could begin to really break free into the life God has for them?

If those things really happened, the impact of such a work of God could bring genuine renewal to individuals, start the process of healing in marriages and families and pave the way for revival in churches! It could pave the way for revival in your heart!

Recognizing that it takes a lifetime to become like Christ and that spiritual maturity does not happen overnight… and certainly not in 40 days… we firmly believe that this intentional, intensive time of seeking God and his truth will be well worth your time and effort. We have been asking God to bring the following changes to the lives of those who work through this study. We've been praying that God will bring you:

- A fresh view of who God is.

- A new joy in understanding how Christ makes you acceptable to God.

- A clear awakening to God's love for you.

- A bright hope in knowing how valuable you are to God.

- A purer understanding of how safe and secure you are in Christ.

- A deep assurance of being at peace with God.

- A real opportunity to live a victorious life!

Please join us fully in this *Journey to Freedom* by investing just 20-30 minutes a day over the next 40 days to begin to pursue this dream. And do yourself a big favor. Resist the urge to skip over some of the questions or applications. What you get out of these six weeks will be proportional to what you put in. A hearty investment of time and energy each day will pay off with huge dividends for you personally at the end of these 40 days.

We are genuinely excited about what God has in store for you as he begins to unlock whatever has held you back from reaching your fullest potential in him. With love shining in his eyes and a warm extended hand, God is inviting you to get to know him… the God of freedom! He says:

No eye has seen, no ear has heard, no mind has conceived what God has prepared for those who love him.

1 Corinthians. 2:9 (NIV)

Like a loving dad playfully chasing his kids around the house, jumping out from around a corner, grabbing the child and giving him a big hug, we know God has some love-surprises in store for you. We're praying you let him "ambush" you with his great love. Because this connection to God is so vital, your journey to freedom will not go uncontested, so we encourage you to join us in prayer:

Dear heavenly Father, in some ways I feel like I'm being asked to "follow the yellow brick road" to a place where people say I'll learn the way home. But I'm not really sure what I'm going to find at the end of that road. I also don't know what I'm going to encounter inside of me or around me as I take these first steps. But I choose to step out in faith anyway, believing deep down in my heart that you are great and you are good and that somehow… though it almost seems too good to be true… somehow you not only love the world, but you love me, too. As only you know how, please give me strength to face and deal with the bondage in my life, knowing that doing so will lead me into the path of freedom. And most importantly, in the process, I'll get to know you, the God of freedom.

Please surround me with your protective hand and don't let me go until you bless me. I want to be free and so I ask these things through Jesus who came to set me free, amen.

Let's get started!

NOTE: Several times in this daily devotional, the authors use scenes from movies to illustrate biblical truth. This usage should in no way be construed as the authors giving their recommendation to view the entire film. Readers are encouraged to exercise prayerful discretion in choosing what they watch or do not watch.

My Covenant

With God's help, I commit the next 40 days of
my life to discovering God's personal liberating
truth for my life.

_____

Your name

_____

Freedom Partner's name

*Two are better off than one, because
together they can work more effectively. If
one of them falls down, the other can help
him up... Two people can resist an attack
that would defeat one person alone. A
rope made of three cords is hard to break.*

Ecclesiastes 4:9 (TEV)

Getting to Know the God of Freedom

Day 1:   The Father You Always Wanted and Needed

Day 2:   Jesus Christ, the Compassionate Healer

Day 3:   Jesus Christ, the Liberating Savior

Day 4:   Jesus Christ, the Risen Lord and Returning King

Day 5:   The Holy Spirit, the Believer's Companion

Day 6:   Sin, the Ultimate Enemy

Day 7:   New Beginnings

Getting to Know the God of Freedom

The Father You Always Wanted and Needed

My (Rich's) parents have spent over 60 years together and my dad is in his mid-eighties. I've got a great relationship with him that started when I was a kid. This story is a snapshot from the "photo album" in my heart of memories of my dad and me. It took place when I was about ten years old.

During this time in my life I was into two things: baseball and animals. Almost any animal that I would see on TV, I would want as a pet – raccoons, foxes, wolves, dolphins, you name it. But I wanted a horse more than anything. I had no idea how much a horse would cost, but I was determined to get the money to buy one.

One Thursday evening temptation took over. I spotted my mom's purse by the hall phone (out of view of my parents who were watching TV). In her wallet was a wad of twenties from my dad's cashed paycheck. I very quietly pulled out one of the $20 bills and began to weave my deceitful plot. .

After school the next day I found an envelope, put the money in it, and took off for the woods near our home. I rubbed the envelope in the dirt to try and make it look like it had been there a while, then, after playing for an hour or so, I rushed into the house all excited.

"Mom, look what I found in the woods! An envelope with $20 in it!"

"You can use that toward your horse," she replied smiling.

The next day was Saturday. It was late spring and I had a Little League baseball game. After it was over I walked toward my dad who had been sitting up on a little hill near the parking lot, watching the game. Although I thought I had committed the "perfect crime," I didn't bank on my conscience bothering me.

The closer I got to my dad, the worse I felt. When I finally reached him, I burst into tears, confessing, *"Dad, I didn't find that money; I stole it!"*

Hugging me close my dad said, *"Son, your mother and I knew that you'd stolen that money. We were just waiting for you to come and tell us."*

Though that incident happened four decades ago, it is still fresh in my mind. It gives me a vivid picture of my heavenly Father who knows full well when I sin but loves his sinning child anyway. And although I don't remember how I did in that particular game, I know that my dad hit a home run that day.

What comes to your mind when you hear the word "father" or "dad"? If we were to survey 1000 people, we'd probably get nearly that many different words to express how people feel about their fathers. Below is just a sampling of adjectives that describe dads.

Check any of the following words that describe your father as you were growing up:			
☐ loving	☐ leaving	☐ angry	☐ affectionate
☐ gone	☐ busy	☐ fun-loving	☐ protective
☐ abusive	☐ drunk	☐ stressed	☐ gentle
☐ kind	☐ weak	☐ cold	☐ involved
☐ distant	☐ hard-working	☐ patient	☐ explosive
☐ passive	☐ strong	☐ unknown	☐ stoned
☐ criminal	☐ helpful	☐ violent	☐ funny
☐ respected	☐ loved	☐ close to God	☐ rigid
☐ critical	☐ scary	☐ smart	☐ wise

WALKING ON

Depending on what kind of a relationship you have or don't have with your dad, you may be experiencing any number of emotions right now – anything from deep sadness to intense anger or warm thankfulness. This is normal. Later in this *Journey to Freedom*, we will lead you in a process toward healing any painful memories you may have. For now, just feel the freedom to acknowledge that any negative emotions you have are there and are very real.

Though none of us does this intentionally, it is very easy to take our view of our earthly dads and project that perception onto our heavenly Father. For example, if your dad was very busy, gone a lot and not very involved in your life, it is very natural to picture your heavenly Father as distant and disinterested in you.

Though your picture of God the Father is very real to you, it may not accurately represent who he really is.

During today's study we'll give God a chance to speak for himself so that we might begin to see him as he is – the Father we have always wanted and needed. Below we have listed some Scripture verses that provide a picture of God the Father. Take some time to think about what they reveal about his character, and see if there is anything he reveals about himself that is contrary to how you view him.

Before we look at how God has revealed himself, let's ask him to open our eyes to the truth of who he really is:

Dear heavenly Father, I want to know you as you really are, but I'm afraid I may not have an accurate picture of your character. Please remove anything from my mind that may be keeping me from seeing the truth and believing it deep in my heart. In Jesus' name I pray, amen.

God is the holy and perfectly pure ruler over all creation

This, in essence, is the message we heard from Christ and are passing on to you: God is light, pure light; there's not a trace of darkness in him.

1 John 1:5 (MSG)

God, the blessed and only Ruler, the King of kings and Lord of lords, who alone is immortal and who lives in unapproachable light...

1 Timothy 6:16 (NIV)

God is a faithful provider

You can be sure that God will take care of everything you need, his generosity exceeding even yours in the glory that pours from Jesus.

Philippians 4:19 (MSG)

God is a strong protector

Because he has loved Me, therefore I will deliver him; I will set him securely on high, because he has known My name.

Psalm 91:14 (NASB)

God is a wise counselor

All this also comes from the Lord Almighty, wonderful in counsel and magnificent in wisdom.

Isaiah 28:29 (NIV)

God is a compassionate healer

but they did not realize it was I who healed them. I led them with cords of human kindness, with ties of love.

Hosea 11:3,4 (NIV)

God is a powerful warrior who delights in us

The Lord your God is in your midst, a victorious warrior. He will exult over you with joy, He will be quiet in His love, He will rejoice over you with shouts of joy.

Zephaniah 3:17 (NASB)

God is a merciful forgiver

I'll forever wipe the slate clean of their sins.

Hebrews 10:17 (MSG)

God is a loving disciplinarian

For those whom the Lord loves He disciplines.

Hebrews 12:6 (NASB)

God is an ever-present encourager

So do not fear, for I am with you; do not be dismayed, for I am your God. I will strengthen you and help you; I will uphold you with my righteous right hand.

Isaiah 41:10 (NIV)

God is a patient teacher

I will instruct you and teach you in the way you should go; I will counsel you and watch over you.

Psalm 32:8 (NIV)

God is a welcoming dad

For you have not received a spirit of slavery leading to fear again, but you have received a spirit of adoption as sons by which we cry out, "Abba! [Daddy!] Father!"

Romans 8:15 (NASB)

Now, in the spaces provided below, write down anything from the verses above about God as your Father that surprised or encouraged you.

_____

_____

_____

_____

_____

_____

_____

_____

_____

What you have just read about God is barely scratching the surface! The Bible is filled with many more descriptions of who God the Father is. Look for them when you read his word!

As you were reading through these descriptions of God, did you find yourself praising him for who he is, or were you struggling with believing these things? Maybe you had mixed emotions; many people do.

The most important part of your "belief system" *(what you are convinced is true)* is your concept of God. Your spiritual health is largely dependent on whether you are filled with truth or swallowing lies about God. The following exercise is designed to expose the lies you may have believed about God the Father, and provide an avenue for you to choose truth.

Renouncing *(verbally rejecting or disowning)* lies and accepting truth is a biblical way to express *repentance.* True repentance is changing your mind to conform to God's truth, and it always results in a change of life. God promises good things for those who repent:

Repent therefore and return, that your sins may be wiped away, in order that times of refreshing may come from the presence of the Lord.

Acts 3:19 (NASB)

That is our desire for you today, that by rejecting lies and receiving truth about God the Father, you might find refreshment with him. Make the following declarations of truth. Say them out loud. Work your way down each list one by one, left to right. Begin each declaration with the statement in **bold print** at the top of the table.

Choosing the Truth About God the Father

I renounce the lie that my Father God is:	I receive the truth that my Father God is...
Distant and disinterested	*Intimate and involved (Ps. 139:1-18)*
Insensitive and uncaring	*Kind and compassionate (Ps. 103:8-14)*
Rejecting, stern or demanding	*Accepting and filled with joy and love (Rom. 15:7; Zeph. 3:17)*
Passive, cold or silent	*Warm, affectionate and communicative (Is. 40:11; Hos. 11:3,4; John 10:16,27)*
Absent, distracted or too busy for me	*Always with me and eager to be with me (Heb. 13:5; Jer. 31:20; Ez. 34:11-16)*
Never satisfied with what I do, impatient or angry	*Patient and slow to anger (Ex. 34:6; 2 Peter 3:9)*
Mean, cruel or abusive	*Loving, gentle and protective of me (Jer. 31:3; Is. 42:3; Ps. 18:2)*
Trying to take all the fun out of life	*Trustworthy and he wants to give me a full life; his will is good, acceptable and perfect for me (Lam. 3:22,23; John 10:10; Rom. 12:1,2)*
Controlling or manipulative	*Full of grace and mercy, and he gives me the freedom to fail (Heb. 4:15,16; Luke 15:11-16)*
Condemning or unforgiving	*Tender-hearted and forgiving; his heart and arms are always open to me (Ps. 130:1-4; Luke 15:17-24)*
Nit-picking, exacting or perfectionistic	*Committed to my growth and proud of me as his growing child (Rom. 8:28,29; Heb. 12:5-11; 2 Cor. 7:4)*

I am the apple of his eye! (See Deut. 32:9,10)

Perhaps some of those truths about our heavenly Father were hard for you to believe. If so, we encourage you to look up the Scripture references in the right hand column, read and think about them, and ask God to make them a part of your belief system. He earnestly desires to do that!

Table taken from Steps to Freedom in Christ *by Neil T. Anderson, p. 13. Copyright © 2004 by Gospel Light, Ventura, CA 93003. Used by Permission*

Our prayer is that you will come to know God the **FATHER** as he really is:

Faithful and true

Actively loving

Tenderhearted and forgiving

Holy and healer of broken hearts

Enthusiastic encourager

Redeemer (the One who wants to buy us out of slavery to sin and death)

Truth Point

We know how much God loves us, and we have put our trust in him.
God is love, and all who live in love live in God, and God lives in them. 1 John 4:16 (NLT)

Application

From the *Choosing The Truth About God the Father* table, make a list of any of the lies that you have believed regarding who Father God is.

Example: "I have believed that God is distant and disinterested in me."

_____

_____

_____

_____

_____

_____

PRAYER

Father God, thank you for speaking up and letting me catch a glimpse of who you really are. I want all my misconceptions replaced with the truth about your character. I'm sorry for believing lies about you. You alone are worthy of worship and I want to worship you with all my heart according to your true character. As I think about it, I wouldn't be surprised if there are things about Jesus that I've been confused about too, so please open my heart to him as well. In Jesus' name I pray, amen.

DECLARATIONS

- **God the Father is the holy and pure ruler of all!**
- **God the Father is love!**
- **God the Father is my faithful provider!**
- **God the Father is my strong protector!**
- **God the Father is my wise counselor!**
- **God the Father is my compassionate healer!**

- **God the Father is a powerful warrior who delights in me!**
- **God the Father is a merciful forgiver!**
- **God the Father is a loving disciplinarian!**
- **God the Father is a patient teacher and encourager!**
- **God the Father is a welcoming dad!**

Special Note To Dads

It is very possible that as you went through the chart of lies and truths about your heavenly Father, the Lord began to speak to you in another way. Perhaps you realized that some of your behavior toward your children was too much like the left-hand column, but you want it to be like the right column. In essence, you want to be the kind of father to your kids that our heavenly Father is to you. If this is your desire, here is a suggested prayer:

Dear heavenly Father, I can see that too often I have failed to reflect your character to my kids. I don't want them to develop a distorted picture of who you are because of how I am. I confess that I have been far too *(be specific in your sins and failings as a dad)* but I want to be like *(be specific in the godly qualities you want to exhibit).* Thank you for your forgiveness. I know that only you can change me and I ask for that in Jesus' name, amen.

Getting to Know the God of Freedom

Jesus Christ, the Compassionate Healer

WARMING UP

I (Christi) had the advantage of being raised by godly parents with solid values and who believed in being in church every time the doors were open. Now, I didn't say that my parents were perfect or that I was the perfect child – that's impossible! Quite honestly, my teenage years were very challenging for both my mom and me.

I had low self-esteem by nature and was easily crushed by even the slightest hint of criticism or negative response from my mom. With two sets of eyes (one of which was in the back of her head!) my mom didn't miss much, and I provided more than enough for her to catch. She took very seriously her role to rear responsible children and seized every opportunity to teach and admonish me. My mom was doing her best to train me and wanted only the best for her daughter.

One problem was that I just couldn't meet her expectations in keeping my room straightened up. Sometimes I just didn't want to. I had one of the messiest rooms in one of the most spotless houses that you can imagine.

I knew my mom loved me but I also believed that she would love me even more if I could just get my act together and keep my room clean. I would always forget to put things away… and she would persistently remind me. This cycle went on for several years.

Unfortunately, I ended up falling into the trap of believing the lie that I had to perform in order to gain my mom's acceptance. It was not true, but that was what I thought.

The lies in my head grew as I allowed the enemy to exploit the situation, especially with negative self-talk. I began expecting people to reject me and even worse, I began to believe the lie that I was unlovable and there was something wrong with me.

I entered marriage waiting for the hammer to fall, for my husband to reject me. I anticipated rejection and that became a self-fulfilling prophecy. It seemed that everywhere I went, people rejected me. I wanted to be loved and accepted so much but the lie that I was unlovable and unacceptable blocked me from being able to receive love and acceptance from anyone.

Finally, God broke through all the lies with his sharp sword of truth. I can honestly say from having had the "disease" of insecurity, rejection and insignificance that there is only one real, lasting antidote – the healing words of Jesus.

If you have been stricken with believing lies about your personal identity, worth or value, take special note of today's devotion. Jesus wants to speak words of life to you that could begin to change your life forever…today!

WALKING ON

You might remember in our Introduction that Jesus said our basic problem – the thing that keeps us from being free – is sin (***John 8:34***). He also said, ***"If therefore the Son shall make you free, you shall be free indeed" (John 8:36)***. In case it's unclear to you, Jesus was talking about himself. He is the Son and he was saying that real, lasting freedom comes from him… and *only* from him! Do you believe him?

The apostle John – who walked with Jesus for three years of his life, watched him live, and who watched him die and watched him come back to life again – had this to say about who he was:

> *In the beginning the Word already existed. He was with God, and he was God.*
>
> *John 1:1 (NLT)*

> *So the Word became human and lived here on earth among us. He was full of unfailing love and faithfulness. And we have seen his glory, the glory of the only Son of the Father.*
>
> *John 1:14 (NLT)*

John called Jesus "the Word", declaring him to be the very expression of God. Make no mistake about it; the Bible proclaims Jesus to be God himself!

During the next three days we are going to take a look at three facets of the God who became human flesh and lived among us, the Lord Jesus Christ, the Messiah, the Anointed One.

All three have great significance when it comes to our freedom:

- His earthly ministry of healing
- His liberating death on the cross
- His powerful life-giving resurrection

Today we will look at Jesus' healing ministry, in both *word* and *deed.* For Jesus healed with the *words of his mouth* as well as with the *touch of his hands.* We'll first focus on what we call *Healing Words from Jesus to You,* a short sampler of some of Jesus' more encouraging words. For this exercise you'll need a Bible. As you look up the Scriptures in the shaded box, fill in the blanks and think about how these truth-treasures apply to you today.

Healing Words from Jesus to You

Matthew 6:8 God knows what you need even before you ask him.

Matthew 6:26,30 You are of much more value to God than even the birds of the air and the flowers of the field.

Matthew 10:30 My Father watches over you; he even knows the number of hairs on (or not on!) your head.

Matthew 11:28-29 You can come to Me to find _____ when you are weary and burdened.

Matthew 11:29,30 I am gentle and humble in heart and My yoke is easy, My load is light.

Matthew 28:20 I will be with you always, even to the end of the age.

John 8:31,32,36 If you continue in My word, you are truly My disciple and you will know the _____ and the _____ will set you free. If I set you free you will be free indeed!

John 10:3,14 If you are one of my sheep (a follower) I lead you, call you by name and I know you…

John 10:10 I have come to give you _____ and to give it _____ _____.

John 10:28,29 No one can snatch you out of My hand or the Father's hand.

John 14:27 I promise you My peace, which is not as the world gives.

From just looking at these things that Jesus taught, is it any wonder that huge crowds followed him? His teaching had authority and power to heal broken hearts and damaged lives, and so people were transformed when they listened to him with open hearts.

Jesus truly was the expert teacher full of wisdom, creativity and love.

Jesus' words have the same power, authority, wisdom, creativity, and love today as they did 2000 years ago. Take a moment and write in the blanks below the most healing or encouraging thing that you learned (or were reminded of) from the 11 Scriptures you just looked at, and explain why that truth is meaningful for you today.

_____

_____

_____

_____

_____

_____

_____

Our desire and prayer in this exercise is that you would be refreshed and renewed in your heart by some of the amazing teachings of the Lord Jesus, and that you would hunger for more of him and his word. Jesus said that freedom would come by continuing in his word and knowing the truth. Do you have a hunger for God's word? If not, why not take a moment and ask God to kindle or rekindle that hunger.

In addition to Jesus healing with his words, Jesus also reached out and touched people, setting them free from disease and from the bondage of Satan. Word got around about what Jesus could do, as you'll see from the following account:

That evening, after the sun was down, they brought sick and evil-afflicted people to him, the whole city lined up at his door! He cured their sick bodies and tormented spirits. Because the demons knew his true identity, he didn't let them say a word.

Mark 1:32-34 (MSG)

In that account from Mark 1, you get a little taste of how self-sacrificing Jesus' love for people was. Right when you and I would be settling down to dinner with plans to watch Wheel of Fortune® and Jeopardy!®, Jesus found the whole town at his door wanting and needing ministry. But he didn't take the phone off the hook and shut the blinds; he reached out and touched many.

Here are a couple examples from Jesus' ministry:

A leper came to him, begging on his knees, "If you want to, you can cleanse me."

Deeply moved, Jesus put out his hand, touched him, and said, "I want to. Be clean."

Then and there the leprosy was gone, his skin smooth and healthy.

Mark 1:40-42 (MSG)

Leprosy was the most dreaded disease of the first century. People were afraid of lepers and wanted them to stay away. Nobody would touch a leper. Nobody but Jesus, that is. Here's another example:

And He was teaching in one of the synagogues on the Sabbath. And behold, there was a woman who for eighteen years had had a sickness caused by a spirit; and she was bent double, and could not straighten up at all. And when Jesus saw her, He called her over and said to her, "Woman, you are freed from your sickness." And He laid hands upon her; and immediately she was made erect again, and began glorifying God.

Luke 13:10-13 (NASB)

Both leprosy and disfigurement were looked upon as a curse from God. The self-righteous religious leaders in Jesus' day would have nothing to do with such dregs of society.

But Jesus was different. Jesus is different.

There is no one in any condition too shameful for Jesus to touch, but Jesus often waits for us to invite him to touch us.

The blind man by the road near Jericho wouldn't stop yelling for Jesus to have mercy on him (see Luke 18:35-43). Gripped by this man's determination, Jesus stopped and asked him a question, "What do you want Me to do for you?" What an invitation! It was as if Jesus were handing the man a blank check and asking him to fill in the amount! But the blind man didn't want money; he wanted to see again. Jesus granted him his request.

What about you? What do you want Jesus to do for you?

What are you secretly hoping you will find by the end of this *Journey to Freedom?*

The following exercise is a private matter between you and the Lord. Below is a list of some heart cries that people through the centuries have voiced to Jesus, the compassionate healer. If you find your needs on the list below, go ahead and underline them. You'll be referencing them in our closing prayer in just a few minutes.

- I want to be free from the haunting guilt and shame in my life.

- I need emotional healing from the deep wounds of abuse.

- I am so driven to achieve success in my life; I need to learn how to love my family more.

- I really need a touch from God in my physical body.

- I am pretty discouraged right now; I need some genuine encouragement.

- I can't seem to shake off this depression that clouds my mind, dulls my senses and drains me of vitality; I need to be able to feel hope again.

- I need to be set free from the tormenting lies and accusations of the evil one.

- I am so anxious and uptight; I can't seem to rest.

- If I'm perfectly honest with myself, I would have to admit I'm a control freak; I need help in learning how to "let go", because I'm alienating my friends and family.

- Bitterness and resentment have a stranglehold on my heart; I need to be free!

- I think I'm pretty close to burnout and I need a refreshing, healing touch.

- I am trapped in an addiction and I don't know how to break free.

- Others the Lord brings to mind:

_____

_____

_____

_____

_____

_____

_____

_____

_____

_____

_____

_____

_____

_____

_____

WINDING DOWN

As we close, there is one more short story from the healing ministry of Jesus that we need to share, because there is the danger of becoming so used to our wounded condition, that we accept a victim rather than victor mentality. :

Inside the city, near the Sheep Gate, was the pool of Bethesda, with five covered porches. Crowds of sick people—blind, lame, or paralyzed—lay on the porches. One of the men lying there had been sick for thirty-eight years. When Jesus saw him and knew how long he had been ill, he asked him, "Would you like to get well?" "I can't, sir," the sick man said, "for I have no one to help me into the pool when the water is stirred up. While I am trying to get there, someone else always gets in ahead of me." Jesus told him, "Stand up, pick up your sleeping mat, and walk!" Instantly, the man was healed! He rolled up the mat and began walking!

John 5:2-9 (NLT)

Perhaps Jesus would ask you the same searching question today:

Do you want to get well?

After all, being wounded has its benefits. People don't expect much out of you and you always have an excuse if things don't work out in your life. There is an increased responsibility to live a whole life when you are whole and healthy. So ... do you want to get well?

Jesus is waiting for your answer.

WRAPPING UP

Truth Point

He forgives your sins—every one. He heals your diseases—every one.

Psalm 103:3 (MSG)

Application

What sins or diseases are you trusting Jesus to forgive or heal you of?

_____

_____

_____

_____

_____

Dear heavenly Father, time after time Jesus heard the cries of wounded people and healed them. Not only did he touch their bodies, but more importantly he touched their hearts. My heart needs your touch, too. I really do want to get well and be whole, so I ask you to touch me by *(tell God now the things your heart cries for him to do based on what you've written down in this day's lesson)*. I don't want to spend the rest of my life lying around the pool making excuses about why my life never really amounted to much for Christ's kingdom. All I can do is come to Jesus like the people in the Bible did and reach out for cleansing and healing of my soul. And if it pleases you to touch my physical body as well, I will give the credit to you. If your answer is for me to find your strength to endure physical suffering, then I receive that grace as well. In Jesus' healing name I pray, amen.

DECLARATIONS

- **Jesus has the power to heal with the words of his mouth!**
- **Jesus has the power to heal with the touch of his hands!**
- **Jesus has the power to set me free from bondage!**
- **No disease or condition of the heart is too shameful for Jesus to touch!**
- **I want to get well!**
- **Jesus has the power to make me well!**

Getting to Know the God of Freedom

Jesus Christ, the Liberating Savior

It's amazing how often real truth, God's truth, shows up in films. One classic example is in the movie, *The Matrix*. In that movie, artificial Intelligence (AI) has become so sophisticated on planet earth that AI clones are able to gain their needed energy from human beings. They have enslaved humans, who are kept in pod-like containers. The AI then keeps the humans alive by feeding data into their minds, making them think that they are actually living life, working, having families, going to church, etc. But the entire human race is living a delusion.

In one of the defining moments of the movie, Morpheus (who has come to understand the plight of the human race) talks to Neo about "the matrix" — the data stream that everyone believes, but doesn't see. He says, "... there's something wrong with the world. You don't know what it is, but it's there... like a splinter in your mind, driving you mad... [It] is the world that has been pulled over your eyes to blind you from the truth... that you are a slave... Like everyone else you were born into bondage, born into a prison that you cannot smell or taste or touch. A prison for your mind."

Millions of people watched that movie and listened to these words but had no clue how true they actually were for them! And the same millions of people watched the film's hero, Neo, (played by Keanu Reeves) beat the odds and begin to set the human race free, while having no clue that Jesus has done that already for them!

What Hollywood made a film about, people on planet earth virtually live out every day. In this true story, an intelligence greater than that of humans has deceived and enslaved the entire race. In this captivity, he lies to them, tortures them and makes false promises. After a while, the captives come to believe that life in captivity is real life and is as good as it gets.

Into this real life scene walks the Lord Jesus Christ, who has truly come to set captives free. But this freedom doesn't come cheaply.

In the movie *The Matrix* a betrayer who sides with the AI causes some of the real humans to die. Freedom never comes easily. There is always a price to pay. The good news is that the price has already been paid. Jesus said,

> *Greater love has no one than this, that one lay down his life for his friends.*
>
> *John 15:13 (NASB)*

Jesus knew what he was talking about, because that is exactly what he ended up doing by dying on the cross to purchase our freedom. Today, we're going to take a fresh look at what Jesus accomplished through his death on the cross. True, that is not new news, for Jesus died nearly 2000 years ago. However, it is incredibly good news because his suffering and death is meant to have a profound impact on your life! (Here. Now. Today.)

Think for a moment about the things in your life that are important to you. Listed below are some of life's treasured possessions. Imagine that each of these items came to be owned by someone else. What would you be willing to pay to get them back? Do your best to place a monetary value on them by filling in the blank with the dollar amount you believe they are worth.

Your car(s)	$_____
Your house	$_____
Your furniture	$_____
Jewelry you own	$_____
Art objects	$_____
Family photos	$_____
Pets	$_____
Friends	$_____
Family members	$_____

If you are like most people, you found it much easier to put a price tag on the first five than you did on the last four, especially the final two – friends and family members. You might even have become offended at being asked to place a dollar value on your loved ones. And rightly so, because the only time people are exchanged for money is in slavery.

The tragedy, however, is that every person without Christ *is* a slave – a slave to sin and death!

Take a moment to reflect on the following Scriptures that tell of mankind's condition as slaves.

Do you not know that when you present yourselves to someone as slaves for obedience, you are slaves of the one whom you obey, either of sin resulting in death, or of obedience resulting in righteousness? ...For when you were slaves of sin, you were free in regard to righteousness. Therefore what benefit were you then deriving from the things of which you are now ashamed? For the outcome of those things is death.

Romans 6:16, 20-21 (NASB)

For we also once were foolish ourselves, disobedient, deceived, enslaved to various lusts and pleasures, spending our life in malice and envy, hateful, hating one another.

Titus 3:3 (NASB)

Jesus said, "I tell you most solemnly that anyone who chooses a life of sin is trapped in a dead-end life and is, in fact, a slave."

John 8:34 (MSG)

The word of God is crystal clear. The human race is in captivity, enslaved to sin, with no hope of escaping *by itself* from sin's clutches. Sin drags its victims closer and closer to eternal separation from God… to spiritual death.

So what does it take to set mankind free from slavery to sin and death?

What is the price God had to pay to ransom captive humanity from slavery?

The answer is equally clear in the Bible. The shed blood of Jesus Christ dying on the cross is the *only payment sufficient* to set captive people free from sin! The writer to the Hebrew believers revealed this truth vividly, contrasting the ultimate futility of the Jewish sacrificial system to forgive sin with the power of Christ's shed blood:

But when the Messiah arrived, high priest of the superior things of this new covenant, he bypassed the old tent and its trappings in this created world and went straight to heaven's "tent" – the true Holy Place – once for all. He also bypassed the sacrifices consisting of goat and calf blood, instead using his own blood as the price to set us free once and for all. If that animal blood and the other rituals of purification were effective in cleaning up certain matters of our religion and behavior, think how much more the blood of Christ cleans up our whole lives, inside and out. Through the Spirit, Christ offered himself as an unblemished sacrifice, freeing us from all those dead-end efforts to make ourselves respectable, so that we can live all out for God.

Hebrews 9:11-14 (MSG)

Paul's letter to the Romans also shows God's way of rescuing us from our futile attempts to free ourselves from slavery to sin:

With the arrival of Jesus, the Messiah, that fateful dilemma is resolved. Those who enter into Christ's being-here-for-us no longer have to live under a continuous, low-lying black cloud. A new power is in operation. The Spirit of life in Christ, like a strong wind, has magnificently cleared the air, freeing you from a fated lifetime of brutal tyranny at the hands of sin and death. God went for the jugular when he sent his own Son. He didn't deal with the problem as something remote and unimportant. In his Son, Jesus, he personally took on the human condition, entered the disordered mess of struggling humanity in order to set it right once and for all. The law code, weakened as it always was by fractured human nature, could never have done that. The law always ended up being used as a band-aid on sin instead of a deep healing of it. And now what the law code asked for but we couldn't deliver is accomplished as we, instead of redoubling our own efforts, simply embrace what the Spirit is doing in us.

Romans 8:1-3 (MSG)

Not surprisingly, the devil himself was behind the whole scheme of keeping people enslaved to sin and death. Jesus' death also became our victory over Satan:

Since the children are made of flesh and blood, it's logical that the Savior took on flesh and blood in order to rescue them by his death. By embracing death, taking it into himself, he destroyed the Devil's hold on death and freed all who cower through life, scared to death of death.

Hebrews 2:14-15 (MSG)

Here's one more incredible Scripture that talks about how Christ's death on the cross has won the victory over sin, death and Satan:

When you were stuck in your old sin-dead life, you were incapable of responding to God. God brought you alive – right along with Christ! Think of it! All sins forgiven, the slate wiped clean, that old arrest warrant canceled and nailed to Christ's cross. He stripped all the spiritual tyrants [demonic powers] *in the universe of their sham authority at the Cross and marched them naked through the streets.*

Colossians 2:13-15 (MSG)

[bracketed comment ours]

We've looked at quite a bit of Scripture in a short time here. Sometimes it's easy to read it so fast that we miss its impact. Choose one of the four Scripture passages above and write it in your own words in the blanks provided below.

_____

_____

_____

_____

_____

_____

_____

_____

_____

_____

_____

_____

In Summary:

- Anyone who lives in sin is a slave to sin!

- We are all helpless to escape from sin's clutches on our own! (See ***Rom. 5:8***)

- Jesus' shed blood is the only thing precious and powerful enough in this universe to buy us out of slavery to sin. (See ***1 Peter 1:18,19***)

- Through Christ's death on the cross, Jesus has provided an open door for us to be set free from slavery to sin, death and Satan!

Before we wrap up today's devotion, it is important for you to realize that God didn't send Christ to die for the sins and sinners of the world because we deserved it — quite the contrary.

For if, when we were enemies, we were reconciled to God by the death of his Son, much more, being reconciled, we shall be saved by his life.

Romans 5:10 (KJV)

Enemies? Yes, enemies. Anyone who is a friend of the world and its sin is an enemy of God (See ***James 4:4***). And that was every one of us without Christ!

So, where does that leave us?

It leaves us with the sobering reality that sin is much more powerful than we are, but also with the good news that the Cross of Christ and his shed blood is much more powerful than sin!

Christ's death is the key that unlocks the chains of our slavery to sin. So let's bring today's devotion to a close by looking at the price tag that hangs from every person who is enslaved to sin, wasting life and waiting for death in the Pawnshop of Lost Mankind. What does that price tag say?

Perhaps an illustration will help answer that question.

We believe it is safe to say that the value of any object can be determined only by one who knows and loves that object. A little boy staring at a Rembrandt or Picasso in an art museum might reach into his pocket and pull out a few coins and try to buy it, thinking he was paying a lot! But the art expert standing next to him would gaze in rapt admiration of the masterpiece and whisper, "Priceless."

What is your value then to God?

What is the value written on the price tag of mankind?

A million dollars in gold or silver…?

No, something far more valuable and precious than all the gold, silver, and gems in the world!

The blood of Jesus!

God the Father believed it was worth the ultimate price -- the shed blood of his only Son, the Lord Jesus Christ -- to purchase you and me out of our slavery to sin. Though others might look at you and consider you worthless… Your true value is determined by the price that your Creator – the One who knows and loves you – was willing to pay in order to have a relationship with you and to spend eternity with you.

That's something to think *hard* about. That's something to thank God for!

Truth Point

This is how much God loved the world: He gave his Son, his one and only Son. And this is why: so that no one need be destroyed; by believing in him, anyone can have a whole and lasting life.

John 3:16 (MSG)

Application

Write a brief description of what Jesus went through so that you and I can be free.

_____

_____

_____

Dear heavenly Father, I'm a bit stunned by all this. First of all, I never realized how deadly sin really was and how totally powerless I am to break its chains in my life. It's also pretty humbling to understand that there was nothing but your great love that motivated Jesus to die for me. It wasn't because I was so great or good (in fact I was not great at all and not the least bit good) that he did that for me. And yet somehow, even though I was your enemy, doing the exact opposite of what you wanted, you still decided I was worth rescuing. Father, it cost you and your Son, Jesus, everything to buy me out of slavery. And for that I say "thank you" and it's in Jesus' name I pray all this, amen.

- **Jesus died a brutal death, so I can live an abundant life!**

- **The work Jesus accomplished on the cross has the power to save me!**

- **This work also has the power to change my life!**

- **Outside of Jesus' accomplishment, I would have no hope at all!**

- **Jesus blood can make the most wicked sinner clean!**

- **The most appalling sinner is worth the shed blood of Jesus to God!**

- **Jesus' death and resurrection has become our victory over Satan!**

- **I choose to be forever grateful for the shed blood of Jesus Christ!**

Getting to Know the God of Freedom

Jesus Christ, the Risen Lord and Returning King

WARMING UP

As a child of God and pastor's wife, I (Christi) have had the opportunity to get down in the dirt with people and listen when they are hurting the most. During counseling, I have heard many personal stories that have both touched my heart and challenged me toward my own personal growth. In all the stories, there seems to be one common element, one nagging question, "How can I break free and truly overcome this certain sinful habit in my life?"

Sinful habits are no stranger to me. For years I struggled with lustful thoughts and actions that controlled my life. I was caught in the trap of getting my needs met through unhealthy relationships. Our culture places so much emphasis on a sexuality that is selfish. So many adults and teens – even Christian ones – fall into this snare. I did.

I wanted to be noticed and desired by the opposite sex even if it was only in my imagination. The soap operas that I watched when I came home from school only fueled these fantasies. They provided images of false romance and false intimacy on which my mind could feed. Being raised in church, I found myself living under a cloud of guilt, shame and what seemed like hopeless bondage. I would pray, try harder, read my Bible more, repent… and then sin anyway… and then cycle through all these steps again and again.

I couldn't understand why God would not take this bondage away from me. I made bargains with him, but temptation would mount and off again I went to sin, like a dog returning to its vomit.

One Sunday morning, the Lord broke through. Contrary to what I might have wanted, or some church traditions might expect, there were no spiritual fireworks or power encounters knocking me to the floor, removing sin's attraction for me. It was a gentle encounter with God and the truth of his word. God opened my eyes to the truth that I, his child, really *am* dead to sin and alive to him. He assured me that the same power that raised Jesus Christ from the dead was living inside me. That meant I no longer had to give in to sin, because I was *dead* to it.

God also gave me some real practical advice concerning things I needed to stay away from to maintain my freedom from sexual-romantic fantasies. The soap operas that fueled my fantasies had to go, along with a bunch of other stuff.

What happened? My surrender + God's unlimited empowerment = freedom!

I learned that surrender is a form of worship (Romans 12:1) and joy came as a result of sacrifice. Each time I was tempted to go back to sin, I would remember that I was *dead to sin.* I would take the temptation straight to God and surrender it to Him as worship. The Lord accepted my worship and gave me the gift of joy in His presence. The result? No more tormenting guilt and shame, because I had the lasting fulfillment that comes from walking in obedience to God in the power of Christ's resurrection!

Yesterday we took a good look at the victory over sin, death and Satan that was purchased by Jesus Christ's shed blood as he died on the cross. Thank God for the blood of Jesus that has the power to buy us out of slavery! But did you know all that Christ sought to accomplish on the cross would have been futile… unless he also rose from the dead? There were thousands of people crucified during the time of the Roman Empire, including Jesus. And those thousands of bodies were taken down off the cross and buried, including Jesus. But there is only ONE who conquered the grave by rising from the dead, and that is **JESUS!**

And Jesus Christ our Lord was shown to be the Son of God when God powerfully raised him from the dead by means of the Holy Spirit.

Romans 1:4 (NLT)

Today we will look at what the Bible has to say about Jesus Christ, the *risen Lord* and *returning King*, and catch a glimpse of how we can experience the power of the resurrection.

Perhaps you are a bit skeptical about the possibility of a man – even a man with the moral integrity of Jesus – coming back to life after three days in the grave.

Let's take a look at some of the evidence for his resurrection.

First, Jesus predicted both his death and resurrection a number of times. For example, he spoke the following words, recorded in Luke:

For I, the Son of Man, must suffer many terrible things," he said. "I will be rejected by the leaders, the leading priests, and the teachers of religious law. I will be killed, but three days later I will be raised from the dead.

Luke 9:22 (NLT)

Even Jesus' enemies had heard him make that prediction. Matthew recorded the Jewish leaders' concern and the precautions taken after Jesus had been crucified and buried:

The next day—on the first day of the Passover ceremonies—the leading priests and Pharisees went to see Pilate. They told him, "Sir, we remember what that deceiver once said while he was still alive: 'After three days I will be raised from the dead.' So we request that you seal the tomb until the third day. This will prevent his disciples from coming and stealing his body and then telling everyone he came back to life! If that happens, we'll be worse off than we were at first." Pilate replied, "Take guards and secure it the best you can." So they sealed the tomb and posted guards to protect it.

Matthew 27:62-66 (NLT)

Consider these things:

- Jesus was dead and buried.

- The disciples had scattered in fear for their lives. (See *Matt. 26:56*)

- Peter, (their leader) was devastated emotionally because of his denial of Jesus. (See *Matt. 26:75*)

- The Romans and Jews had teamed up by placing a well-armed, well-trained guard in addition to an "extremely large" stone to secure Jesus' cave-like tomb (See *Mark 16:4*)

Then three days later the lives of the disciples were suddenly transformed from timid and trembling losers into joyous and ecstatic men who eventually turned the world upside down by their faith.

How did this happen? Did the disciples somehow overtake the guard unit and steal the body to make it look like Jesus had risen from the dead?! That was the story fabricated and circulated after Jesus' resurrection!!! (See *Matthew 28:11-15*)

But that bogus story simply makes no sense. People do not willingly put their lives at risk, suffer and die (like many of the disciples of Jesus eventually did) for something they know is a lie! The only legitimate explanation for what had happened is that which the apostle Paul declared in *1 Corinthians 15:3-8 (NLT):*

I passed on to you what was most important and what had also been passed on to me—that Christ died for our sins, just as the Scriptures said.

He was buried, and he was raised from the dead on the third day, as the Scriptures said.

- *He was seen by Peter and then by the twelve apostles.*

- *After that, he was seen by more than five hundred of his followers at one time, most of whom are still alive, though some have died by now.*

- *Then he was seen by James and later by all the apostles.*

- *Last of all, I saw him, too, long after the others, as though I had been born at the wrong time.*

Do you see what Paul is claiming?

In essence, Paul was saying that had there been a trial in court to determine whether Jesus actually rose from the grave or not, hundreds of eyewitnesses for the defense could have taken the witness stand. And many of them eventually suffered terribly and even died for the truth of what their eyes had seen and their hands had touched!

The only reasonable explanation for the totally transformed lives of the disciples was this: **Jesus rose from the dead and they knew it because they saw him!**

One example is from Luke's gospel:

While they were still talking about this, Jesus himself stood among them and said to them, 'Peace be with you.' They were startled and frightened, *thinking they saw a ghost. He said to them, 'Why are you troubled, and why do doubts rise in your minds? Look at my hands and my feet. It is I myself! Touch me and see; a ghost does not have flesh and bones, as you see I have.' When he had said this, he showed them his hands and feet. And while they still did not believe it because of joy and amazement, he asked them, 'Do you have anything here to eat?' They gave him a piece of broiled fish, and he took it and ate it in their presence.*

Luke 24:36-43 (NIV)

Jesus did everything he could to show the disciples that 1) it was really him, 2) he was truly alive from the dead and 3) he had risen in bodily form and was not a ghost or hallucination. With all the opposition from "scholars" over the years concerning Jesus' bodily resurrection, there's one thing that the prosecution has never been able to produce… the one thing that forever would silence those proclaiming the resurrection… **the body of Jesus!**

The reason for that is very simple. Jesus, who has been taken up into heaven *(in bodily form)*, **will return** in just the same way as they watched him go into heaven *(Acts 1:9-11)*. Jesus rose in bodily form from the dead. He ascended in bodily form into heaven. He now sits at the Father's right hand, in bodily form reigning as Lord. And one day He will return in bodily form as the whole earth witnesses the true return of the King! God's word plainly declares that one day, every knee will bow and every tongue will confess that Jesus Christ is the risen Lord.

What an incredible piece of truth we've studied today!

The entire universe, all of history, and the fate of every human being *(including you!)* are hanging in the balance, depending on the reality of the death, burial and resurrection of Jesus Christ.

To further experience how world-transforming the person of Jesus Christ is, take a few minutes to describe in the blanks below what you think the world would be like *(or not like)* if Jesus had **not** risen from the dead, and there were no Christian faith. For example, how many more people would be homeless, starving and hopeless without the ministry of the Salvation Army! Take your time on this one; you'll be amazed at what you come up with.

_____

_____

_____

_____

_____

_____

_____

It staggers the imagination, doesn't it, to think of a world without the risen Christ and the Christian faith – a world with no Christian mercy, no compassion in life and no concrete hope of life after death. How many clinics, hospitals, schools and orphanages around the world would never have been built? How many individuals, families, tribes and even nations would still be bound by the powers of darkness, fearful in life and terrified of death? How much more crime, disease, famine and war would there have been? It is overwhelming to think about.

The apostle Paul knew from firsthand experience how transforming the resurrected life of Christ was for him. If the resurrection were not true, Paul announced in *1 Corinthians 15: 13-19,* we are doomed for sure. We might as well *"…eat and drink, for tomorrow we die" (1 Cor. 15:32).* The only thing that makes sense – if Christ has not risen from the dead – is to live fast, die young and leave a good-looking corpse!

But did Paul give in to that despair? Never! His words resound from the pen of one who saw the risen Christ and was miraculously transformed from murderer to missionary, vicious persecutor to vigorous proclaimer of the resurrection of Christ. Paul's final conclusion:

…the fact is that Christ <u>has</u> been raised from the dead. He has become the first of a great harvest of those who will be raised to life again.

1 Corinthians 15:20 (NLT)

It's not a sham! The good news of Christ's resurrection is TRUTH!

Circle the statements below that you are convinced are true:

- Christ has been raised from the dead!

- Those who believe in him will spend eternity in heaven with him!

- Sin has been paid for!

- Death has been conquered!

- Satan has been defeated!

- Believers in Christ have truly been set free!

- Service in the name of Christ is not in vain!

This may all seem too good to be true… but it is good and it is true!

You and I are not going to wake up one day to discover "faith in Jesus" was just a dream, fable or fairy tale! You and I and every person who has ever lived will instead one day stand before the risen Lord Jesus Christ and give an account of our lives!

Later in this *Journey to Freedom* you will learn more about how to experience the power of God in your life. But before that "feast," we want to give you a hors d'oeuvre to whet your appetite. Check this out:

I keep asking that the God of our Lord Jesus Christ, the glorious Father, may give to you the Spirit of wisdom and revelation so that you may know Him better. I pray also that the eyes of your heart may be enlightened in order that you may know... his incomparably great power for us who believe. That power is like the working of his mighty strength, which he exerted in Christ when he raised him from the dead and seated him at his right hand... Now to him who is able to do immeasurably more than all we ask or imagine, according to his power that is at work within us...

Ephesians 1:17-20; 3:20 (NIV)

Take a moment and write down what those verses in Ephesians are saying about God's power at work in you!

_____

_____

_____

Truth Point

It stands to reason, doesn't it, that if the alive-and-present God who raised Jesus from the dead moves into your life, he'll do the same thing in you that he did in Jesus, bringing you alive to himself? When God lives and breathes in you (and he does, as surely as he did in Jesus), you are delivered from that dead life. With his Spirit living in you, your body will be as alive as Christ's!

Romans 8:11 (MSG)

Application

God's power enabled Jesus to overcome death, hell and the grave. If you are a believer in Christ, the same power that raised Jesus from the dead is living inside of you.

Make a list of problems in your life that you need God's power to help you overcome. In our prayer at the end of this day's devotional tell God about those areas of need, asking him to work on your behalf.

_____

_____

_____

The resurrection of Christ is a historical fact, but it doesn't belong in the dusty annals of ancient history somewhere.... because he is alive today and wants to be active in your life!

Dear heavenly Father, when I think about the incredible power that raised Jesus from the dead, I stand amazed. Jesus is not just a great religious teacher who loved people and then died for a good cause. He is the risen, reigning and returning King! I want all the power of His risen life to transform me so that I can walk in freedom from sin, death and Satan. I need your power, Lord, to tackle these problems in my life: (list the ones you just wrote down). Continue to show me how to experience your power and transformation in my daily life – for your sake and glory, Jesus, amen.

- **There is only ONE who has conquered death, and that is JESUS!**

- **The body of Jesus Christ is no longer in the tomb!**

- **Jesus is alive and well, and is seated at the right hand of the Father!**

- **The same power that raised Jesus from the dead is available to live in me!**

- **Sin has been paid for and Satan has been defeated!**

- **One day Jesus will return to earth in bodily form!**

- **Every knee will bow and every tongue will confess that Jesus is Lord!**

Getting to Know the God of Freedom

The Holy Spirit, the Believer's Companion

Is it possible for real change to come to a life? Is it possible for a person to be set free and transformed from sinful selfishness to such an extent that an entirely new life opens up for him or her? You may be wondering if this kind of radical change is possible *for you!*

The following story should give you hope… hope in the transforming presence and power of the Holy Spirit as he works in the life of a true follower of Christ.

As a teenager, Michael (Christi's husband) was so painfully shy that he would literally sit in church *on his hands*, to keep people from trying to shake hands with him! If approached by someone, he would drop his head and turn as red as a beet. The more forward and aggressive people were in their greetings, the more he wanted to crawl under the seat.

Being an intellectual introvert, Michael headed off to Virginia Tech to study engineering. Though he was very shy and reserved around people, deep inside his heart was a burning passion to receive more of God's presence and power. Each day he would walk across campus talking with God and asking him to fill him with the Holy Spirit. (NOTE: Being filled with the Holy Spirit involves the presence and power of God taking over a person surrendered to him. This enables a person to defeat sin, love supernaturally and to boldly reach out to people with Christ's truth.)

One Monday Michael found himself in the War Memorial chapel three different times, sensing that God was trying to get his attention. On his last trip, Michael sensed God saying to his spirit, *"Just say that you accept My will for your life."* When Michael agreed, surrendering his entire life to the Lord, something happened. He felt as if a huge rock was lifted off him and he knew from that moment on that God was calling him into ministry.

But Michael was still Michael. How could this shy, introverted person who was terrified of people be able to minister to them? Michael could relate to the Bible story of Jesus calling His disciple, Peter, to come out and walk on the water with Him! And Michael, too, would have sunk if God had not equipped him.

While checking his mail that Wednesday he noticed a poster hanging on the wall that read *Faith Alive Revival.* When he read those words, Michael knew he was supposed to attend that service. When he went he heard a message about being filled with the Holy Spirit. The preacher shared about stepping out into the waters and going deeper with God. He used this passage about water flowing from God's throne:

Measuring as he went, he led me along the stream for 1,750 feet and told me to go across. At that point the water was up to my ankles. He measured off another 1,750 feet and told me to go across again. This time the water was up to my knees. After another 1,750 feet, it was up to my waist. Then he measured another 1,750 feet, and the river was too deep to cross without swimming.

Ezekiel 47:3-5 (NLT)

At the end of the service, Michael made his way to the front of the church to pray and ask God to fill him full of the Spirit. But being shy, he hid behind a plant so that hopefully no one would notice him and come over and pray with him. But the pastor found him and as they prayed together, there was such a powerful moving of God's Spirit upon Michael that he became a changed man… *really changed!*

Michael received a new boldness from God as the Holy Spirit began equipping him for full-time ministry. On his way back to the dorm, lying spirits (demons) whispered harsh accusations into his mind, trying to get him to believe he wasn't really any different. Before Michael even realized it, he heard himself saying out loud, *"Satan, you are a liar! I am changed!!"* The new spiritual boldness was already kicking in.

When Michael went home that weekend, as soon as he walked in the door, his mom noticed the difference. The following Sunday morning, Michael got up and for the first time played his guitar in church. Before long, Michael was serving the Lord full-time as a traveling evangelist, preaching the good news of Christ.

When Michael shares this story with people now, they can hardly believe that he used to be so shy! There is no way he could ever pastor a church – as he is doing now – without having been empowered by the Holy Spirit, God's wonderful companion to all true believers in Christ.

We complete our brief introductory discussion of God by looking at the third person of the one true God, the Holy Spirit.

WALKING ON

Understanding who God is can be a bit confusing, even to Christians. Jews, Christians, and even Muslims adamantly affirm that there is only one God. Yet only Christians talk about God as Father, Son and Holy Spirit. Sometimes it can sound like Christians believe in three gods. Nothing could be further from the truth!

What has been called "the Trinity" simply means that there is one eternal, living God who exists in three persons: Father, Son and Holy Spirit. How can three be one or one, three? No one but God himself fully understands this, but should it surprise us that there is some mystery surrounding the nature of God? After all, if we could comprehend everything about God, that would make us God. That's a scary thought!

It is sufficient to say that the Scriptures reveal that the Father is God (see **Eph. 1:2,3** e.g.), the Son is God (see **Titus 2:13** e.g.) and the Holy Spirit is God (see **Acts 5:3,4** e.g.)… the same God. Whatever the Father thinks, feels or does, the Son and Spirit are in complete agreement. They are in complete unity of nature and harmony of purpose.

To prepare us to receive an important truth, we've designed a short exercise. Take a minute and think about how your response to challenging circumstances would change if you could literally see the Lord Jesus Christ walking next to you, as opposed to being on your own.

Record your thoughts below:

- Having to confront a boss or coworker for unethical behavior.

With Jesus _____

Without Jesus _____

- Experiencing the loss of a loved one.

With Jesus _____

Without Jesus _____

- Getting laid off from work.

With Jesus _____

Without Jesus _____

- Chronic or life-threatening illness.

With Jesus _____

Without Jesus _____

- Sharing your faith with a neighbor.

With Jesus _____

Without Jesus _____

You may be thinking at the moment, this is all well and good, but I don't happen to live in the first century and so I don't have the luxury of having Jesus walk around with me. True enough. We need to realize, however, that though the Lord Jesus Christ has ascended to the right hand of God the Father, believers in Christ are not alone here on earth.

Jesus, only hours before his betrayal, arrest and crucifixion spoke these comforting words:

I will talk to the Father, and he'll provide you another Friend so that you will always have someone with you. This Friend is the Spirit of Truth. The godless world can't take him in because it doesn't have eyes to see him, doesn't know what to look for. But you know him already because he has been staying with you, and will even be in you! I will not leave you orphaned. I'm coming back.

John 14:16-18 (MSG)

What an incredible promise!

Jesus loved his followers so much that though it was time for him to leave, he was asking the Father to make special provision for them. And it was going to happen!

The Father, at Jesus' request, was going to send a helper (sometimes translated as Friend, Comforter, Counselor or Advocate), one who was called alongside to help. The word "another" in the above Scripture means "another just like Me." Jesus was saying that the Spirit of truth or Holy Spirit would be just like him without the human body. Everything that was true of the heart of Jesus would also be true of the Spirit, with one additional advantage: the best Jesus could offer while in a human body was to be *with* his followers. The Holy Spirit would actually come to live *in* them!

It was really to our advantage that Jesus left and the Spirit came. As a man, Jesus could only be in one place at a time. If he went with Peter in one direction, he could not go with Paul in another. By sending the Holy Spirit, however, he could be "omnipresent" or everywhere, with every believer, all at once.

Get the picture?

Having Jesus literally walk with us through life would give us great supernatural courage, peace, security and comfort. Just knowing that he was right by our side in the midst of all our experiences would be great. But what if that same Christ, in the person of the Holy Spirit, were in you? The boldness, strength, serenity and encouragement you could tap into because of his inner Presence would allow you to live life at a whole new level..

Maybe you're not convinced that having the Spirit in you is better than having Jesus beside you.

Let's see what Jesus had to say on that issue:

So let me say it again, this truth: It's better for you that I leave. If I don't leave, the Friend won't come. But if I go, I'll send him to you.

John 16:7 (MSG)

Any sentimental longings we might have to walk with Jesus on the dusty roads of Galilee are misplaced. It is better to walk with the Holy Spirit in you now than it was to walk with Jesus next to you then! Wow!

With this awesome truth in mind, it would be to our advantage to get to know more about who this Holy Spirit (the One who dwells inside Christians) truly is. By the way, if your Bible happens to call him the "Holy Ghost", don't be afraid. In Old English the word "ghost" meant "spirit" in the sense of an invisible (but very alive) person.

One of the main ways that God reveals himself to us in the Bible is through his names.

So let's look at some of the names of the Spirit.

He is called the Holy Spirit (John 14:26)

What does it mean to be "holy"? The writer of Hebrews, speaking of the Lord Jesus, gives us a good description of holiness when he wrote:

> *He is the kind of high priest we need because he is holy and blameless, unstained by sin. He has now been set apart from sinners, and he has been given the highest place of honor in heaven.*
>
> Hebrews 7:26 (NLT)

Holiness means being separated from or "set apart" from sin and impurity. So, the Holy Spirit is completely pure, untainted by sin, incapable of even being tempted to sin. Therefore, the Holy Spirit will never lead us into temptation or any kind of sin. He prompts us and empowers us to live holy lives.

He is called the Spirit of truth (John 14:17)

Truth lies at the very core of the Spirit's character and nature. That should not surprise us because Jesus identified himself as being "the way, the truth and the life" *(John 14:6).* Since the Holy Spirit is the Spirit of truth, what he says will always be true. He is incapable of lying, deceiving or misleading. He will lead us into all truth as opposed to the devil who is a liar and deceiver. Since the Scriptures are truth *(John 17:17),* the Spirit of truth will never direct someone to act contrary to the Word of God.

He is called the Spirit of Christ (1 Peter 1:11)

This one is pretty self-explanatory. Basically this name assures us that what Jesus is, the Holy Spirit is also. They are identical in nature, because the essence of who or what a person is will be their *spirit.* The Spirit of Christ will reveal to us the wonderful person of the Lord Jesus Christ.

He is called the Spirit of grace (Hebrews 10:29)

Jesus came full of grace and truth (John 1:14). So has the Holy Spirit. We are accepted and acceptable to God because of an extravagantly generous and free gift of God *(grace),* not because of the good works we do or sins we do not do. The Holy Spirit yearns to broadcast that message loud and clear to every believer in Christ. In the heart of the Spirit of grace, there is absolutely no condemnation or accusation designed to make us feel like dirt. He will show us when we've sinned, but it is always with the longing that we again experience the forgiveness and cleansing purchased for us at the Cross.

He is called the Helper (John 14:16)

We sing, and rightfully so, "*What a Friend We Have in Jesus…***"** The same is true of the Holy Spirit. He is our friend and helper in many ways. He is our companion to walk with us (actually *in* us!) through every circumstance of life. He is our comforter to grant strength to our souls when we are weary, downcast or grieving. He is our counselor, giving the wisest, most relevant advice when we are confused or uncertain. He is our advocate, standing at our defense when the railing accusations of the devil seek to drown us in guilt or shame. He is our filler, the one who fills and empowers us with moral strength to stand against temptation and sin. and he fills us with boldness to speak about Jesus. He is our prayer-teacher who shows us what to pray for and how to pray according to the will of God.

There is much more that can be said of the wonderful Spirit of God but we'll reserve a full study of that to another book… *the Bible!*

Identity Reminder:

I am God's child.

Jn. 1:12

In the spaces below, write down the character qualities you appreciate about the Lord Jesus Christ. For each one, take a moment and thank God that the Holy Spirit is the same in nature as Jesus. And (if you are a true believer in Christ), thank God that this same Spirit is *in* you!

_____

_____

Truth Point

For his Holy Spirit speaks to us deep in our hearts and tells us that we are God's children.

Romans 8:16 (NLT)

Application

Look back over the brief discussions about the names of the Spirit and think about your life right now. How do you need the Holy Spirit to be "himself" to you… today?

Holy Spirit:

_____

Spirit of truth:

_____

Spirit of Christ:

_____

Spirit of grace:

_____

Helper:

_____

Dear heavenly Father, thank you for answering Jesus' request to send the Holy Spirit. I don't know where I'd be without him. Actually I do. I'd be nowhere. Thank you for giving such a faithful friend to me, the Holy Spirit. I want to get to know him better even as I realize he will always be pointing me to Jesus. I desire him to remove the obstacles that keep me from having his full release and full reign in my life. I need his strength to keep going on this journey to freedom. Thank you, Father, for giving me the strength that I need through the Holy Spirit. In Jesus' name I pray, amen.

DECLARATIONS

(For true believers in Christ)

- **It was better for Christ to leave so the Holy Spirit could live in me!**
- **The Holy Spirit, who is in me, is pure and holy!**
- **The Holy Spirit, who is in me, will lead me into all truth!**
- **The Holy Spirit, who is in me, is the Spirit of Christ!**
- **The Holy Spirit, who is in me, is full of grace and mercy!**
- **The Holy Spirit is my helper, friend, comforter, counselor, and advocate!**
- **I am not alone!**

Special note

It is possible that much of what we have looked at in these first five days has seemed foreign to you, or has gone in one ear and out the other. It is possible that all this talk of a relationship with God the Father, Son, and Holy Spirit sounds like a foreign language to you.

Maybe you've looked inside and you're not sure that the Holy Spirit or a holy anything is there!

First, let us commend you for hanging in there until now. Not everyone would do that. Second, let us encourage you to hang in there a little longer. We believe that the next two days may very well bring some things into focus for you, and could be two of the most important days of your life!

Getting to Know the God of Freedom

Sin, the Ultimate Enemy

I (Rich) asked my wife, Shirley, if she wanted to contribute today's personal story on the subject of sin. For some strange reason she declined the invitation. *I* could probably come up with one about her… but then again I value my marriage too much for that!

There are a million stories I could tell about myself. I know you could, too. Maybe you could come up with some real whoppers that would top my stories in a second. Or maybe you have lived a relatively clean life and would think that my episodes of drunkenness, carousing, swearing, rebellion, fascination with the occult, bitterness and so forth were pretty sick. Either way, we all sin and the root of sin is pride – hopping up on our little throne and being lord of our own little kingdom. So here's my sad tale about a time when I thought I had it all together and the Lord used a knock at the door to reveal the depths of my own self-righteousness. And, by the way, when it comes to things that turn God's stomach, self-righteousness is pretty high on the list.

Back in the early 1980s I became a rabid Keith Green fan. He was a popular Christian musical artist at that time. I would often take my very minimal singing ability and even paltrier piano-playing talent and hang out at our church late at night. I would bang away on the piano and sing with prophetic power, pretending I was performing before a large, and of course deeply moved, audience.

One night, very late… I heard a knock at the church door. A little unnerved I opened the door and found a vagrant looking for money. Frightened a little bit, I quickly told him to come back during normal business hours, shut and locked the door and went back to my virtual concert. The next song of Keith's that I started playing was about how people needed Christ and our help but we often turn them away.

I jumped from the piano bench and burst out the door, desperately looking for some sign of the man. Across the street from the church was a Christian school and so I raced frantically around the campus, hoping to catch up with him. I must have looked like a lunatic. I felt like a hypocrite. Deeply broken, I realized that my Christianity went about as deep as my musical talent and that I was really fervent in my faith – just so long as I didn't have to get close to people who made me feel uncomfortable. Sadly I never did find the guy.

And somehow I didn't have the heart to go back and finish the concert.

WALKING ON

This has been a full week... of getting to know the God of freedom. You may be tempted to take a few days off. Don't do that. These final two days are last but definitely not least!

In the first five days, we have prayed that you would catch a glimpse of God that would deeply satisfy you while also causing you to hunger and thirst for more of him. God is like that.

"O taste and see that the Lord is good;"

Psalm 34:8 (NIV)

God invites you and wants you to experience him on that kind of level – the level of the heart. And that's exactly the problem… our hearts. Today and tomorrow form a kind of "bad news, good news" scenario. As much as we might prefer not to, we've got to look at the bad news before the good news makes sense.

A person generally won't seek out a doctor unless he suspects he's sick. A lifeguard is largely ignored until swimmers find themselves caught in a rip tide. Most people don't even think about the fire department until the sirens wail alerting them to a fire somewhere. Human nature is such that we won't call out for help from God unless and until we see that we're in trouble. The Bible tells us the human race is in trouble. Big trouble.

It wasn't always the case for mankind. There was a time when things were not so bad; in fact, they couldn't have been better. Let's do a quick rewind of history and see how things started… and then how they went sour.

The first book of the Bible, Genesis, tells us that at first man's (and woman's!) needs were completely taken care of by God in a perfect environment.

- All their physical and emotional needs were met. The Garden of Eden was filled with every kind of fruit and vegetable they could want! It was all there for them to pick and eat. Meat wasn't part of their diet because there was no such thing as death. The climate was such (no cold, no rain) that houses and clothing weren't needed. Adam and Eve "were naked and not ashamed." There were no barriers in their relationship. It was totally open, honest and healthy. Talk about paradise! *(See **Gen. 1:29,39; 2:25**)*

- All their needs for meaningful work were met. God assigned them to be gardeners and "zookeepers" – taking care of the garden and overseeing the animal kingdom. Can you imagine in the morning planting and pruning a garden that never had weeds and in the afternoon playing with your pet lions, tigers and bears – and living to tell about it? *(See **Gen. 2:15; 1:28**)*

- All their spiritual needs were met through an intimate friendship with God. He spoke to them and blessed them. *(See **Gen. 2:15-17; 1:28**)*

Adam and Eve were fully human and had many of the same needs as we have now. The difference is that their perfect union with God, each other and their world perfectly met all those needs. But the presence of needs made them susceptible to temptation. Since their "flesh" had not yet been trained to look in the wrong places for satisfaction, Satan had to come along with his sinister suggestions to spark the fires of temptation.

Before we see how things fell apart, take a quick inventory of your life in terms of how your needs are currently being (or not being) met.

Rate yourself from Low to High, 1 2 3 4 5 regarding how well these needs are currently being met, and circle your answer.

Physical needs (clean air, water, healthy food, shelter, clothing)

1   2   3   4   5

Emotional needs (open, honest, clean, satisfying relationships with family & friends)

1   2   3   4   5

Fulfillment-related needs (meaningful, challenging, consistent work)

1   2   3   4   5

Spiritual needs (intimate, joyful, worshipful relationship with God individually and in church)

1   2   3   4   5

Moral needs (consistent victory over temptation and sin - a fresh capacity to love others)

1   2   3   4   5

How'd you do?

The fact is that none of us lives perfect lives with perfect relationships in perfect happiness. To be perfectly honest, life on this planet can be pretty messed up.

Amazingly, Adam and Eve would have scored a perfect 5 on all counts. Until… Sin.

The S Word!!!

Sin is not a four-letter word, but it should be. You can check out the whole story in Genesis 3, but here's a summary of what happened when sin stepped in.

- God told Adam and Eve that one tree and its fruit were off limits. It was in the center of the Garden of Eden and was called the tree of the knowledge of good and evil. To eat of it meant that man and woman had determined that they didn't really need God to be the determiner of right and wrong; they could do that very nicely themselves, thank you. God told Adam that they would die on the very day that they ate from that tree.

- The devil, speaking through a snake, told them they were missing out on the ultimate party by not trying that fruit. It was pretty and delicious (or so Eve thought) plus it would make them wise just like God (or so the devil lied).

- Adam and Eve focused on the "benefits" of eating the fruit and forgot the consequences. So Eve took the bait and so did Adam and the trap was sprung and they were hooked.

The party was over. Sin always does that. Sin is the ultimate enemy, the ultimate party pooper.

But what is sin? Sin is buying Satan's lie that we can be our own god and this results in acts of independence from God (called sins) that deeply offend him and hurt us and usually others too.

In Adam and Eve's case, sin resulted in death, just like God had warned:

But the Lord God gave him this warning: "You may freely eat any fruit in the garden [Can you see God's big, generous, life-loving heart?] ***except fruit from the tree of the knowledge of good and evil. If you eat of its fruit, you will surely die.*** [Can you likewise see God's caring, protective heart?]

Genesis 2:16-17 (NLT)

[bracketed comments ours]

"Wait a minute," you may be protesting! I read my Bible enough to know that Adam and Eve didn't drop dead after they ate the fruit. They lived a long time after that. True enough. They didn't die *physically* that day. That came later, though the process began that day. In light of the fact that "death" means a "*separation from*" we will see how they did die in other ways:

- They died spiritually. They lost their intimate union with God and so hid from him in fear and guilt. *(Gen. 3:8)*

- They died personally. They lost their self-respect and dignity. They were now naked and ashamed, as shown by their lame attempts to make fig-leaf underwear. *(Gen. 3:7)*

- They died relationally. They played the blame game with each other and their perfect, open, honest relationship was shattered. *(Gen. 3:11-13)*

The sin of Adam and Eve caused a negative chain of events that continues in the daily flood of evil in the world. The Bible is peppered with descriptions of sin that read like today's newspaper. You can check out a few of them in *Galatians 5:19-21* and *Romans 1:18-32* for starters.

Our environment is not the primary cause of sin, by the way, but – as we indicated earlier in today's devotion– the problem is with our hearts.

He [Jesus] went on: "It's what comes out of a person that pollutes: obscenities, lusts, thefts, murders, adulteries, greed, depravity, deceptive dealings, carousing, mean looks, slander, arrogance, foolishness – all these vomit from the heart. There is the source of your pollution."

Mark 7:20-23 (MSG)

The apostle Paul was equally clear in his announcement that matters of the heart would get worse, not better, as time passed.

Don't be naïve. There are difficult times ahead. As the end approaches, people are going to be self-absorbed, money-hungry, self-promoting, stuck-up, profane, contemptuous of parents, crude, coarse, dog-eat-dog, unbending, slanderers, impulsively wild, savage, cynical, treacherous, ruthless, bloated windbags, addicted to lust, and allergic to God. They'll make a show of religion, but behind the scenes they're animals.

2 Timothy 3:1-5 (MSG)

Feel like somebody has been reading your mail? We warned you. The bad news had to come first. And here's the clincher: Apart from Christ, we're all in the same boat...and it's the Titanic!!!

WINDING DOWN

One of the primary building blocks of Freedom in Christ Ministries is understanding who we are in Christ. We will talk about that next week. But we can't fully appreciate who we are in Christ without realizing who we *were* apart from Christ. Here's just a sampling:

Our hearts were deceitful and desperately wicked	Jeremiah 17:9
Our hearts were like stone – cold and hard	Ezekiel 36:26
Our minds were set on what our sin nature wanted	Romans 8:5; Ephesians 2:3
Our minds were death, locking us into an existence separated from God	Rom. 8:6; Eph. 2:12; Colossians 1:21

Our minds were blinded by Satan; we were unable to see the truth of the gospel	2 Corinthians 4:4; Eph. 2:2
Our minds were hostile to God	Rom. 8:7
We were enemies of God	Rom. 5:10; Col. 1:21
Our minds were rebellious – unwilling and unable to submit to God	Rom. 8:7
We were unable to please God	Rom. 8:8
We were slaves to sin	Rom. 6:20,21
We were captive slaves of Satan	2 Timothy 2:26
We used to follow the sinful ways of this world	Eph. 2:2
We were spiritually dead in our sins	Eph. 2:1
We were separated from God	Isaiah 59:1,2; Eph. 2:12
We were under God's wrath and without hope	Eph. 2:3; John 3:36; Eph. 2:12

Truth Point

For all have sinned; all fall short of God's glorious standard.

Romans 3:23 (NLT)

For the wages of sin is death, but the free gift of God is eternal life through Christ Jesus our Lord.

Romans 6:23 (NLT)

All means all!

We're all *(apart from Christ)* born and raised sinners with only one destiny. Death! The ultimate meaning of death is separation from God on earth and separation from God for all eternity. Hell *(eternal separation from God)* is what the Bible often refers to as "the second death," and is the place of God's judgment where all who reject Christ will go. No exceptions.

If you are working through today's devotion and you are absolutely certain that you know Jesus, and you have experienced his cleansing blood for your sins, just take a few minutes to thank God for his forgiveness.

For those who are not so sure of God's forgiveness of sin in your lives, coming to the realization that you are spiritually sick and dying and in need of the Doctor is a very good thing.

Application

Take a few moments and acknowledge to God that you have indeed committed the sins that you are remembering right now. Perhaps while you were reading the Scriptures today, some things started coming to mind. If so, don't blame others. Don't excuse yourself. Just agree with the Holy Spirit who brought them to your mind. Simply say, *God, you're right and I'm wrong.* List any sins that God is bringing to your mind right now.

—————————————————————

—————————————————————

—————————————————————

—————————————————————

—————————————————————

Take as much time as you need to face whatever he shows you…

Don't run from the Light. The Light heals!!!

PRAYER

Lord, you <u>are</u> right. I <u>was</u> wrong for doing/saying/believing (Confess the sins listed above: _____ _____) Thank you for dying on the cross so I could be forgiven. Show me the way to Christ so that I can live my life in your forgiveness, free from sin's stranglehold in my life. Amen.

DECLARATIONS

- **Sin is buying Satan's lie that we can be our own god!**

- **Sin IS the ultimate enemy!**

- **Because of sin, the life God had originally planned for me fell apart!**

- **Sin kills life spiritually, personally and relationally!**

- **Sin deeply offends God and ultimately hurts others and us!**

- **Apart from Christ, there is no hope, only eternal separation from God!**

- **God sent a rescue Vessel to save me; his name is JESUS!**

- **Because Jesus lives I can have a wonderful future!**

Identity Reminder:

I am Christ's friend.

Jn. 15:15

Getting to Know the God of Freedom

New Beginnings!

I (Rich) did not grow up in a Christian or even religious home. Like the old cliché, however, I was a regular church attender. I went twice a year... Christmas and Easter! I grew to doubt the existence of God and considered science to be the way, the truth and the life. I was a staunch evolutionist who viewed the "myths and fables" of the Bible with contempt.

No wonder my recently-converted brother had a tough time getting up the gumption to tell me the good news of the gospel when I was 18 years old! But he did. Once he finished, God embarked on a six-month relentless process of showing me what a mess I'd made of my life. I fought back with all my "intellectual" questions, but there was one thing I could not deny: the presence of a quality of life in my brother, his friends, and other Christians that I could not explain away. It was the presence of God's love.

On Christmas Eve during my freshman year in college, I was at home. The house seemed empty to me. My brother was off somewhere, Dad was probably wrapping presents in a back bedroom and Mom was most likely in the kitchen preparing for the next day's feast. I wandered around the house trying to figure out what to do and I found a book of Christmas carols. In one of them were the words, "To save us all from Satan's power when we were gone astray. O tidings of comfort and joy..."

Suddenly my mind was working at warp speed. I started thinking about how commercialized Christmas had become and how we'd lost the simplicity of just celebrating Jesus' birth. This thought process scared me to death. I thought, What in the world is happening to me? I sound like my brother! I went back to my room and was overwhelmed by the conviction of God's Spirit, showing me my need for that Jesus.

Before I knew what was going on I found myself being swept into God's presence, crying out to him to come into my life, change me and give me the kind of love my brother had.

And he did.

I went running around the house like a maniac, so joyful and excited that this thousand pound weight of guilt had been pulled off my shoulders.

O tidings of comfort and joy!

Identity Reminder:

I have been justified.

Rom 5:1

WALKING ON

Are *you* ready for some good news? Good! So was a lady that Jesus met one day after he had been walking all morning in the hot sun. Jesus was headed north toward his home country of Galilee and he stopped at a well to rest. His followers took off to a nearby town to pick up some Big Mac's®… Jesus was left all alone to talk to this lonely woman who had come to the same well to get some water. Jesus asked her for a drink. She was a Samaritan woman and was shocked that Jesus even talked to her since that was a cultural no-no for a Jewish man like Jesus to do in that day and age. She asked Jesus why in the world he was even speaking with her.

Let's pick up the story starting in John, chapter 4:

Jesus answered, "If you knew the generosity of God and who I am, you would be asking me for a drink, and I would give you fresh, living water." The woman said, "Sir, you don't even have a bucket to draw with, and this well is deep. So how are you going to get this living water?" … Jesus said, "Everyone who drinks this water will get thirsty again and again. Anyone who drinks the water I give will never thirst – not ever. The water I give will be an artesian spring within, gushing fountains of endless life."

John 4:10-14 (MSG)

You've probably figured out by now that Jesus was on a different wavelength than this woman. She wanted bottled water instead of the dirty stuff she usually pulled out of the well; but Jesus wanted to give her living water (forgiveness and eternal life). But whatever Jesus had, she definitely wanted!

The woman said, "Sir, give me this water so I won't ever get thirsty, won't ever have to come back to this well again!" He said, "Go call your husband and then come back." "I have no husband," she said. "That's nicely put: 'I have no husband.' You've had five husbands, and the man you're living with now isn't even your husband. You spoke the truth there, sure enough." [The woman replied] "Oh, so you're a prophet! Well, tell me this: Our ancestors worshiped God at this mountain, but you Jews insist that Jerusalem is the only place for worship, right?"

John 4:15-20 (MSG)

Whoa! How in the world did this conversation go from water to husbands to where you should worship… all in less than a minute? First, Jesus was making his move toward her soul. Remember that a sick person won't go to a doctor unless he or she suspects illness? Well, Jesus is the Doctor and the woman was unaware that she was very soul-sick. Jesus was helping her see that she had a need by reminding her of her search for love in all the wrong places. Second, the woman responded the way a lot of us might when the heat is on. She asked a religious question to change the subject. She asked the Samaritan version of *"Okay, if you're so smart, what church am I supposed to go to?"* It is human nature to think that we can wipe the stain of our sin away by *doing something religious.*

In the following exercise, check any of the "good works" listed below that you have believed would earn you "Brownie points" with God.

Good works

☐ Going to church	☐ Reading the Bible	☐ Fasting
☐ Going to church a lot	☐ Helping the poor	☐ Giving up some bad habit or questionable behavior for a period of time
☐ Praying	☐ Getting baptized	
☐ Giving to the church	☐ Going to the church altar (maybe many times!)	
☐ Giving to the church a lot		☐ Helping old ladies across the street

☐ Being a "good, moral" person

☐ Not being as bad as some people

☐ Being a patriotic person

A lot of people think that it only takes enough *(How many?)* good works in order to stack the spiritual deck in their favor to buy a one-way ticket into heaven. They believe that God has some sort of scales in heaven to weigh deeds and sins; if the good deeds "weigh more" than the sins, they'll get in. **Wrong!**

The Bible sheds light on that deadly misunderstanding:

> *For by grace you have been saved through faith; and that not of yourselves, it is the gift of God; not as a result of works, that no one should boast.*
>
> *Ephesians 2:8,9 (NASB)*

Grace is a gift that is undeserved. It can't be bought or earned. You see, no amount of good works that you do for God will cleanse you of your sin and bring you eternal life. The "weight" of our sin is too great, so to speak. In fact, *James 2:10* tells us that even if we kept every part of God's law and just messed up once *(and we have all messed up too many times to count!)*, we would be as guilty as if we went out and deliberately broke every commandment.

Not convinced that you're guilty of sin? Have you ever lied? *(Be careful you don't lie when you answer!)* Of course you have. The prosecution rests.

So if our being saved from the horrible penalty of our sin (spiritual separation from God now and forever) isn't based on our good deeds, what is it based on?

You are saved by a free gift from God, believing that Jesus died for YOUR sins and rose from the dead to give YOU life, and by faith trusting him alone to save YOU.

Now back to the story…

Jesus explained to the woman that it is not the place where your body is located when you worship that matters. It is Who you worship and the condition of your heart that really matters. Let's pick up the conversation again…

The woman said, "I know the Messiah will come—the one who is called Christ. When he comes, he will explain everything to us." Then Jesus told her, "I am the Messiah!"

John 4:25,26 (NLT)

And she believed.

She got so excited that she left her water pot and ran back to town. She told everybody everything that Jesus had said and the whole town came out to see! And Jesus was excited, too, because he knew many Samaritans were going to be forgiven, just like the woman. Listen to the excitement in Jesus' voice:

> *As you look around right now, wouldn't you say that in about four months it will be time to harvest? Well, I'm telling you to open your eyes and take a good look at what's right in front of you. These Samaritan fields are ripe. It's harvest time!*
>
> *John 4:35 (MSG)*

The main theme of today's lesson has been to help those outside of Christ see how to get in. But many who are already "in Christ" live life unsure of how forgiven they really are. Guilt remains an unwelcome companion that dogs their steps as they try and grow in Christ. If you consider yourself a Christian, circle the statement(s) that best describes how you feel about your life at the moment:

- I hope that God will let me into heaven one day.

- When I am doing good, I know I'm forgiven, but when I sin a lot I wonder…

- I'm certain that all the sins I committed before I became a Christian are forgiven, but I'm not as sure about the ones since…

- I need to confess my sins in order to be forgiven.

- I have sinned in certain ways so many times, I know God is fed up with me.

- I have no doubt that every one of my sins – past, present and future – has been totally forgiven by Christ.

- My being forgiven and going to heaven is dependent upon how much I keep away from sin.

Some of the most beautiful pictures in Scripture are painted with the colors of God's forgiveness of his people. Here's a sampler:

"Come now, let us reason together," says the LORD. "Though your sins are like scarlet, they shall be as white as snow; though they are red like crimson, they shall be like wool."

Isaiah 1:18,19 (NIV)

You will once again have mercy on us; you will conquer our evil deeds; you will throw our sins into the depths of the sea.

Micah 7:19 (NET)

For as high as the heavens are above the earth, so great is His lovingkindness toward those who fear Him. As far as the east is from the west, so far has He removed our transgressions from us.

Psalm 103:11,12 (NASB)

I'll forever wipe the slate clean of their sins.

Hebrews 10:17 (MSG)

It is as though the Lord were exhausting human language in his effort to make clear the depth, totality and finality of forgiveness! *Ephesians 1:7* echoes the above verses by proclaiming that in Christ we have redemption through Christ's blood, which is the forgiveness of our sins. Notice the verse says "have," not "will have." In other words, forgiveness is a done deal! How many sins are forgiven? *Colossians 2:13* removes any and all doubt by saying, *"He made you alive together with him, having forgiven us all our transgressions."*

All means all. Every sin of a true believer in Christ has been washed away through the blood of Jesus!

So what about *1 John 1:9* and the role of confession? Since *1 John* was written that we might have fellowship with God and other believers *(1 John 1:3)*, not that we might be saved, confession becomes a means of experiencing fellowship. When believers clam up about their sins or deny their reality, the cleansing and intimacy of fellowship with Jesus and other Christians is blocked. The relationship remains but the blessing of it is not experienced. Confession of sin (admitting we did it) cleanses our souls and opens up the way to honest, real communion with God and community with other believers.

WINDING DOWN

There is a great feast that has been planned by God, an ultimate bash, a celebration of the harvest and you and I are invited! God Almighty has requested that you and I join him in a time of rejoicing over all who have been forgiven! There will be many Samaritans at that banquet table.

How about you? Will you be there?

Jesus told us in *Luke 15:7,* in heaven they are so excited for this big day; that they throw a warm-up party every time anyone is forgiven!

Have you been forgiven?

Jesus said, "I am the Bread of Life. The person who aligns with me hungers no more and thirsts no more, ever.

John 6:35 (MSG)

We'd love for you to join us at that great wedding feast with Jesus in heaven one day, but that decision is yours to make, not ours. We can lay out the truth as God tells us in his Word. We can pray for you. We can urge you to come to Jesus. But the first step is yours.

Waiting for "just the right time"?

There's no time like the present. If you sense God speaking to you, drawing you to himself, then *now* is "just the right time." The Bible urges… and warns us… not to wait.

Therefore, just as the Holy Spirit says, "Today, if you hear his voice, do not harden your hearts…"

Hebrews 3:7 (NASB)

As God's partners, we beg you not to reject this marvelous message of God's great kindness. For God says, "At just the right time, I heard you. On the day of salvation, I helped you." Indeed, God is ready to help you right now. Today is the day of salvation.

2 Cor. 6:1-2 (NLT)

God wants to make some exchanges with you - how about it?

- Darkness to light.

- Bondage to freedom.

- Sin stains to forgiveness.

- Separation from God to union with God.

- Death to new life.

The choice is yours.

If you want this good news to become real to you, it must be received by faith – trusting God that what he says is true. Though prayer is not what saves you, praying a prayer of faith to God is a great way to open your heart to Jesus. We'll give you an opportunity to express your desires to God in prayer in just a moment.

Truth Point

And now you also have heard the truth, the Good News that God saves you. And when you believed in Christ, he identified you as his own by giving you the Holy Spirit, whom he promised long ago.

Ephesians 1:13 (NLT)

Application

Tell God exactly what you are thinking and feeling right now concerning your relationship (or lack of relationship) with him.

_____

_____

_____

_____

_____

_____

Dear heavenly Father, you have done it all for me, haven't you? You loved me even while I was breaking your laws and sinning against you. You sent Jesus to die for my sins even while I was your enemy. You raised Jesus from the dead to show that he is the way to you and to open the way for me to have new life. I want it. I want Jesus. More than anything I've ever needed, I need him to forgive me and give me life. Jesus, I receive you into my dark, sinful heart. Please give me a new, clean heart and give me your eternal life even now. Thank you for doing that for me. I believe. And now, Father, in this new relationship with you as your child, guide me through this upcoming journey of freedom so that I can begin to walk with you all the days of my life. Through the incredible, saving name of Jesus I pray, amen.

DECLARATIONS

- **By grace alone I can be saved through faith!**

- **I could never earn my way into heaven!**

- **Good works or "brownie points" cannot buy me eternal life!**

- **Salvation is a free gift from God and not a result of work on my part!**

- **In Jesus Christ all sins are deeply, totally and forever forgiven!**

Who In the World Am I?

Who In The World Am I?

Reflections on our Identity

WARMING UP

I (Rich) was pretty miserable from about age 11 through 15. Just thinking about those years makes me curl up in the fetal position. In fact, if someone came to my front door and offered me one of those gigantic sweepstakes checks for a million dollars on the condition I had to go back and live out those "middle school" years again, I'd say, "Keep your money!" In one year I went from about 5'6" and 120 lb. to 6'2"… and 120 lb. I wasn't skinny, I was skeletal. World War III broke out on my face, I got braces, and to be perfectly honest, about every commercial product on TV, I could use!

Because of my gangly, pimply, clumsy appearance and behavior, I got picked on a lot. Not fun. Rejection was what I was "fed" in school and for "dessert" I had hours of anger and self-loathing at home. What I saw in the mirror made me sick and caused me to wonder if there was any hope for change. And the attitudes about myself spawned during the painful circumstances of life in those critical, identity-forming years have taken a lot of time and the grace of God to heal.

How about you? Look at the words below and circle the ones that you'd use to describe yourself during your pre-adult years.

- ☐ confident
- ☐ mean
- ☐ awkward
- ☐ angry
- ☐ insecure
- ☐ partier
- ☐ active
- ☐ talented
- ☐ happy
- ☐ nervous
- ☐ athletic
- ☐ well-liked
- ☐ moody
- ☐ moral
- ☐ respected
- ☐ confused
- ☐ despairing
- ☐ spiritual
- ☐ sinful
- ☐ smart

When we think about our identity – who in the world we are – we have a variety of mirrors that we can choose to look into. We can look at TV or in magazines and see whether we are in vogue. We can compare ourselves to the people around us. We can judge ourselves in relation to our parents or siblings or people at church or at the fitness center or school or at work or… you get the picture. Every one of those "mirrors" can be very convincing. In the exercise below, rate yourself on a one to ten scale (low level of "success" to high level of "success") based on each of the "mirrors" mentioned:

The Money Mirror (Do you have plenty of money left at the end of the month or do you always seem to have too much month left at the end of the money?)

1   2   3   4   5   6   7   8   9   10

The Stuff Mirror (Are you struggling to "keep up with the Joneses" or are the Joneses struggling to keep up with you?)

1   2   3   4   5   6   7   8   9   10

The Popularity Mirror (Is your phone ringing off the hook from friends or is a call from a telemarketer a welcome event?)

1   2   3   4   5   6   7   8   9   10

The Health & Beauty Mirror (Mirror, mirror on the wall, who's the fairest…?)

1   2   3   4   5   6   7   8   9   10

The Success Mirror (Can you see the top of the ladder from where you are or are you still trying to find the ladder?)

1   2   3   4   5   6   7   8   9   10

Every one of us has an opinion about ourselves that has been formed as a result of information we received from good, bad and ugly sources. These sources act like mirrors that reflect back to us an image of ourselves that may or may not accurately represent the real you and me.

Have you ever been to a "fun house" at a circus or carnival? If so, you probably remember laughing at yourself as you looked into all those distorted mirrors. One mirror made you look like a string bean, another like a pear, another like a pumpkin, and so on. Finally, when you got to the end the last mirror confirmed your true appearance… a nut! Just kidding.

A fun house is a fun house because you know the distorted mirrors are just that… distorted. They don't represent reality. They can't trick you and aren't even designed to do so. But discerning a distorted image on the inside of us is not so easy.

The funny thing about life is that you may score yourself really high on these "mirrors" in the shaded box but still not be happy. The reverse could be true also. You may have scored low in these five areas but find yourself living with a high level of inner joy.

Are you simply a product of how much money you make or don't make, how much stuff you have or don't have, the opinions of other people, how good looking or successful you are in the eyes of the world? Or is there something more?

There's one more mirror that you need to take a look in today. It's the mirror of God's word. Like the last mirror in the fun house that shows you who you really are on the outside, God's word shows you who you really are on the inside… *the real you.*

If you are a true believer in Christ, the following Scripture is for you!

"I will dwell in them and walk among them; and I will be their God, and they shall be My people. Therefore, come out from their midst and be separate," says the Lord, "and do not touch what is unclean; and I will welcome you. And I will be a father to you, and you shall be sons and daughters to Me," says the Lord Almighty.

2 Corinthians 6:16-18 (NASB)

According to the above Scripture, who are you? _____

And who does God say he will be to us? _____

Our true identity as believers in Jesus is all wrapped up in our relationship with God. By the way, Jesus himself would have scored very low on most of those five mirrors listed above, yet he was totally secure in who he was as God's Son.

Jesus had no money. When he wanted to use a coin to teach about paying taxes, he had to borrow one *(Luke 20:24)*. As for possessions, he had no house *(Luke 9:58)* and all he owned were the clothes on his back that were taken by the Roman soldiers at his crucifixion. True, he was very popular for a while, but eventually the crowds turned against him and most of his disciples deserted him. He died with just a scant gathering of family and friends by his side. His health was likely good, but he would never have made the cover of *Jerusalem Quarterly* magazine. Isaiah predicted of Christ that

He has no stately form or majesty that we should look upon Him, nor appearance that we should be attracted to Him.

Isaiah 53:2 (NASB)

And as far as worldly success was concerned… he was a carpenter turned itinerant preacher with no formal education, no degrees, and no professional awards. He did the work of the humblest servant and died a despised criminal's death.

The ways of God are very different, in fact supremely higher than the ways of man in this world **(Isaiah 55:8,9).** You can try and find a secure, satisfying identity in the five distorted mirrors mentioned earlier, and you will fail. Or you can pursue God and truly find yourself, who you *really* are in this world in him. Take it from God himself:

Truth Point

Thus says the LORD, "Let not a wise man boast of his wisdom, and let not the mighty man boast of his might, let not a rich man boast of his riches; but let him who boasts boast of this, that he understands and knows Me, that I am the LORD who exercises loving kindness, justice, and righteousness on earth; for I delight in these things," declares the LORD.

Jeremiah 9:23,24 (NASB)

Application

Many times we fall into the trap of believing that those mirrors listed earlier in this devotion are the key to who we are and the secret to happiness. Have you believed any of these distorted mirrors? Check any boxes that reflect your beliefs:

☐   Great body + admiration from others = a person to be envied.

☐   Accomplishments + awards + praise from people = a person truly valuable to society.

☐   Money + power + position + popularity = a life worth striving for.

Identity Reminder:

I am united with the Lord (one spirit).

Jn. 1:12

Father God, I trust you as my Creator to open my eyes to see your true and clear image of myself. I welcome you to help me not only see the truth but also receive it deep into my heart. Enable me to make your view of me my view of me. Give me courage to let go of all false opinions I have had of myself so that I can experience your freedom. Draw me into your heart in the days ahead. In Jesus' name I pray, amen.

- **My personal worth does not come from money, power or achievements in life!**
- **My value as a person is NOT DETERMINED by other people's opinions of me!**

Identity Reminder:

I am bought with a price; I
belong to God.

1 Cor. 6:19-20

Who In The World Am I?

The Door's Open to Home

Yesterday we opened the door a bit to my (Rich's) past dealings with *rejection*. Rejection and its offspring, *isolation*, are friends to no one and can be agonizing when there is no place for God in the picture. I was rejected by my peers, and rejected by the one that stared back at me in the mirror. And I had rejected the One who held all the solutions to my pain in his hands.

God has uniquely beautiful and powerful ways of revealing his love to us. One day he gave me a picture that revolutionized my life. The scene begins with a house reminiscent of a Thomas Kinkade painting.. It is dusk at Thanksgiving and there is a joyful, noisy, family reunion going on inside. Light pours out through the windows. Cheerful music and inviting cooking aromas waft out of the open front door. The father of the family is at the door, welcoming relatives in with hugs and warm greetings. When a new family member enters the house, everyone inside stops what they're doing to greet the new arrival with a heaping plate of food, then includes him or her into their games and conversations.

People walking down the street either stop to gaze with curiosity or longing, while others retreat into their overcoats, lower their heads and hasten to pass by. There are a few little boys with their runny noses and grimy hands pressed against the outside of the large living room window, fogging up the window and smearing it with their muddy fingers. They envy those on the inside.

The father turns and smiles at them.

As I was thinking of this picture, one of the little boys left the window and walked slowly to the front door. He had been reluctant to come in because he didn't feel worthy, didn't feel like anybody really wanted him. But as he approached the door, the father scooped him up, kissed him and cleaned him up. Before the boy knew what had happened, he was ushered inside and welcomed into the family as warmly as the rest.

That day, with healing power, the Father revealed that the little boy was me.

Where would you put yourself in that painting?

Would you be on the inside or on the outside? Would you be wrapped up in the Father's arms or hurrying down the street? That's definitely food for thought. Below we have listed some descriptive words. Put an "x" by the ones that best depict how you currently perceive God the Father's attitude toward you. Be honest! Then put a "check mark" by the ones you wish were true.

- ☐ uninterested
- ☐ angry
- ☐ excited to see me
- ☐ ignoring
- ☐ warm

- ☐ annoyed
- ☐ smiling
- ☐ frowning
- ☐ pursuing
- ☐ proud

- ☐ delighted
- ☐ fed up
- ☐ cold
- ☐ withdrawing
- ☐ embarrassed

- ☐ tolerant
- ☐ welcoming
- ☐ accepting
- ☐ shaking his head
- ☐ impatient

WALKING ON

What if your Father in heaven is really like that father in the story above? What if he actually is warm, caring, loving and welcoming and that he accepts you… just as you are? What if all your perceptions of a God who is annoyed, irritated, impatient or angry with you are wrong? What if your sense that God is barely tolerating you or that he has already dismissed you as not worth his time, attention, energy or help is 180 degrees off from the way he really is?

We've got great news for you. God is actually warm, caring, loving and welcoming. he accepts you just as you are. He is not annoyed, irritated, impatient or angry with you. In fact, he delights in you. That's amazing news, incredible news. Maybe unbelievable news for you as you think about how sinful your life has been… or maybe is right now.

Let's take a look at what it took for the Father to welcome you as his forgiven, clean, loved, accepted child…

First, the stain of sin had to be removed.

It cost God plenty to get you out of that dead-end, empty-headed life you grew up in. He paid with Christ's sacred blood, you know. He died like an unblemished, sacrificial lamb.

1 Peter 1:18,19 (MSG)

"Come now, let us reason together," says the LORD. "Though your sins are like scarlet, they shall be as white as snow; though they are red as crimson, they shall be like wool."

Isaiah 1:18 (NIV)

When you trusted in the Lord Jesus Christ as your Savior and accepted his blood sacrifice on the cross as full payment for your sins, those Scriptures listed above instantly became true for you! All your sins – past, present and future – were stricken from the record!

In Christ, you are clean	*(John 15:3)*
In Christ, you are forgiven	*(Eph.1:7; Col. 1:13,14; 2:13,14)*

Second, you had to be made righteous and holy.

He made Him who knew no sin to be sin on our behalf, that we might become the righteousness of God in Him.

2 Corinthians 5:21 (NASB)

Paul, called as an apostle of Jesus Christ by the will of God, and Sosthenes our brother, to the church of God which is at Corinth, to those who have been sanctified in Christ Jesus, saints by calling, with all who in every place call upon the name of our Lord Jesus Christ, their Lord and ours:

1 Corinthians 1:2 (NASB)

Because you are *in Christ* (placed in him at the moment of salvation – see 1 *Cor. 12:13*), you have been made righteous, holy, and a saint (a holy one)! Not *will be* but *are*. Not *in heaven*, but *in Christ* — *now!* So the next time you wear a name tag, pull it out and put an St. (for "saint") in front of your name.

In Christ, you are righteous	(1 Peter 3:12)
In Christ, you are holy	(Heb. 10:10)
In Christ, you are a saint	(Eph. 1:1; 6:18)

Third, the Father welcomed you into his family as an undeserved gift and act of kindness.

Saving is all his idea, and all his work. All we do is trust him enough to let him

do it. It's God's gift from start to finish! We don't play the major role. If we did,

we'd probably go around bragging that we'd done the whole thing! No, we

neither make nor save ourselves.

Ephesians 2:8,9 (MSG)

He chose us in Him before the foundation of the world, that we should be holy

and blameless before Him. In love He predestined us to adoption as sons through

Jesus Christ to Himself, according to the kind intention of His will to the praise

of the glory of His grace which He freely bestowed on us in the Beloved.

Ephesians 1:4-6 (NASB)

How great is the love the Father has lavished on us, that we should be called children of God! And that is what we are!

1 John 3:1 (NIV)

Welcome to the family of God! The Father is standing at the door, welcoming you in!! He has accepted you and loves you as much as he loves the Lord Jesus Christ (*John 15:9; 17:23*). There is nothing that you can do today to "buy" God's love or cause it to increase – because it is a free gift and already perfect! There is nothing you can do that will cause God's love to waver or decrease, because God is love (*1 John 4:8*) and God does not change (*James 1:17; Malachi 3:6*).

In Christ you are saved	(Titus 3:5)
In Christ you are chosen	(Col. 3:12)
In Christ you are at peace with God	(Romans 5:1)
In Christ you are accepted	(John 6:37)
In Christ you have received God's lavish grace	(Rom 5:2; Titus 3:6,7)
In Christ you have been adopted into his family	(Rom. 8:15)
In Christ you are a child of God	(Rom. 8:16,17; John 1:12)

WINDING DOWN

WRAPPING UP

Clean. Forgiven. Righteous. Holy. A saint. Saved. Chosen. At peace with God. Accepted. Recipient of God's lavish grace. Adopted into his family. Embraced as God's child. That is who you are in Christ. No strings attached, no small print, no escape clause. It's a done deal for all who have turned to Christ alone to save them. Bottom line: If you are born again by the Spirit, that means *you!* In the space below, tell God what is on your heart right now, in light of the truths from this lesson.

Knowing who you are *in Christ* brings healing. Perhaps you have experienced rejection from an even more painful source than peers. Maybe you have been rejected – either overtly or covertly – by your parents. If so, let God be the Parent you have been longing for. We don't know exactly *how* King David experienced rejection from his parents, but we know he did. We also know where he found the antidote to that pain:

Truth Point

For my father and my mother have forsaken me, but the LORD will take me up. Teach me Thy way, O LORD, and lead me in a level path, because of my foes. Do not deliver me over to the desire of my adversaries; for false witnesses have risen against me, and such as breathe out violence. I would have despaired unless I had believed that I would see the goodness of the LORD in the land of the living. Wait for the LORD; be strong, and let your heart take courage; yes, wait for the LORD.

Psalm 27:10-14 (NASB)

Application

Do you truly see yourself as you are *in Christ* or are you experiencing a crisis of belief concerning your true identity? On each of the spectrums in the following box, put an "x" at the point between each column that best describes how you currently perceive yourself.

Totally forgiven	Guilty for sin
Completely clean in God's eyes	Dirty and evil
Really righteous	I can't do anything good and right
Holy	Still living under sin's control
A saint	A sinner
Saved	Unsure of my salvation
Chosen by God	Ignored or barely tolerated by God
At peace with God	Feeling like God is mad at me
Accepted by God	Trying to gain God's acceptance
Lavished with God's grace	Driven by religious rules
Adopted by God	A fearful slave of God
God's child	Feeling like a spiritual outsider

[Suggestion: For any areas above where you are placed yourself toward the right-hand column, go back and study the Scriptures in this day's devotional on that topic. Ask God to take the truth and begin to set you free in that area.]

PRAYER

Dear heavenly Father, I can tell that my view of you is still diluted and polluted by lots of junk in my mind and from my past. I can see what your word says about you and about me and yet I can hear another voice whisper, "Yeah, but…" I believe; help my unbelief. Set me free to embrace who you are and who I am in you, not only with a learning mind but with a yearning heart. In Jesus' name I pray, amen.

DECLARATIONS

• **By faith, regardless of my feelings, I declare the truth that because I am in Christ I am NOT guilty for sin. I am not dirty or evil, incapable of doing right, or a sinner still living under sin's control. Neither am I unsaved, ignored or barely tolerated by God. I am NOT a spiritual outsider or a fearful slave trying to gain the acceptance of an angry God!**

• **By faith, regardless of my feelings, I declare the truth that because I am in Christ I am a completely forgiven, clean and righteous. I am a holy saint, saved, chosen, at peace with, accepted and adopted by God as his child, lavished with his amazing grace!**

Who In The World Am I?

Friends Forever

WARMING UP

In Simon and Garfunkel's classic song, *I Am a Rock, I Am an Island,* the singers proudly declare that they have no need of friendships, because friendships cause pain. They disdain laughter and loving. They affirm that their books and poetry protect them, that they are shielded in their armor, safe and secure in the "womb" of their room – touching no one and allowing no one to touch them either.

That song was my (Rich's) theme song as a teenager.

If it weren't for Jesus invading my world to become my friend, my room which served as my safe "womb" could very well have become my *tomb.* Having learned to cope with pain through withdrawal and isolation, I needed to renounce (verbally reject) the lie that "I am a rock." I have come to understand that *the Lord Jesus* is the rock (**Psalm 18:2; 1 Corinthians 10:4**)! He is *my* rock, and he is yours, too!

One early morning recently, while walking I had the distinct sense that Jesus was walking with me. He seemed to impress on my heart three distinct ways relationally that God the Father, Son and Holy Spirit wanted to connect with me. One of them we'll discuss later this week. Another we discussed yesterday – as Father to child, delighting in just being with me. The Scripture that has become so meaningful in that area is

Zephaniah 3:17 (NIV), The LORD your God is with you, he is mighty to save. He will take great delight in you, he will quiet you with his love, he will rejoice over you with singing. God is a powerful warrior, waging war on our behalf. But he is also an exuberant Father, delighting in being with us, quieting us down when we're upset and singing triumphantly over us when we succeed.

The other relational connection Jesus mentioned to me was *friend to friend.* In the spaces below, jot down the words you would use to describe a true friend. Later on in today's lesson we'll see specifically what Jesus' friendship means to us:

_____

_____

_____

_____

_____

_____

_____

_____

_____

WALKING ON

What makes a true friend?

Proverbs 17:17 (NIV) says, *"A friend loves at all times and a brother is born for adversity."*

True friends are loyal. They stick with you through thick or thin.

Proverbs 27:9b (NIV) says, *"the pleasantness of one's friend springs from his earnest counsel."*

True friends are involved. They care enough to talk to you about what's going on in your life. This is one of the great joys of friendship; friends share burdens.

Proverbs 27:6 (NIV) says, *"Wounds from a friend can be trusted, but an enemy multiplies kisses."*

True friends don't flatter but they speak the truth in love to us, even if it hurts.

To have a friend like that is a treasure! And that treasure is available to you! You've probably sung the song, What a Friend We Have in Jesus. But what kind of friend is he? Does he qualify as a true friend?

Jesus Christ is loyal. He himself said that he would be with us always, even to the end of the age (*Matthew 28:20*). No one can snatch us out of his or the Father's hand (*John 10:28,29*). *Psalm 139* describes our always-present Lord:

Is there anyplace I can go to avoid your Spirit? to be out of your sight? If I climb to the sky, you're there! If I go underground, you're there! If I flew on morning's wings to the far western horizon, you'd find me in a minute – you're already there waiting! Then I said to myself, "Oh, he even sees me in the dark! At night I'm immersed in the light!"

Psalm 139:7-11 (MSG)

Jesus Christ is involved. He actually dwells in our hearts (*Ephesians 3:17*); you can't get any more involved than that! Like a long-time friend that

knows what you are thinking and can even finish your sentences for you, Jesus is that close. This is a picture of how intimately involved he really is!

God, investigate my life; get all the facts firsthand. I'm an open book to you; even from a distance, you know what I'm thinking. You know when I leave and when I get back; I'm never out of your sight. You know everything I'm going to say before I start the first sentence. I look behind me and you're there, then up ahead and you're there, too – your reassuring presence, coming and going.

Psalm 139:1-5 (MSG)

Jesus Christ speaks truth in love. He is called "Wonderful Counselor" and "Prince of Peace" in *Isaiah 9:6.* He tells us everything he has learned from his Father (see *John 15:15*). Whatever we need to hear, he is there to confide in us and advise us. Sometimes what he says isn't what we want to hear, but if we follow his counsel we are always better off because he knows what is best for us.

You can tell a lot about a person by the friends he chooses and by those who choose to be his friends!

Jesus chose you to be his friend	*John 15:16*
Jesus calls you his friend	*John 15:15*
Jesus enjoys being with friends like you	*Mark 3:13.14*
Jesus will never leave you	*Hebrews 13:5*
Jesus will never stop loving you	*Romans 8:38,39*
Jesus is always available to listen	*Phil. 4:6,7; 1 Thess. 5:17*

> **Complete the following sentences in light of Jesus' friendship with you:**
>
> (ex.) When I am lonely, Jesus <u>is right here with me so I'm never alone.</u>
>
> When I am confused, Jesus _____
>
> When I am rejected by people, Jesus _____
>
> When I am excited, Jesus _____
>
> When I am worried, Jesus _____
>
> When I just need to talk, Jesus _____

Think about the people on this planet that you highly respect but don't know personally. We're talking about people you would really like to meet. Depending on your areas of interest, you might be thinking of athletes, entertainers, musicians, writers, political figures (we know, in most cases this is a stretch!), military personnel, etc. Now pick out the top three people.

Imagine for a moment that not only did you have the chance to meet these three people, but that they became close friends. How would you feel about yourself? Wouldn't you feel important? If you're like us, you would not be able to keep these new friendships a secret! You'd tell everybody you knew and you'd be beaming with a sense of pride the whole time!

Capture this thought: **The King of kings and Lord of lords, who created all that there is and who is the Sovereign Lord of the entire universe has chosen you to be his friend.**

As humans, one of our deepest needs is for companionship.. Even in the perfect pre-sin world of the Garden of Eden, God pronounced it "not good" for man to be alone. All the animals on the planet might have made wonderful pets for Adam, but he needed another human to meet his deepest relational needs. So God created Eve. But there is an even deeper need that has been placed in our hearts by God himself. It is the need for friendship with God. And in Christ, who laid down his life for us, that need has been fulfilled!

Truth Point

Greater love has no one than this, that one lay down his life for his friends. We know love by this, that he laid down his life for us...

John 15:13; 1 John 3:16a (NASB)

Application

Let's review the six summary statements regarding Jesus' friendship with you:

Jesus chose you to be his friend.

Jesus calls you his friend.

Jesus enjoys being with friends like you.

Jesus will never leave you.

Jesus will never stop loving you.

Jesus is always available to listen.

Choose the statement above that is most meaningful to you during this season of your life. Then write a short prayer of thanksgiving in the spaces below, based on that statement.

_____

_____

_____

Father in heaven, you are so kind, good and generous. You sent your Son to die on the cross for my sins so that I could come into the greatest friendship humanly possible – with Jesus himself. I thank you that I didn't have to... in fact, I couldn't... initiate this with you. You took the initiative with me. You sought me out and saved me just so that we could spend all eternity hanging out together. What a friend I have in Jesus! Open up the doors to the fullness of all you have designed that friendship to be... both for Jesus and for me! And it's in the name of my Best Friend, Jesus, I pray, amen.

- **Jesus, you chose me to be your friend. I accept your friendship!**

- **Jesus, you call me your friend and I am honored. I will not be ashamed of you!**

- **Jesus, you really like me and like being with me. I will pursue getting to know you better!**

- **Jesus, you will never leave me. I want to stay close to you, too.**

- **Jesus, you will never stop loving me. Open my eyes to your love.**

- **Jesus, you are always available to listen to me. Lord, teach me to pray!**

Who In The World Am I?

In Good Hands

WARMING UP

I (Rich) can't possibly count the number of times I have asked Jesus into my heart. The first time was on Christmas Eve, 1972, as I mentioned at the end of Week One. I am convinced I became a true believer in Christ at that moment.

But, as you probably know, those early baby steps as a Christian are filled with many stumbles and falls. I didn't really know how to stand against temptation and so I caved in and sinned many times. So I invited Jesus into my life time and time again, just to make sure… just in case he had left in disgust over my sin. After all, I WAS pretty sinful.

I'm not sure when it finally dawned on me that I was inviting Someone into my life that was already there and who had no intention of giving up on me, no matter how hard I struggled or how much I failed. But when I came to see that my safety and security in Christ is a matter of *his power* and *not my performance*, freedom came.

However, before freedom came there was an intense battle. I went through a period of time believing I might even have committed the "unpardonable sin." I was scared to death that I had crossed over some line and could never get back. Fortunately the truth set me free and continues to keep me free today.

Maybe you can relate to some of my struggles. Most Christians can.

On a scale of 1 to 10 (1 being sure you are not forgiven for your sin and are not on your way to heaven and 10 being absolutely certain you are spiritually safe and secure in Jesus), rate yourself below. Then explain why you answered as you did in the blank lines following.

| 1 | 2 | 3 | 4 | 5 | 6 | 7 | 8 | 9 | 10 |

_____

_____

_____

_____

_____

Most Christians will put themselves toward the high end of that scale, but many are reluctant to circle the "10". Why is that? The primary reason, we believe, is that they tend to base their sense of spiritual safety and security on their current religious performance rather than on the grace of God. That is, if they feel like they are doing pretty well – staying away from gross sin, going to church, reading the Bible (at least some), then God is pleased with them and their salvation seems fairly secure, at least for the moment. But if things recently have gone a bit awry spiritually, they can view God as raising a suspicious eyebrow and keeping a wary eye on them. In that place of spiritual "angst" it is easy to wonder if they might get "cut" from the team.

Let's take a look at some Scriptures and draw some conclusions about how safe and secure we are spiritually.

It is because of him [God] that you are in Christ Jesus, who has become for us wisdom from God – that is, our righteousness, holiness, and redemption. Therefore, as it is written, "Let him who boasts boast in the Lord."

1 Corinthians 1:30,31 (NIV)

According to this Scripture, who is responsible for us being in Christ?

_____

Now it is God who makes both us and you stand firm in Christ. He anointed us, set his seal of ownership on us, and put his Spirit in our hearts as a deposit, guaranteeing what is to come.

2 Corinthians 2:21,22 (NIV)

From those verses above, who is responsible for *keeping us* in Christ?

_____

_____

_____

According to that Scripture, what has God done to show he intends to follow through with his promise to keep us?

_____

_____

_____

Blessed be the God and Father of our Lord Jesus Christ, who according to his great mercy has caused us to be born again to a living hope through the resurrection of Jesus Christ from the dead, to obtain an inheritance which is imperishable and undefiled and will not fade away, reserved in heaven for you, who are protected by the power of God through faith for a salvation ready to be revealed in the last time.

1 Peter 1:3-5 (NASB)

What is protecting us in our salvation? _____

_____

_____

God put us in Christ. God keeps us in Christ. And God protects us in Christ by his power so that we will be saved to the end! Is there anything in these verses about our religious performance? Not a word! The only prerequisite for us who are born again (as mentioned in *1 Peter 1:3-5*) is that we have faith in Christ. That's it!

Here are some other truths to help you know you are spiritually safe and secure in Christ:

- God will never condemn you for your sins! In fact, you have been set free from sin and death's control through Christ! (*Romans 8:1,2*)

- You are already considered by God to be a citizen of heaven! You just aren't home yet! (*Philippians 3:20*)

- God will never leave you or forsake you! (*Hebrews 13:5*)

- In that place of your spirit, deep down inside, even the devil himself cannot touch you there or succeed in removing you from being in Christ. (*1 John 5:18*)

- God is for you and even if others are against you, he never will be! (*Romans 8:31-34*)

What can we say about such wonderful things as these? If God is for us, who can ever be against us? Since God did not spare even his own Son but gave him up for us all, won't God, who gave us Christ, also give us everything else? Who dares accuse us whom God has chosen for his own? Will God? No! He is the one who has given us right standing with himself. Who then will condemn us? Will Christ Jesus? No, for he is the one who died for us and was raised to life for us and is sitting at the place of highest honor next to God, pleading for us.

Romans 8:31-34 (NLT)

That seals the deal. Jesus Christ himself refuses to condemn us. He died for us. He was raised from the dead for us. Now he sits at the right hand of God the Father praying for us – and he will not stop until we are safely home. Can anything be more secure than that?

It just seems fitting here to take a brief break and thank God for some of the liberating truths we've looked at already today. As the Lord leads you, complete the statements below with expressions of gratitude to God. Let it come from your heart.

Thank You, Lord, for _____

_____

Thank You, Lord, for _____

_____

Thank You, Lord, for _____

_____

Thank You, Lord, for _____

_____

One of the things we have tried to do this week is keep our identity in Christ (who we are) in the context of our relationship with God. We looked at our acceptance in Christ as part of the Father-child relationship. We looked at our companionship with Christ friend to friend. In this lesson we wanted to take a brief glimpse at our safety and security in Christ as part of his being our Shepherd.

Shepherds love their sheep intensely, and will even risk their lives if necessary to protect them. Sheep are basically helpless creatures and need someone strong to take care of them. David was a shepherd before he was a king and he risked his life, fighting a lion and a bear, in order to save his sheep. Jesus is the Good Shepherd who gave his life for his sheep – his followers (*John 10:11*). That's you and me! Jesus' words to us as our Shepherd are immensely comforting:

My sheep hear My voice, and I know them and they follow Me; and I give eternal life to them, and they shall never perish; and no one shall snatch them out of My hand. My Father, who has given them to Me, is greater than all; and no one is able to snatch them out of the Father's hand.

John 10:27-30 (NASB)

The apostle Paul echoed those truths about God's protective love – even though we may suffer great trials (see *John 16:33*) – when he wrote:

Do you think anyone is going to be able to drive a wedge between us and Christ's love for us?

There is no way! Not trouble, not hard times, not hatred, not hunger, not homelessness, not bullying threats, not backstabbing, not even the worst sins listed in Scripture: "They kill us in cold blood because they hate you. We're sitting ducks; they pick us off one by one." None of this fazes us because Jesus loves us. I'm absolutely convinced that nothing – nothing living or dead, angelic or demonic, today or tomorrow, high or low, thinkable or unthinkable – absolutely nothing can get between us and God's love because of the way that Jesus our Master has embraced us.

Romans 8:35-39 (MSG)

Though we will suffer pain in this fallen world, God has promised to never stop loving us. He placed us in Christ. He keeps us in Christ. And he will bring us safely home *to Christ*. His power – which is unmatched – will accomplish this!

In today's *Warming Up* section, we mentioned the struggles with fear that I (Rich) might have committed the unpardonable sin. What is that exactly? Jesus spoke about it in Matthew

Therefore I say to you, any sin and blasphemy shall be forgiven men, but blasphemy against the Spirit shall not be forgiven. And whoever shall speak a word against the Son of Man, it shall be forgiven him; but whoever shall speak against the Holy Spirit, it shall not be forgiven him, either in this age or in the age to come.

Matt. 12:31,32 (NASB)

Strong words. Without understanding what Jesus was talking about, they could be very scary words.

The "unpardonable sin" Jesus referred to is "blasphemy of the Holy Spirit." The context of Jesus' stern rebuke of the unbelieving Pharisees was that they had accused Jesus of casting out demons by the power of Satan (*Matt. 12:24*). In actuality, Jesus had cast out the demons by the Spirit of God (*12:28*). This accusation by the Pharisees, Jesus declared, was indicative of a heart so cold and hard against him that there was no forgiveness for them.

In reality, these Pharisees had rejected Jesus as Messiah and would never turn to him. In essence, *that* is the unpardonable sin – to forever reject Jesus Christ as Savior and Lord.

So don't let the enemy accuse you and scare you into thinking that you have committed the unpardonable sin. The mere fact that you would be concerned that you *might* have done so (as I was) is sure evidence that you haven't!

Identity Reminder:

I am a member of Christ's Body.

1 Cor. 12:27

Our relationship to God as sheep to Shepherd is powerfully expressed in Psalm 23. In the blanks below write out what each phrase means to you. Some of them are filled in already to give you an idea of what we're asking you to do

The LORD is my Shepherd <u>The King of all is watching over my life with great care.</u>

I shall not be in want. _____

_____

He makes me lie down in green pastures. <u>He puts me in safe resting places where I can grow</u>

He leads me beside quiet waters. _____

_____

He restores my soul. _____

_____

He guides me in paths of righteousness for his name's sake. _____

_____

Even though I walk through the valley of the shadow of death, I will fear no evil, for you are with me.

_____

_____

Your rod and your staff, they comfort me. <u>Your rod protects me from danger and your staff rescues me when I'm trapped.</u>

You prepare a table before me in the presence of my enemies. <u>You bless me in full view of those who are against me.</u>

You anoint my head with oil; my cup overflows. <u>You treat me like royalty!</u>

Surely goodness and love will follow me all the days of my life. _____

_____

_____

And I will dwell in the house of the LORD forever.

_____

_____

God is committed to us for the rest of our lives – to care for us, protect us and provide all we need (*Phil. 4:19*). No matter how much you struggle in your Christian life, you can be confident that *"He who began a good work in you will perfect it until the day of Christ Jesus"* (Phil. 1:6).

Identity Reminder:

I am a saint.

Eph. 1:1

What are you anxious about today? Your salvation? You can trust him to finish what he started with you and to bring you to himself! Your future? Your times are in his hands, and they are good hands! (*Psalm 31:14,15*). Your finances? He will supply all your needs according to his riches in glory in Christ Jesus! (*Phil. 4:19*). Your health, your family, your job, your…? Whatever it might be, will you put your trust in the good hands of the Good Shepherd? He already gave his life for you to save you from your sins; can't he be trusted to supply whatever else you may need?

Truth Point

So, what do you think? With God on our side like this, how can we lose? If God didn't hesitate to put everything on the line for us, embracing our condition and exposing himself to the worst by sending his own Son, is there anything else he wouldn't gladly and freely do for us?

Rom. 8:31,32 (MSG)

Application

Complete the following statements based on the truths of today's lesson:

I can trust God to save me because _____

_____

I can trust God to keep me saved because _____

_____

I can trust God to bring me safely to heaven because

_____

I can trust God to take care of me today because ____

_____

Dear heavenly Father, I love you because you are my strength. You are my rock and my fortress and my deliverer. You are my rock in whom I take refuge. You are my shield and the horn of my salvation, my stronghold. Thank you, Lord, for protecting me. Thank you for placing me in the palm of your hand and keeping me safely and securely in Christ. I choose to accept your word as true and I refuse to gauge my spiritual security on my religious performance. I am yours and you are mine and I am secure in you by your grace alone. I say thank you in the name of Jesus, amen.

- **I am safe and secure in Jesus' and the Father's hands.**

- **I am forever free from condemnation.**

- **I am God's work in progress, his masterpiece.**

- **God will not stop working on me until Christ returns.**

- **Absolutely nothing, including the devil himself, can ever yank, pull, sneak, smuggle or kidnap me out of God's family or away from his love!**

Who In The World Am I?

Jesus Christ, the Compassionate Healer

I (Rich) had finally achieved my goal and with it the reality of total "coolness." I had not only passed the rigorous Senior Lifesaving course at Penn State University, but I also was qualified as a Water Safety Instructor. I was a lifeguard and I could teach swimming lessons (where the better money was). I had a great tan, a position of authority where people had to do what I said, and the admiration of the girls… sort of. I felt like a king when I ascended my "throne" above the pool. Once I even had the chance to rescue a boy sputtering for air in the deep end. I had it "all"… almost.

Being a lifeguard is not nearly as glamorous as you might think. It's actually pretty mundane and monotonous. And when you're working at a swim club as I did, sometimes it's downright disgusting.

One of the jobs the guards had to do when we rotated off the lifeguard stands was to make sure the bathrooms were clean. Unfortunately, more often than not some little kid would miss the toilet and we'd have to clean it up. I was not a happy Christian when that would happen.

One day before going to work, I happened to read in Colossians:

> **Whatever you do, do your work heartily, as for the Lord rather than for men; knowing that from the Lord you will receive the reward of the inheritance. It is the Lord Christ whom you serve.**
>
> **Colossians 3:23,24 (NASB)**

It's one thing to rescue a drowning boy heartily for the Lord. That's easy. But cleaning another boy's waste material off a wet bathroom floor? That's different, I thought. But I was wrong. That day, after reading those verses in Colossians, God changed my attitude. I went into that bathroom and cleaned up the mess as if the Lord himself were going to walk in there next. It didn't make the mess any less messy, but it sure made a difference in my attitude.

I began to understand that I could honor the Lord even in the smallest or most unpleasant tasks, and that he would reward me for that. I started to realize that God could infuse a touch of his glory in everything I do. In his Majesty's service, *everything* is significant.

Before we look at some Scriptures that further reveal how significant our lives are *in Christ,* it's time for some honesty. Listed on the next page are a variety of tasks that could show up in a Christian's life. Where would you place yourself on the "Grumble-Humble" scale? Grumble means just that, you *grumble* when you have to do it; *humble* means you undertake the task with thanksgiving and experience God's joy and strength. Maybe you fall somewhere in between. Put an "x" where you honestly land most of the time.

	Grumble	Humble
Changing a diaper	....	
Attending a Sunday School class	....	
Cooking dinner	....	
Going to work Monday morning	....	
Balancing your checkbook	....	
Mowing the grass	....	
Teaching a Sunday School class	....	
Reading the Bible	....	
Cleaning up after the pet	....	

Don't feel too badly if you ended up on the "Grumble" side more than you'd care to admit. Every one of those items was picked because at times we've been more filled with groaning than grace when faced with doing them!

What motivates you to get out of bed in the morning? Is it simply the incessant demands of work and the relentless noise of the alarm clock? Or is it a passion that comes from knowing that your life counts for something meaningful because of Christ? Many Christians might mutter at this point, "Well, sure, if I was Billy Graham or somebody, I'd feel like my life is significant, but all I do is _____."

Or maybe you'd say, "With the salary I make and the bills I have to pay and the debt I'm trying to get rid of, what's so significant about all that?"

Good questions. Fortunately the Bible has some good answers, and the key to discovering the treasure of our great significance in Christ is to understand our relationship to who is in charge. Isaiah tells us clearly:

But now, thus says the LORD, your Creator, O Jacob, and He who formed you, O Israel… for I am the LORD your God, the Holy One of Israel, your Savior…Bring My sons from afar, and My daughters from the ends of the earth, everyone who is called by My name, and whom I have created for My glory, whom I have formed, even whom I have made… "You are My witnesses, declares the LORD, "and My servant whom I have chosen, in order that you may know and believe Me, and understand that I am He. Before Me there was no God formed, and there will be none after Me. I, even I, am the LORD; and there is no savior besides Me.

Isaiah 43:1, 3, 6,7, 10,11 (NASB)

Based on the Scripture above, who is charge? What are the titles he uses for himself? _____

_____

_____

_____

What does *Isaiah 43* say *we* are? _____

_____

_____

_____

God is in charge. That's what LORD means. There is no one higher. He calls the shots. He runs things. He also created us and formed us and he is not only God but he is *our* God. Beyond that, he is the Holy One, our Savior, and our Father. And there will be no substitutes or pinch hitters for him. He is the Lord and there never was and never will be another. So what he says, goes!

But notice who we are in relation to him. We are not robots or automatons that have no heart, will or choice. Nor are we fearful slaves (see **Romans 8:15**). We have been made by God to know, believe and understand him. We are sons and daughters, called by his very name. We have the honor of being his witnesses and his servants.

He is the Lord and we are called into the high honor of being in his Majesty's service. That is significance!

Here's the clincher. Do you know why we were created? We were created for God's *glory.* That means, when we fulfill our God-given calling, we make God shine. We make God look so good that people see him as he is and turn to him. Then they can find their God-given calling in life, too! Jesus put it this way:

You are the light of the world. A city on a hill cannot be hidden. Neither do people light a lamp and put it under a bowl. Instead they put it on its stand, and it gives light to everyone in the house. In the same way, let your light shine before men, that they may see your good deeds and praise your Father in heaven.

Matthew 5:14,15 (NIV)

It's at this point that most people start compartmentalizing their lives. They think, "Okay, when I share my faith or lead a home fellowship group or help out on a church work day, I feel like my light is shining…" But they scratch their heads wondering how that happens when driving in rush hour traffic or checking emails or doing all the other everyday work, school or home tasks. It's easy to conclude wrongly that God's not all that concerned about that "non-spiritual" stuff. But the apostle Paul wrote:

So eat your meals heartily, not worrying about what others say about you – you're eating to God's glory, after all, not to please them. As a matter of fact, do everything that way, heartily and freely to God's glory. At the same time, don't be callous in your exercise of freedom, thoughtlessly stepping on the toes of those who aren't as free as you are. I try my best to be considerate of everyone's feelings in all these matters; I hope you will be, too.

1 Corinthians 10:31-33 (MSG)

Did you catch it? We are to do *everything* in our lives heartily and freely to God's glory. This is so the light shines on God and he looks so good and attractive that people turn to him. When you live that way (and say "no" to sin!) *nothing* is unspiritual.

The exercise below is designed to stretch your thinking. Ask the Lord to give you his wisdom to know how the following things can be done to his glory. Then write your responses in the blanks provided.

Driving a car <u>example: obey the traffic laws and</u> <u>speed limits; be courteous to other drivers; leave in</u> <u>plenty of time so that you're not anxious or easily</u> <u>irritated.</u>

Talking on the phone _____

_____

_____

Doing paperwork _____

_____

_____

Eating a meal_____

_____

_____

Cleaning house _____

_____

_____

Doing everyday stuff at work _____

_____

_____

Earning a large income _____

_____

_____

Just "getting by" financially _____

_____

_____

One aspect of Christ being Lord and our being his servants involves understanding that Jesus is the head of his body, the church (*Ephesians 1:22,23*). As the head of the church, Jesus has not only assigned work for each one of us to do, but he has also given every one of us at least one gift from the Holy Spirit to give us the power to do that work. These gifts are different from natural talents (which even unbelievers have.) They are supernatural endowments for fruitful service for the kingdom of God. You will discover your gift or gifts by taking the opportunity to serve Christ in ways he leads you. Watch for areas of service that seem to come (super)naturally, that bring you satisfaction, and that yield fruit (changed lives for Christ). Be especially aware of times when other members of the body of Christ comment on how much they were benefited by your ministry. Spiritual gifts can be used at work, at home, in the community, in the church, at school… anywhere *you* are!

If you want to study what those spiritual gifts are, check out the following Scriptures:

1 Corinthians 12, 14; Ephesians 4; Romans 12

Identity Reminder:

I have been adopted as God's child.

Eph. 1:5

WINDING DOWN

The key to living life with a sense of significance is knowing that what you are doing is pleasing the Lord and that it matters in his kingdom plans. *Remember that God is not only concerned about what you do, but why you do it.*

A janitor joyfully, contentedly cleaning toilets at a megachurch —if that is what God has called him to do, is living life at a far more significant level than the senior pastor of that church, if that pastor is ministering because he desperately needs people to think he's important. A housewife faithfully raising three toddlers may be living life at a far more significant level than her "climbing to the top of the corporate ladder" workaholic, money-hungry husband… no matter how "respected" he might be.

You see, man looks at the outward appearance, but God looks at the heart (see *1 Samuel 16:7*). People see what we do outwardly. God looks at the motivation.

What has God called you to do? Jesus said that when you discover what God wants you to do and you do it through Christ, you will experience real joy. In fact, you will bask in the love of God and have the same joy that Jesus had (see *John 15:10,11*).

WRAPPING UP

All of us will be amazed at what will be rewarded in heaven. Perhaps when we see all God's people crowded around the throne of Christ… the ones closest to him could very well end up being those who on earth were shut-ins and could do nothing but pray. Their prayers made the domain of darkness shudder and explosively propelled the kingdom of light forward!

God will judge not only the "what's" of our work here on earth but the "why's" as well. What is done for his glory will be a precious treasure; what is not will be burned up (see *1 Corinthians 3:10-15*).

Don't live for the applause of men but for the applause of heaven.

Truth Point

For we are God's workmanship, created in Christ Jesus to do good works, which God prepared in advance for us to do.

Ephesians 2:10 (NIV)

Application

Take a minute and prayerfully evaluate what you are doing in life. Is it what the Lord is calling you to do? If it is, how can you glorify God even more through what you do? If not, what is keeping you from doing the good works he has prepared for you to do? Write your thoughts below.

_____

_____

_____

_____

Dear heavenly Father, it is knowing you and bringing glory to you that makes life satisfying and meaningful. It is knowing that I am called to be your child, your servant and your witness that gets me out of bed in the morning. I am sorry for the ways I have tried to live life for the applause of men rather than for the applause of heaven. You are the LORD and I want to discover what pleases you. Thank you for the privilege of walking with you and bearing fruit for your kingdom. In Jesus' name I pray, amen.

- **God is my Creator, Savior and Lord. Seeking and serving him is the source of my significance!**

- **I am a light that shines on God and points people to him!**

- **I am God's workmanship, his masterpiece, created to discover and walk in his good works!**

- **I am chosen by God to be his witness!**

- **I will live for the applause of heaven, not for the applause of men!**

Who In The World Am I?

A Marriage Made in Heaven

WARMING UP

I (Rich) was okay when Jesus invited me into a deeper son to Father relationship to God and a closer friend to Friend relationship with him. But when he told me he wanted to love me with the intense love of Groom to bride, it shook me up a bit. There's nothing sexual about this relationship at all, though there is something very romantic. Christi's story is powerful and poignant here.

Several years ago, through a series of painful events, I (Christi) wound up believing that God loved everyone else but me. In my deception, I stepped out of his good plans for my life and thought I was stamped with a big red "REJECTED" mark by God. Feelings of helplessness, grief and despair overwhelmed me and I sank into a deep pit of emptiness and depression.

My loving husband, Michael, was not about to stand by and watch this happen, so he took me to counseling, a conference and bought me a book from Freedom in Christ Ministries. Each night he read to me and had me repeat out loud the truths about my new identity in Christ. I didn't like doing this because I did not really believe those things were true of me.

One day the question came to mind, "Is it possible that God really hasn't given up on me and that he does still love me?" The question wouldn't leave my mind, so I decided to ask God for myself, "God do you still love me? If you do, would you somehow let me know?"

Several days went by and I heard nothing but silence. Each day the pain of rejection grew stronger. One day during my normal routine of questioning God, "God do you love me?" He opened my spiritual eyes and allowed me to see his hand reach down and lift my chin to see his glory. Out of the brightness I heard his strong voice say to me, "Do I love you? You are my BRIDE!"

My heart was overwhelmed and I immediately went to the back of the house and pulled out my wedding dress. I put it on – zipping it up as far as I could – and leaped through the house shouting:

I am the bride of CHRIST!

I AM the bride of Christ!

I am the BRIDE of Christ!

That's the image we want to develop for you in this fifth and final relational picture of our relationship to God and identity in Christ: Christ is the Groom and we are his beloved bride!

Identity Reminder:

I have access to God thru the Holy Spirit.

Eph. 2:18

This idea of relating to Christ as a bride to the Groom may be a paradigm shift for you. Many Christians have never considered this reality; it's not even on their radar screens. To them the Christian life is more of a *thing to do or a commitment to keep* rather than an *intimate relationship to enjoy.*

For others who have felt the sting of marriage turned sour or bitter, the idea of being wedded to Jesus may raise some uncomfortable questions. *Is Jesus really in this for the long haul? Is it truly for better or for worse, knowing that he's better and I'm worse? Is he going to be a controlling abusive husband? I've seen some very religious people who claimed to be close to Jesus and I wouldn't trust them with my pet, let alone my life. Is Jesus really trustworthy?*

As always, it's best to let God speak for himself. Take a few minutes and soak in these Scriptures and then respond afterwards with your own description of the kind of Groom Jesus is and how beautiful we are as his bride.

> *You will also be a crown of beauty in the hand of the LORD, and a royal diadem in the hand of your God. It will no longer be said to you, "Forsaken," nor to your land will it any longer be said, "Desolate"; but you will be called, "My delight is in her," and your land, "Married"; for the LORD delights in you, and to Him your land will be married. For as a young man marries a virgin, so your sons will marry you; and as a bridegroom rejoices over the bride, so your God will rejoice over you.*

> *Isaiah 62:3-5 (NASB)*

> *And I saw the holy city, new Jerusalem, coming down out of heaven from God, made ready as a bride adorned for her husband. And I heard a loud voice from the throne saying, "Behold, the tabernacle of God is among men, and He shall dwell among them, and they shall be His people and God Himself shall be among them, and He shall wipe away every tear from their eyes; and there shall no longer be any death; there shall no longer be any mourning, or crying, or pain; the first things have passed away... And one of the seven angels who had the seven bowls full of the seven last plagues, came and spoke with me, saying, "Come here, I shall show you the bride, the wife of the Lamb." And he carried me away in the Spirit to a great and high mountain, and showed me the holy city, Jerusalem, coming down out of heaven from God, having the glory of God. Her brilliance was like a very costly stone...*

> *Revelation 21:2-4, 9-11 (NASB)*

From these Scriptures, write your own description of Jesus as a Groom and the church as his precious bride:

_____

_____

_____

_____

_____

_____

Can you picture this: Jesus dancing and singing over you (see also *Zephaniah 3:17*), shouting with joy when he sees you, then tenderly taking you in his arms and wiping away all the tears of pain, grief, illness and death? Can you see him adorning you with his glory and bestowing on you brilliance and beauty like the most precious gem? This is pure love and love that is pure. This is love that is uninhibited, unhindered, unbounded and undying. It is the love that is "as strong as death" burning with a holy jealousy that is "as severe as the grave." "Its flashes are flashes of fire, the very flame of the LORD. Many waters cannot quench love, nor will rivers overflow it." It is so pure and powerful that "if a man were to give all the riches of his house" to try and buy it, that price "would be utterly despised" (see *Song of Solomon 8:6,7*).

A little scary isn't it? To be loved that intensely – especially if your experience with Christ has consisted of checking in on Sunday morning at 10:30 or 11 and checking out at noon with a wave and a promise to "see ya' next week!"

But this kind of love is what we were made for and what makes life worth living.

Once you begin to realize how treasured you are by Jesus, the doors for real freedom and healing swing wide open.

To further understand this kind of love, we need to take a look at three aspects of Jesus' passionate love for his bride. Before we do that, we need to clear up some confusion about the word "passion."

The definition of passion is a deep desire, but at its root it means to endure or suffer. Christ's passion for us then refers to his intense love and desire for us shown by his agonizing, excruciating suffering and death as payment for our sins. So when we talk about Christ's "passionate love," there's nothing sexual implied at all. It means he yearned for us so deeply that he sweat, he bled, he agonized; he died to purchase us as his bride.

That is why the famous play in Oberammergau, Germany is called "The Passion Play." Even the passion fruit (despite inevitable efforts by secular media to eroticize it) reflects the Cross. The passion flower – from which the passion fruit comes – has its parts configured in such a way that it resembles Christ's wounds.

So when you think of Christ's passion for you think deep desire but more than that, think *pain.* Jesus suffered brutal and cruel treatment because he would

not be stopped in his longing to make you his bride and bring you into union with himself.

First, Jesus loves us so much that he not only is *near* us, but he is in *union* with us.

On that day, you will realize that I am in my Father, and you are in me, and I am in you.

> *Jesus' words in John 14:20 (NIV)*

Do you not know that he who unites himself with a prostitute is one with her in body? For it is said, "The two will become one flesh." But he who unites himself with the Lord, is one with him in spirit.

> *1 Corinthians 6:16,17 (NASB)*

The closest illustration in human life of the union of Christ and his church is the sexual union of a man and woman, especially in marriage (see *Ephesians 5:22-33*). What the apostle Paul calls "a profound mystery" is that the union of the believer's spirit with the Spirit of Christ is at least as real and intimate as the bodily union of man and woman! And that union is a *tender union*, for Jesus "feeds and cares for" his church far better than the best mortal husband could ever do.

Second, Jesus loves us so much that he is coming back one day to take us home.

In a Jewish wedding, the woman is betrothed to the man and then he goes off to get their house ready. Once all is prepared and the father of the groom says it's time, the groom returns to the bride's family home and announces his arrival with a shout. Then she joins him, the wedding feast begins and they live together in the new home he has prepared for her. Check out these Scriptures:

Don't let this throw you. You trust God, don't you? Trust me. There is plenty of room for you in my Father's home. If that weren't so, would I have told you that I'm on my way to get a room ready for you? And if I'm on my way to get your room ready, I'll come back and get you so you can live where I live.

> *Jesus in John 14:1-3 (MSG)*

No one knows about that day or hour [when Jesus will return], not even the angels in heaven, nor the Son, but only the Father.

Matthew 24:36 (NIV)

For the Lord Himself will descend from heaven with a shout, with the voice of the archangel, and with the trumpet of God; and the dead in Christ shall rise first. Then we who are alive and remain shall be caught up together with them in the clouds to meet the Lord in the air, and thus we shall always be with the Lord.

1 Thess. 4:16,17 (NASB)

Finally, Jesus loves us so much that he expects and deserves our whole-hearted devotion to him.

In most of life, jealousy is looked upon as an evil thing, and indeed most of the time it is. It is a deed of the sinful flesh (**Galatians 5:20**) and more fierce and overwhelming than wrath and anger (**Proverbs 27:4**). But God is a jealous God (**Exodus 20:5**) and a jealous husband in the most pure and holy way. It is the same kind of jealousy that would cause a true, loving husband to risk his life if necessary to protect his wife from a rapist or win her back from another lover. That is the *good* kind of jealousy, the kind that God has. In fact, his name *is* Jealous (see **Exodus 34:14**).

The apostle Paul, filled with the Spirit of God, wrote of this godly jealousy and our need for whole-hearted devotion to Christ:

I am jealous for you with a godly jealousy. I promised you to one husband, to Christ, so that I might present you as a pure virgin to him. But I am afraid that just as Eve was deceived by the serpent's cunning, your minds may somehow be led astray from your sincere and pure devotion to Christ.

2 Corinthians 11:2,3 (NIV)

I (Rich) was speaking at a church that had recently been through a workshop on worship. The speaker had rightly pointed out to the congregation that there are a number of biblically-approved postures for worship including standing, lifting your hands, kneeling, bowing down, etc. Noting a group of unresponsive and apparently quite disgruntled attendees in the back, the speaker added, "There is one biblically-*unapproved* posture for worship – sitting down with your arms folded and a scowl on your face!"

Freedom means you are not inhibited by the fear of man (pleasing people) in your worship. Freedom means you are able to express your love for the Groom in a way that honors him and is led by the Spirit of God – even if other people around you don't join in. In fact, if you make the choice to pour out your love, attention and affection on Jesus in public worship, you can almost count on some people not approving.

The following Scripture passages tell of three incidents where worshipers expressed their bride-Groom devotion and delight, in spite of opposition. We trust as you read them you will be encouraged to worship Jesus in spirit and in truth… freely!

- Martha's sister, Mary, and her quiet devotion – **Luke 10:38-42**

- King David's exuberant public worship – **2 Samuel 6:16-23**

- Mary anointing Jesus with perfume – **John 12:1-8**

Identity Reminder:

I have been redeemed and forgiven.

Col. 1:14

As you no doubt can tell, there is a war going on – a battle for your heart (your deepest affections) and that battle is being waged in your mind. It is a battle between the enemies of God — the things of this world — and Christ. It is a battle between the cunning, scheming lies of the devil and the pure, unadulterated truth of God. It is a war of the worlds, between the domain of darkness and the alluring temptations of life around you, and the kingdom of Christ and his light. Who's winning in your life? Who do you *want* to win? Take a minute and write your honest answer below.

_____

_____

_____

_____

Every one of us needs to be loved like the Lord Jesus Christ loves us. Our sincere prayer is that you will open yourself up to the fullness of Jesus' love for you. These yearning words of Paul are from God's heart to you, too:

Truth Point

We have spoken freely to you… and opened wide our hearts to you. We are not withholding our affection from you, but you are withholding yours from us. As a fair exchange – I speak as to my children – open wide your hearts also.

2 Corinthians 6:11-13 (NIV)

Application

In order to remember, reflect and be renewed in who you are in Christ, take a few moments to summarize what the Lord has said to you regarding the following relational identities you have in Christ. Review previous lessons if necessary.

Father to child (acceptance) _____

_____

_____

_____

Friend to friend (companionship) _____

_____

_____

_____

Shepherd to sheep (safety and security) _____

_____

_____

_____

Lord to servant (significance) _____

_____

_____

_____

Groom to bride (passionate love) _____

_____

_____

_____

Identity Reminder:

I am complete in Christ.

Col. 2:10

Dear heavenly Father, it is kind of unnerving to be loved like the Lord Jesus loves me, and yet it's also the most wonderful thing imaginable. Thank you for being a God that so freely and tenderly pursues, envelops, cares for, comforts and revels in me. It is a wild, untamable love that yearns to sweep me off my feet. Yet there is much in me that restrains that love from fully breaking over me. Break down those walls, Lord, and flood me with your relentless love. In Jesus' name I pray, amen.

- **Christ's passion on the Cross showed the fervency of his love for me!**
- **I am now one with Jesus in spirit!**
- **My body is his very own temple!**
- **I am Christ's bride and fervently loved by him!**
- **I am filled with his glory and I am a royally beautiful treasure to Jesus!**

Who In The World Am I?

All Together Now

WARMING UP

After becoming a Christian early in college, I (Rich) struggled for about a year and a half to get my "spiritual balance." Mostly what kept me off balance was my own proud self-will and independent spirit. My first pride-generated mistake was my refusal to tell my older brother that I had trusted Christ. I didn't want him to think he had "gotten me." I had (false) visions of my becoming just another notch on his spiritual conquest belt.

Once I told him the good news, he was genuinely thrilled and invited me to some Christian meetings on campus. I went, but I was always afraid he would one day be unable to contain himself and during the "sharing time" would burst out with something like, "My brother has become a Christian! Tell everybody what happened, Rich!" Although giving public testimony of one's faith in Christ is a very good and very necessary thing, for me as a young, insecure believer, I would have been scared to death to speak!

My second mistake was born of an intellectual arrogance that made me think I was "above" the stuff they were teaching me at those meetings. This was in spite of the fact that I had a ton of unanswered questions. I was wrestling deep down with fundamental issues like, *How can you actually believe all these Bible stories?* and *Hasn't science proven that evolution actually occurred?* I've since come to fully believe the Bible and now know that good science will always end up

vindicating and not contradicting biblical truth. But at that time my mind was swimming with conflicts, and the Christians I knew seemed to be on some kind of continual "spiritual high." I wasn't. I just couldn't relate. What they were experiencing is called *joy.* It wasn't a big part of my vocabulary at that time and it certainly was not a consistent part of my life.

So I dropped out and started hanging out with my non-Christian friends. I got deep into the partying scene and tried to numb my guilt and shame with alcohol. Still the nagging questions and gnawing conflicts wouldn't go away. I would often spend hours late at night walking the grounds of the Penn State golf course yelling (and yes, at times, swearing) at God.

My main problem was that I was trying to figure everything out on my own. I was trying to understand God, trying to comprehend what had happened to me and who I really was now as a believer in Christ — but I was trying to do it all by myself.

That is never God's plan.

Although we have talked a lot this week about who *you* are in Christ, the picture would be very incomplete without understanding your relationship to other believers. That is, your *individual identity* in Christ is not the whole story, not by a long shot. You are not alone; we're all in this together. We are part of a family, a community of believers and that is a very healthy thing.

Before we go any further, answer the question *What do you think about church?* Go ahead and respond by circling the words below that best describe your experience with church(es) so far:

satisfying	controlling	worshipful	abusive
legalistic	free	joyful	rigid
edifying	warm	relational	cold
liberal	wishy-washy	money-focused	loving
Spirit-filled	biblical	cliquish	political
secretive	real	mission-minded	healthy
wearying	social club	life-changing	family

As human beings we are social creatures. Some of us are more relational than others but we all need other people – whether we are willing to admit it or not. God created us with deep relational needs and he knows that we will reach our fullest potential in him when we relate to other Christians in healthy ways. The following Scripture makes the reality of our *corporate identity* in Christ very clear:

As you come to him [Christ], *the living Stone – rejected by men but chosen by God and precious to him – you also, like living stones, are being built into a spiritual house to be a holy priesthood, offering spiritual sacrifices acceptable to God through Jesus Christ… you are a chosen people, a royal priesthood, a holy nation, a people belonging to God, that you may declare the praises of him who called you out of darkness into his wonderful light. Once you were not a people, but now you are the people of God; once you had not received mercy, but now you have received mercy.*

1 Peter 2:4,5, 9,10 (NIV)

Let's take a look at the words that Peter used to describe our corporate identity:

- **Living stones** – *we are building blocks, alive and growing together in Christ, part of God's building project.*

- **Spiritual house** – *we are under Masterful construction, being built into a temple of worship to God… together with other brothers and sisters in Christ.*

- **Holy priesthood** – *set apart from sin, we are now set apart for God to minister to him in prayer and worship, offering our lives as living sacrifices to God.* **(Rom. 12:1)**

- **Chosen people** – *God hand-picked each of us to be together as a community following him and called by his name.*

- **Royal priesthood** – *we are the royal family of God and every true believer in Christ is a priestly prince or princess!*

- **Holy nation** – *as saints we comprise a new "country" with God as King.*

- **People belonging to God** – *we are not alone, abandoned or homeless; we are a company of people that are God's treasured possession.*

Which of those descriptions above is most meaningful to you? Why?

_____

_____

Experiencing joy is a huge theme in Scripture. We were newly created in Christ with a newly-birthed capacity for joy at a deep heart level. The following words of Jesus show us that God wants us to experience the richness of joy — joy that can never be experienced apart from the love of God and his people.

> *As the Father has loved me, so have I loved you. Now remain in my love. If you obey my commands you will remain in my love, just as I have obeyed my Father's commands and remain in his love. I have told you this so that my joy may be in you and that your joy may be complete. My command is this: Love each other as I have loved you.*
>
> *John 15:9-12 (NIV)*

The most familiar imagery in Scripture about our corporate identity is that of the church, the body of Christ, with Jesus being the Head. Just as the head (which contains the brain) calls the shots in your physical body, Jesus, the Head of the church, is in charge of all of us.

> *At the center of all this, Christ rules the church. The church, you see, is not peripheral to the world, the world is peripheral to the church. The church is Christ's body, in which he speaks and acts, by which he fills everything with his presence.*
>
> *Ephesians 1:22 (MSG)*

As Head of the church, Christ has instructed his body to act together in a coordinated way under his rule, in order to accomplish a number of objectives. Here are three of them:

First, Christ created his body to work together so we will all be healthy spiritually and grow up in love.

> *He [Christ] handed out gifts of apostle, prophet, evangelist, and pastor-teacher to train Christians in skilled servant work, working within Christ's body, the church, until we're all moving rhythmically and easily with each other, efficient and graceful in response to God's Son, fully mature adults, fully developed within and without, fully alive in Christ. No prolonged infancies among us, please. We'll not tolerate babes in the woods, small children who are*

an easy mark for impostors. God wants us to grow up, to know the whole truth and tell it in love – like Christ in everything. We take our lead from Christ, who is the source of everything we do. He keeps us in step with each other. His very breath and blood flow through us, nourishing us so that we will grow up healthy in God, robust in love.

> *Ephesians 4:11-16 (MSG)*

'Lone Ranger' Christians never grow up spiritually. It is only when we are rightly related to one another, and using the spiritual gifts we've been given that we as his body can be built up and grown up. A healthy, growing, grace-filled church where there is God-honoring worship, Bible-based, Spirit-filled preaching and active, relational, prayerful small groups is like a greenhouse for spiritual growth.

Second, we need to be in healthy community together in order to stay strong against sin.

> *See to it, brothers, that none of you has a sinful, unbelieving heart that turns away from the living God. But encourage one another daily, as long as it is called Today, so that none of you may be hardened by sin's deceitfulness. We have come to share in Christ if we hold firmly till the end the confidence we had at first.*
>
> *Hebrews 3:12,14 (NIV)*

Sin lies. It never delivers what it promises. We need other brothers and sisters in Christ to encourage us or "put courage in" so that our hearts don't turn cold and hard against God. We need the courage to speak truth in love, warning each other against sin and gently correcting one another when we fall into sin snares. We do this together by considering "how we may spur one another on toward love and good deeds" and by not giving up "meeting together, as some are in the habit of doing" (*Hebrews 10:24,25*).

Third, we desperately need to stand together to firmly resist the schemes of the devil.

There is protection in numbers. Isolated Christians are easy targets for the lies, temptations and discouragement of Satan and his demons. Just as grazing animals under attack huddle together with the young inside the circle, so we need to "circle the wagons" to protect each other – especially the young, spiritually immature, weak and hurting.

Part of the problem of realizing our need for each other comes from our interpretation of Scripture. As part of a highly "me-oriented" western culture, we tend to see commands and exhortations in the Bible using the word "you" as being for us as *individuals*. Some are, but many are directed toward the Christian *community* as a whole. *Ephesians 6:10-18* is one of them. We'll examine it in more depth later in our *Journey to Freedom*, but for now understand that this passage is not referring to single soldiers, but is an urgent call to the army of God… together! We encourage you to read the following Scripture with that in mind.

> *Finally, be strong in the Lord, and in the strength of His might. Put on the full armor of God, that you may be able to stand firm against the schemes of the devil.*
>
> *Ephesians 6:10,11 (NASB)*

We need to lock our arms and armor together!

WINDING DOWN

We've spent this whole week looking at snapshots of our identity in Christ – both as individuals and now in community together. The question is, *Are you living life in accordance with who you really are… in Christ? Or are you living below your means?*

The apostle Paul's exhortation to the Ephesian believers is our exhortation as well:

> *As a prisoner of the Lord, then, I urge you to live life worthy of the calling you have received.*
>
> *Ephesians 4:1 (NIV)*

God wants us to live out the reality of our new identity in him on a daily basis.

Before we wrap up this week, we think it would be a good idea to pause and have prayerful reflection on those two questions: *Are you living life in accordance with who you really are… in Christ? Or are you living below your means?*. Be honest with yourself. If you are currently living out the joy of your new life and identity in Christ, then say so. If you know that you're not and you have a pretty good idea why, then write it down. If you're confused and frustrated, acknowledge that. If you're afraid of getting your hopes up again… then express that. If you know that your heart is in lock-down mode because of past pain, describe your situation. If a glimmer of new hope is starting to dawn, then put that down.

No denial. No pretense. No reason to perform for anybody else. Just be real.

_____

_____

_____

_____

_____

This book, *Journey to Freedom* and the entire *40 Days of Freedom* campaign is designed to:

- Build a foundation of acquainting you with your new and true identity… **in Christ.**

- Provide an environment where the Holy Spirit can begin to shake loose the things in your life that are keeping you from living according to that new identity.

Our first task is concluding, though we pray that everything we say from here on out will be infused with the grace, truth and life of our new identity in Christ. Starting tomorrow we will invite the gentle, firm Spirit of God to plow up the soil of our lives. This will enable us to receive the sun, rain and fertilizer of his love, and bear the fruit he's created us to bear. We trust you'll journey on with us.

Truth Point

That's plain enough, isn't it? You're no longer wandering exiles. This kingdom of faith is now your home country. You're no longer strangers or outsiders. You belong here, with as much right to the name Christian as anyone. God is building a home. He's using us all – irrespective of how we got here – in what he is building. He used the apostles and prophets for the foundation. Now he's using you, fitting you in brick by brick, stone by stone, with Christ Jesus as the cornerstone that holds all the parts together. We see it taking shape, day after day – a holy temple built by God, all of us built into it, a temple in which God is quite at home.

Ephesians 2:19-22 (MSG)

Application

Think about the lessons this week. Which one was most meaningful to you? Go back and skim through that lesson and pick a Scripture verse from it to memorize. Write it down on an index card and carry it with you today, taking a look at it every once in a while. By bedtime, you'll have it memorized!

Identity Reminder:

I am free forever from condemnation.

Rom . 8:1-2

Dear heavenly Father, thank you. Thank you for totally transforming my life. Before you came in, I was separated from Christ, dead in my sins, a stranger to your covenants of promise, peace and grace. I was without hope and without you in this world. But all that has changed. I am yours and you are mine. And you've given me a great family around the world to keep me company. Teach me to live a life worthy of this new calling in loving community with my brothers and sisters in Christ, in Jesus' name, amen.

- **We have been completely accepted and adopted into God's family in Christ!**

- **We have been chosen by Jesus to be his friends!**

- **We are safe and secure under the gentle, powerful protective care of the Good Shepherd!**

- **We have been given lives brimming over with meaning and importance by the Lord who calls us his servants!**

- **We have been betrothed to a husband who suffered excruciatingly for us and out of his deep passion, we are his beloved bride!**

- **We are part of a great nation of royal priests, kingly warriors on a mission of worship and warfare!**

Hurt Yet Healed

Week 3

Hurt Yet Healed

The Painful Truth

My (Rich's) street has about eight houses on it. It is a quiet street with neighbors who actually know and care about one another. We've had parties and Bible studies in each others' homes and bonfires in backyards and nearby fields. We've gone Christmas caroling together and we've held Easter sunrise services for most of the time we've lived here. Just about everybody in the neighborhood comes to these gatherings. Don't get me wrong. Not everyone on the street is a follower of Christ, but we are truly a *neighbor*hood.

Despite the outward peacefulness of our street, there have been a lot of tears shed in recent years. The man across the street returned from a golf vacation to discover his wife had left and basically cleaned him out. After she left him and took his money, our neighbor spent most of his free time alone watching TV. Their divorce is now finalized and he has had to sell his house for financial reasons.

A dear lady down the street lost her husband to Alzheimer's and four months later lost a grown son in a biking accident. We sat with her silently hour after hour while she poured out her heart with all the "why?" questions that have no answers this side of eternity. Her other son lives in another state in a residential facility, diagnosed with schizophrenia.

Perhaps our closest friends on the street I'll call Jim and Donna (not their real names). Jim can fix anything, which is good since I need all the help I

can get. We watch their house and pets and they do likewise for us. They bring back presents for our kids when they go away on trips. Jim is in the meteorology field which gives us common ground (that was my major in college).

Jim and Donna's son, "Jeff", has had many troubles in life. His mom and dad did all they could to help him but he kept hanging out with the wrong crowd. Late one Sunday night when they came home from a weekend away, Jim found Jeff upstairs — dead of a drug overdose. Probably meth.

In addition to the obvious grief on our street, there are six couples we care about whose marriages are all disintegrating right before our eyes. Reflecting on all the pain that people we love are experiencing, all we can say is sometimes life on earth just plain stinks. That may not sound very spiritual but that's the way it is.

How does God meet us in our pain? And how can we be free from the chains of anger and bitterness that so often wrap themselves around our hearts as we stagger from the wounds life deals us? That's what this week is all about.

We're not going to pull any punches here. This is the real, raw stuff of life and unless we grab hold of the lifelines God throws to us, we can drown in our pain. Don't let that happen. There really is freedom in the midst of pain.

WALKING ON

The suffering on our street is not isolated. Pain is an unwelcome intruder for us all and an inevitable fact of life in a world fallen because of sin. The Bible gives example after example of good people getting a raw deal and bad people getting off easy… for a while. There were also good men (even kings!) who walked with God for a long time and then, in a moment of utter stupidity and deception, blew it completely. And their sin caused suffering for many (see *2 Samuel 11,12 esp. 12:7-12*).

Maybe you are going through a period of suffering right now. If not, you certainly know someone who is. Either way, pain has entered your world. When we begin to go through a time of suffering, we don't want and don't need advice on how to cope. We all recoil at the pious platitudes thrown our way by well-meaning people. What we really want and need is the quiet presence of someone who loves us and has been down that road… our road of suffering… before. Ultimately that One is Jesus.

The following verses will help you see that Jesus knows and understands pain and suffering. After each verse there are blanks for you to respond, as you desire, to what Jesus went through. Maybe you'll be moved to thank him for what he did. Maybe you'll want to tell him about your pain. Maybe you'll feel the need to cry out to him for help. If you need more paper, use it. It's okay… no it's necessary… to be real.

[A prophecy of Jesus] *"Just as there were many who were appalled at him – his appearance was so disfigured beyond that of any man and his form marred beyond human likeness –; He was despised and rejected by men, a man of sorrows, and familiar with suffering. Like one from whom men hide their faces he was despised, and we esteemed him not."*

Isaiah 52:14; 53:3 (NIV)

_____

_____

_____

_____

[A prophecy of Jesus] *"Surely he took up our infirmities and carried our sorrows, yet we considered him stricken by God, smitten by him, and afflicted. But he was pierced for our transgressions, he was crushed for our iniquities; the punishment that brought us peace was upon him, and by his wounds we are healed."*

Isaiah 53:4,5 (NIV)

_____

_____

_____

In the days of His flesh, He offered up both prayers and supplications with loud crying and tears to the One able to save Him from death, and He was heard because of His piety.

Hebrews 5:7 (NASB)

_____

_____

_____

[At the tomb of his dear friend Lazarus] *Jesus wept.*

John 11:35 (NIV)

_____

_____

For we do not have a high priest who cannot sympathize with our weaknesses, but one who has been tempted in all things as we are, yet without sin. Let us therefore draw near with confidence to the throne of grace, that we may receive mercy and may find grace to help in time of need.

Hebrews 4:15,16 (NASB)

_____

_____

_____

There's a lot more we're going to say this week about dealing with the pain, suffering and anger that accompanies hurt. But it is important as we begin this week of facing the pain in our lives that we remember these things about God:

God is not a detached, dispassionate spectator, observing suffering as though it were some curious scientific experiment. This should be clear from how involved Jesus Christ became, entering into our suffering through His work on the cross. Jesus said, *"He who has seen me has seen the Father" (John 14:9 NASB).* So everything we see in the heart of Jesus is also in God the Father's heart. He is our *"strength every morning, our salvation in the time of distress" (Isaiah 33:2 NASB). "The LORD is near to the brokenhearted, and saves those who are crushed in spirit. Many are the afflictions of the righteous; but the LORD delivers him out of them all" (Psalm 34:18,19 NASB).* In one of the most astounding passages in all Scripture, God's tender heart is laid bare:

I will tell of the kindnesses of the LORD, the deeds for which he is to be praised, according to all the LORD has done for us – yes, the many good things he has done… according to his compassion and many kindnesses. He said, "Surely they are my people, sons who will not be false to me"; and so he became their Savior. In all their distress he too was distressed, and the angel of his presence saved them. In his love and mercy he redeemed them; he lifted them up and carried them all the days of old.

Isaiah 63:7-9 (NIV)

In the New Testament the apostle Paul worshiped God for his compassionate heart. He wrote, *"Praise be to the God and Father of our Lord Jesus Christ, the Father of compassion and the God of all comfort, who comforts us in all our troubles, so that we can comfort those in any trouble with the comfort we ourselves have received from God" (2 Corinthians 1:3,4 NIV).* God has a big heart and he wants to express his heart through the people of God around us. You're not in this alone.

God promises to one day put his people in a place where suffering and pain are a forgotten thing of the past. Though we may wish for that to happen today, we can take comfort knowing that the pain of the present will not last forever. Two times in the final book of the Bible, *Revelation,* God made that point very clear:

Therefore, "they are before the throne of God and serve him day and night in his temple; and he who sits on the throne will spread his tent over them. Never again will they hunger, never again will they thirst. The sun will not beat upon them, nor any scorching heat. For the Lamb at the center of the throne will be their shepherd; he will lead them to springs of living water, and God will wipe away every tear from their eyes.'"

Rev. 7:15-17 (NIV)

"And I heard a loud voice from the throne, saying, 'Behold, the tabernacle of God is among men, and He shall dwell among them, and they shall be His people, and God Himself shall be among them, and He shall wipe away every tear from their eyes; and there shall no longer be any mourning, or crying, or pain; the first things have passed away."

Rev. 21:3,4 (NASB)

God is just. And even though justice is often difficult to find or experience in this world, in the end God will make sure justice prevails… in every case. Scripture is filled with reminders of the promise that *"the Lord of hosts will have a day of reckoning against everyone who is proud and lofty" (Isaiah 2:12).* God declares that *"Vengeance is Mine, I will repay." And again,*

"The Lord will judge his people" (Hebrews 10:30). The chilling truth (for all who reject God) is that *"it is a terrifying thing to fall into the hands of the living God" (Hebrews 10:31).* The danger is that we may be tempted to pay back evil for evil or take our own revenge, as Scripture warns us *never* to do (see *Romans 12:17-19).* We must not grow impatient with God or take matters into our own hands now. The reason God delays the final judgment is because he is patient, waiting for the rest of his family to finally come home. (see *2 Pet. 3:9*)

Identity Reminder:

I am assured all works together for good.

Rom. 8:28

WINDING DOWN

Have you honestly come to the point of trusting God in the midst of your pain? Can you see that *"He who did not spare his own Son, but gave him up for us all – how will he not also, along with him, graciously give us all things?" (Romans 8:32 NIV).* Or are you blaming God for your suffering?

A real and present danger to our freedom is that we turn against God himself in our bitterness and anger. Not understanding (none of us do!) why he has allowed certain painful things in our lives, we can harbor anger and hatred toward him. That would be a grave mistake, because God is the only One who understands our pain and the only One who can walk us through it.

We want to give you an opportunity today to talk things out with God, expressing to him your *feelings* (getting real with him) but also your *faith* (seeing what's real to him). You can be brutally honest with God; he can take it. Tell him about your pain. Complain to him about how you don't understand why he has allowed it. But then humble yourself and give up fighting. Let the Lord who daily bears our burdens (*Psalm 68:19a*) bear yours. Let the God who is our salvation (*Psalm*

68:19b) be yours. *"He who believes in him will not be disappointed" (Romans 9:33b).*

We encourage you to write out your prayer of pain, of confusion, of confession and of surrender below. It will be a huge step on your journey to freedom, and a big load off your mind.

_____

_____

_____

_____

_____

_____

_____

_____

_____

_____

_____

WRAPPING UP

Truth Point

"When my heart was grieved and my spirit embittered, I was senseless and ignorant; I was a brute beast before you. Yet I am always with you; you hold me by my right hand. You guide me with your counsel, and afterward you will take me into glory. Whom have I in heaven but you? And earth has nothing I desire besides you. My flesh and my heart may fail, but God is the strength of my heart and my portion forever."

(Psalm 73:21-26 NIV)

Application

Sometimes it is really helpful to get things down on paper. In the blanks below, write out the main areas of pain and suffering in your life right now. For example, you might write: *chronic illness; parental abuse as a child; our kids rebelling against God*, etc. In the next few days we're going to look at the wrong ways we often deal (or *don't* deal!) with pain as well as God's way. This will help you get started.

_____

_____

_____

_____

_____

_____

_____

_____

_____

_____

_____

_____

Identity Reminder:

I am free from any charge against me.

Rom 8:31-34

PRAYER

Dear heavenly Father, I guess if I truly was honest and saw myself the way you see me, I would have to admit that I spend a good portion of my time trying to avoid pain. And when pain comes my way, I get mad because it messes up my plans, knocks me off balance and just plain hurts. Some of my pain is deep stuff and I need help to face it. Who I really need is you, Jesus, because you know how to do that. I don't. I'm sorry I've been mad at you for somehow not rushing in at the last second to spare me from the suffering in my life. I choose to stop battling you over the "why's" of it all and choose instead to let you into the wounded places in my life so you can touch with your freeing, healing power. As for all the answers to my questions, I'll look forward to talking to you in heaven about those things. In Jesus' name I pray, amen.

DECLARATIONS

- **I know that pain is inevitable in a fallen world.**
- **I accept the truth that God is grieved over my pain.**
- **I will not slam the door in God's face, blaming him for my suffering.**
- **I recognize that God alone has the strength I need to face my pain.**
- **I welcome Jesus Christ into my wounded places to touch with his power.**

Hurt Yet Healed

Every Which Way but Loose

It is both amazing and tragic to see all the ways human beings will try to cope with (without really facing) their pain. I (Rich) received an email from a woman distraught over her husband's descent into deeper and deeper torment. Some time ago the man had been going through the *Steps to Freedom in Christ* with his wife but halted the process when he came face-to-face with difficult memories from his past. He refused to go farther. He also refused to humble himself and seek out help from a male counselor.

According to his wife, the man has "buried his need for freedom in Christ" even as he struggled with anxiety and depression. The stress on his life from his job was too much and he had to resign his position. He was a pastor.

A series of tough circumstances – the loss of a dear friend, the loss of another job due to state funding cuts and the death of his mother – were met with little emotion, at least outwardly. A month or so later he started drinking heavily, using over-the-counter stimulants and taking Prozac given to him by a "friend."

Things are not getting better, as both panic attacks and paranoia have set in. He believes people are watching him, whispering about him and plotting with doctors to have him taken away in an ambulance.

His doctor changed his medication, but the man kept taking the former pills while also taking more of the new medication than prescribed. He now hides his pills.

The poor man cries all the time and when his family tries to help him he bolts and runs away. When he returns he is quiet and moody and acts as if nothing has happened. The moods have become quite dark lately and his wife is very scared.

What would cause a man who once had a real devotion to God, to run 180 degrees in the opposite direction from the help he needs? That is the subject of today's devotional. And though your situation may not necessarily be as extreme as the man in this story, every one of us engages in fearful self-protection at times. To the same extent we run, we will fail to receive the grace we need or experience the freedom we want.

All of us have a very strong pull toward self-preservation and self-protection. Some of this is good and healthy. We are hungry so we eat; thirsty and we drink, cold and we dress more warmly, and so on. If we're threatened with physical harm, the "fight or flight" instinct kicks into action in self-defense. These are good things, God things.

There can be, however, a "dark side" to self-protection. It all depends on what we are protecting and how we are going about doing it. Listed below are some ways in which we can engage in *unhealthy* self-protection. Each of them is ultimately a defense mechanism designed to protect a false god or idol – usually ourselves – and in so doing they rob of us a fuller worship of God and deeper relationships with people. Ironically, the final result of using these techniques is that we are starved of the very thing we need… God's healing touch.

Though it may be painful to admit, it is a healthy first step to confess we have a problem in a certain area. Go ahead and honestly rate yourself for each practice below by circling the response that best describes you. You may want to have a spouse or close friend look over your work to see how clearly you are seeing yourself:

• *Denial (refusing to admit you have a problem or pain; NOTE: If this is a problem for you, you are going to deny you are in denial! Here's some help: Do people close to you get frustrated when they try and point out something wrong in your life because you won't listen? Do people ever tell you that you are in denial?)*				
Never	Rarely	Sometimes	Often	Always
• *Putting on a mask (pretending everything is under control, and life is good; lying to cover your tracks for fear of being discovered or exposed or rejected)*				
Never	Rarely	Sometimes	Often	Always
• *Self-medicating (using alcohol, tobacco, food, drugs, etc. in order to numb your pain)*				
Never	Rarely	Sometimes	Often	Always
• *Trying to escape reality (overusing TV, movies, books, video games, computer games, etc. in order to put off facing the tough realities of life)*				
Never	Rarely	Sometimes	Often	Always
• *Workaholism (spending an inordinate amount of time on the job in order to avoid confronting the other difficult areas of life, e.g. marriage and family)*				
Never	Rarely	Sometimes	Often	Always
• *Materialism (avidly pursuing the accumulation of wealth and possessions in the vain effort to fill up an empty heart)*				
Never	Rarely	Sometimes	Often	Always

● *Reluctance to engage in real, face-to-face relationships (often shown by avoiding people and being absorbed with "things" or "tasks", participating in pornography, overuse of "chat rooms"and other "Internet relationships", etc. that are in reality a false intimacy)*				
Never	*Rarely*	*Sometimes*	*Often*	*Always*
● *Rationalizing or projecting (making excuses for poor behavior or blaming others for your problems; unwillingness to admit you have sinned)*				
Never	*Rarely*	*Sometimes*	*Often*	*Always*
● *Holding onto your anger and expressing it to people (through words, tone of voice, facial expressions, body language, other actions) in order to try and protect yourself from further pain or just be left alone).*				
Never	*Rarely*	*Sometimes*	*Often*	*Always*

Scripture says, *"There is a way which seems right to a man, but its end is the way of death" (Proverbs 14:12).* If you engage in any of the behaviors listed above "sometimes, often or always," you are being seriously deceived. That self-protective behavior looks like it is helping or feels like it is keeping you safe, but it's not. It's a death trap. It leads to the death of intimacy with God. It kills healthy relationships, including marriages and families. It suffocates your own soul.

These are hard words, we know, but they are said in love. God has so much more for you. He wants you to be free! And freedom begins with coming out of the darkness and being honest or "walking in the light." In the light you find God and the help you need from other people.

> *This is the message we have heard from him and declare to you: God is light; in him there is no darkness at all. If we claim to have fellowship with him yet walk in the darkness, we lie and do not live by the truth. But if we walk in the light, as he is in the light, we have fellowship with one another, and the blood of Jesus, his Son, purifies us from all sin. If we claim to be without sin, we deceive ourselves and the truth is not in us. If we confess our sins, he is faithful and just and will forgive us our sins and purify us from all unrighteousness. If we claim we have not sinned, we make him out to be a liar and his word has no place in our lives. My*

> *dear children, I write this to you so that you will not sin. But if anybody does sin, we have one who speaks to the Father in our defense – Jesus Christ, the Righteous One. He is the atoning sacrifice for our sins, and not only for ours but also for the sins of the whole world.*

> *1 John 1:5-2:2 (NIV)*

Why do we engage in these self-protective behaviors in response to our own pain?

The bottom line is that no healthy person enjoys pain. We are afraid of it and generally do everything in our power to avoid it. Nothing profound there. But the fear of not being able to handle our pain (if we face it) and the fear of not being able to handle more pain (if we encounter it) often drives us underground. *Fear* is a main barrier to facing our pain.

Another enemy is *pride*. Pride tells us that we can handle things very well by ourselves, in our own strength. Pride tells us that it would be self-damaging to admit any need, so we keep quiet and try to work things out on our own. To the proud, "image" and "appearances" *are* everything.

A third hindrance to facing our pain in a healthy way is *shame*. When we fall prey to the "*less* mess" – feeling help*less*, hope*less*, worth*less*, point*less* – we feel we can't handle one more whisper of rejection or sense of failure, and though we know we are dying on the inside, we put on a happy face on the outside.

The following checklist is another diagnostic tool to help you discover in what ways you might be allowing *fear, pride* and *shame* to dictate how you try and hide or avoid the pain in your life. Check off the ones that are characteristic of your life:

- Defensiveness – self-protective, attacking others.

- Critical spirit – being quick to see and point out the faults of others.

- Self-righteousness – looking down on others.

- Independence – self-sufficient ways.

- Having to prove you are right.

- Having a demanding spirit.

- Having a consuming desire to win or be a success (as our culture defines it).

- Being driven to be recognized and appreciated.

- Quickness to blame others.

- Unapproachability – staying aloof and isolated.

- Having difficulty sharing your needs with others.

- Overly concerned about reputation and image.

- Having difficulty saying "I was wrong".

- Tendency to confess sins vaguely or generically.

- Concerned about being found out.

- Convinced that everyone but you has problems.

If you want to examine biblically more of the defense mechanisms that people engage in for the purpose of doing everything BUT coming clean regarding the sin and facing the pain in their lives, you might want to check out *Jeremiah 2 and 3*. As best we know, there is no other place in the Scriptures where the self-protective practices of men are better exposed. Just a warning, however: If you go into those chapters, go with the prayer, *Search me O God, and know my heart. Try me and know my anxious thoughts, and see if there be any hurtful way in me. And lead me in the everlasting way. (Psalm 139)*

Let the word of God reveal any unhealthy self-protective strategies that you have been employing. Don't go to the Bible to find all the bad things your spouse does or your boss does or your… You get the picture! *Jeremiah 2:12,13* (quoted as our *Truth Point*) is a very clear summary of that whole section of Scripture.

There is a great beginning of freedom birthed when we repent. To repent means simply to "change your mind." You have believed one way and now you choose another (God's) way. True repentance will always result in a genuine change of behavior (see *Matthew 3:8*). It may sound simple, but the ability to do so is clearly a gift from God (see *2 Timothy 2:25*). *It is God's kindness that leads us to repentance (Romans 2:4).* When we see his mercy and the power of his tender, healing touch we are moved to say "no" to our old ways of thinking and acting and to say "yes" to his truth and his power to change us.

Has the Lord shown you any faulty self-generated practices of self-preservation and self-protection in this lesson? If so, what will you do with them?

Truth Point

My people have committed two sins: they have forsaken me, the spring of living water, and have dug their own cisterns, broken cisterns that cannot hold water.

Jeremiah 2:12, 13 (NIV)

Application

Ask the Lord to shine his light on your life and then, in the blanks below, write down at least two circumstances in which you tend to put on a mask and hide the fact you are hurting. Consider also destructive ways you are trying to "numb" your pain. You might want to consider how you relate to your spouse, your kids, your fellow employees, your friends at church, and your "hang out" friends. See if you can identify if *fear*, *pride* or *shame* (or more than one) are involved.

_____

_____

_____

_____

_____

_____

_____

_____

_____

_____

Dear heavenly Father, it's funny how we haven't learned a whole lot since the Garden of Eden. We're still putting on fig leaves and hiding behind bushes in our fear, pride and shame. And we're still blaming each other like Adam and Eve did. I am truly sorry for the ways I have tried to hide my pain and hide from people and you. I confess that I have (*name the fleshly ways of protecting yourself the Lord has revealed to you*). These are the "broken cisterns" that I have made that hold no water. I turn away from these cracked pots and turn back to you, the fountain of living waters. Continue to peel back the protective layers over my heart so you can perform your open heart surgery in my life. Thank you that you are indeed the healer, Jesus. In your name, amen.

- **I renounce all self-centered ways of protecting myself.**

- **I announce my need for God and for the help of loving people.**

- **I renounce hiding, masking and self-medicating.**

- **I announce my openness to all of God's resources to face and heal my pain.**

Hurt Yet Healed
The Path to Healing

WARMING UP

When I (Rich) met Jeffrey he was 19 years old. I first noticed him when I was speaking to a church group in Long Island, NY. The subject of the message was "*Forgiving from the Heart*." Jeffrey was in a wheelchair and he was crying. Some of his friends were gathered around him as I spoke, trying to comfort him. I was curious about what was going on with him, and so I was glad when he wheeled up to me after the message was over.

"Tonight has been the most important night of my life," he said.

Since he had to go I asked if we could get together the next morning along with his youth pastor. I wanted to hear his story.

The next morning Jeffrey began, "I was born prematurely and as I was being transferred from one medical facility to another, I didn't get the oxygen I needed. That's why I'm this way."

Jeffrey could not walk. In addition, his arms were pencil thin and his hands were locked in a claw-like position. He explained that it was pretty humiliating to have to have everything done for him, including helping him use the bathroom. He even had to have people set him upright again if he tilted over.

"Why was last night so important for you?" I asked after listening to his story.

"Because I was finally able to forgive the people that did this to me."

Jeffrey told me he had won a huge settlement financially because of the neglect of the medical technicians. But all that money did nothing to heal his heart. That couldn't begin until he cancelled the debt by forgiving them.

In his pain, Jeffrey had been very angry with God so letting go of that resentment was huge, too. He couldn't understand why God had healed his sister of an injury suffered while working in a factory, but didn't heal him.

I had no answers and the last thing I wanted to do was spout off some kind of religious cliché. As I prayed, I did sense the Lord prompting me to have Jeffrey do something.

"Jeffrey, would you be willing to thank the Lord for the parts of your body that don't work very well?"

To my relief he did that eagerly and even went so far as to ask God to glorify himself through those same body parts.

We all rejoiced in the Lord.

"Jeffrey," I concluded, "there are millions of able-bodied young men and women out there who can walk around freely and use their hands and arms unhindered. But you are more free than many of them. You may feel trapped in this wheelchair, but they are trapped in their hearts, bound up by their own anger and bitterness."

And that's the truth.

At Freedom in Christ Ministries, we have seen a wide variety of spiritual and emotional afflictions. But one of the most prevalent is the harboring of resentment and bitterness. Nursing grudges, hanging on to offenses suffered, allowing unresolved anger to fester and boil inside — all these create an internal environment where bitterness can breed and grow, causing an epidemic of problems in the body of Christ.

This week we are looking at the subject of pain in our lives. Two days ago we faced the reality that pain is a part of life. Yesterday we examined some of the primary wrong ways we deal with that pain. Today we want to begin looking at God's way of facing pain. Forgiveness.

Before we look at God's word, take a minute to jot down what you believe it means to forgive. Then we'll check and see if you and God are on the same page.

Forgiveness is… _____

_____

_____

_____

_____

_____

Intuitively, you probably realize forgiveness *is* something that God wants us to do, but let's clear the air of any possible confusion first. Forgiveness is clearly God's idea and plan.

Go ahead and be angry. You do well to be angry – but don't use your anger as fuel for revenge. And don't stay angry. Don't go to bed angry. Don't give the Devil that kind of foothold in your life…

Watch the way you talk. Let nothing foul or dirty come out of your mouth. Say only what helps, each word a gift. Don't grieve God. Don't break his heart. His Holy Spirit, moving and breathing in you, is the most intimate part of your life, making you fit for himself. Don't take such a gift for granted. Make a clean break with all cutting, backbiting, profane talk. Be gentle with one another, sensitive. Forgive one another as quickly and thoroughly as God in Christ forgave you.

Ephesians 4:26,27, 29-32 (MSG)

Other Scriptures echo the same message, reminding us that forgiving others is part of the "new you" in Christ:

So, chosen by God for this new life of love, dress in the wardrobe God picked out for you: compassion, kindness, humility, quiet strength, discipline. Be even-tempered, content with second place, quick to forgive an offense. Forgive as quickly and completely as the Master forgave you. And regardless of what else you put on, wear love. It's your basic, all-purpose garment. Never be without it.

Colossians 3:12-14 (MSG)

Okay, it's clear. Whatever forgiveness is, God wants us to exercise it toward those who have hurt us. Let's see then what the Bible says forgiveness is.

We'll tell the story Jesus told in *Matthew 18* in a slightly updated version. It's all about a king who decided it was "pay day"… or really "pay up day." Everybody in the kingdom that owed him money was supposed to empty their pockets and pay off their debts. One guy that owed him the equivalent of about $20 million was brought before the king.

"Pay up!" the king demanded.

The poor guy knew he was in trouble. Despite pulling out his checkbook, his wallet, his piggy bank, his savings account, his investment portfolio and the cookie jar, he was still about $19,999,000 short.

The king, realizing the guy was not going to come through with the dough, decided to sell him, his wife and his children into slavery and sell all the guy's stuff in an auction.

He fell down before the king horrified. He knew he only had one chance, to plead for mercy. And so he did. Amazingly, the king cancelled the entire debt. It was as if he had never owed a penny. The man got to keep his family, his farm and most importantly, his freedom.

Now, you might think the guy would have gone around the countryside proclaiming what an incredibly merciful thing the king had done. But noooo…

The guy grabbed one of his buddies who owed him a couple thousand bucks and threatened to throw him in the slammer if he didn't pay up. His buddy was in no better shape financially than the man the king had forgiven. So he begged his friend for mercy.

Unbelievably, the forgiven man was unwilling to forgive his friend's debt and had him thrown in jail. Word got back to the king, who was understandably upset.

Here's the end of the story:

Then summoning him, his lord said to him [the one he had forgiven], "You wicked slave, I forgave you all that debt because you entreated me. Should you not also have had mercy on your fellow slave, even as I had mercy on you? And his lord, moved with anger, handed him over to the torturers until he should repay all that was owed him. So shall My heavenly Father also do to you, if each of you does not forgive his brother from your heart.

Matthew 18:32-35 (NASB)

We can pull out some important points about forgiveness from this whole story:

- Forgiveness means to cancel a debt that someone owes you.

- Forgiveness is an act of mercy.

- The debt that we owed God (pictured by the first guy's debt to the king) is astronomical; there's no way we can pay what we owe God because of our sins against him.

- God's forgiveness is complete and sets us totally free from the immeasurably huge debt we owed him.

- The debt that others owe us – though significant – is nothing compared to what we owed God and which God forgave us.

- God's expectation is that because of how great a debt he has forgiven us, we also ought to forgive those who have hurt us… and we should do it with all our heart, really meaning it deep down.

- If we choose not to forgive, the pain and suffering we have experienced from the hurt caused by others' sin will only be multiplied in the torment we feel inside because of our bitterness and resentment.

Knowing how tough it can seem to really forgive people, maybe you are now beginning to play what we call the ***Yeah, but…*** game. Check any of the following statements below that express how you're feeling at this point…

1 ☐ Yeah, but you don't realize how much pain I feel.

2 ☐ Yeah, but if you knew what this person did to me, you wouldn't be expecting me to forgive.

3 ☐ Yeah, but they have never apologized.

4 ☐ Yeah, but if I forgive them, that means they're getting off scot-free.

5 ☐ Yeah, but I don't feel like forgiving; I don't want to be a hypocrite.

6 ☐ Yeah, but I've lost track of this person; I have no way to talk to him.

7 ☐ Yeah, but I've already done this and I'm still angry.

We'll give a brief response to each objection.

1. You're right. We don't know how much pain you feel, but why perpetuate the pain by refusing to forgive? God has made a way out of the pain and into healing, but the first step is to forgive. Time does not heal all wounds. The grace of God + our choice to forgive + time will heal many of them, however.

2. It is not that we expect you to forgive, it is God, and he knows exactly what was done to you. What you're really saying is, "This person doesn't deserve forgiveness." And you're absolutely right. Neither did you, and yet God gave it. Forgiveness, at its essence, is an act of mercy (not giving people what they deserve) and grace (giving them what they don't deserve.) That's how God relates to us in Christ and that's how he expects us to relate to others. We know you've been hurt, but isn't it time to stop the pain? God has made one way toward that end: forgiveness.

3. It's unfortunate when people hurt us and don't acknowledge it. But it happens all the time. Sometimes they simply are not aware, other times they don't care or maybe they're even glad they hurt us. Jesus is our example of forgiveness. Even while dying on the cross (and those who did that to him did not apologize either) he prayed, *"Father, forgive them, for they don't know what they're doing" (Luke 23:34)*. Even Stephen, when he was being stoned to death by the Jewish leaders (again with no one apologizing,) he prayed, *"Lord, do not hold this sin against them!" (Acts 7:60)*.

4. No, it doesn't. It means you are giving up the right to exact justice from them, but it doesn't mean God won't bring judgment (if they refuse to accept Christ) or discipline (if they are believers.) *"Vengeance is Mine, I will repay," says the Lord. (Romans 12:19)* When we forgive, we let God be God and stop trying to play God ourselves.

5. That's an honest objection. Many times we don't feel like doing the right thing. We don't feel like praying, but we make the choice to pray and we're glad we did. We don't feel like reading the Bible, but after God ministers to us through his word, we're so glad we made that choice. Forgiveness is a choice based on obedience to God, doing what's right. If you push on and do what's right even in the face of how you feel, God will bring joy to you on the other side of obedience (see *John 15:10,11*.) Hypocrisy is acting differently than who you really are; it is not acting differently than how you feel. At your core, you are a child of God and Christ dwells in your heart. When you choose to forgive, you are choosing to allow the Christ who is your life to express his life through you. That is not being false; it's being true to the true you!

6. Your forgiveness of that person is not contingent upon their being around. Forgiveness is expressed directly to God. If the other person is not alive or available, it doesn't matter. Reconciliation, or the restoration of the relationship, does require "two to tango," but forgiveness does not. You can make the choice to forgive someone before God **today**, even if you never see them again!

7. Chances are you've just mouthed the words "I forgive" but not really connected with the pain and emotions (anger, humiliation, betrayal, hatred, etc.) deep down inside. If you quickly skim over forgiveness and don't get real with how you really feel, it's not really forgiveness. We'll give you a chance in the next few days to, by the grace of God, process through forgiveness more completely.

In the book of Jonah, God asked the prophet a very penetrating question, *Do you have a right to be angry?* Considering how nasty and cruel the Assyrians were and how cruelly they had treated God's people, you might be inclined to think Jonah *did* have a right to be mad. After all, God was choosing to forgive them not blast them! They deserved the wrath of God, not His mercy and so Jonah was really upset with God.

Jonah is a book about God's forgiveness and one man's struggle with the justice of it all. If that's an area of struggle for you, we encourage you to read the book of Jonah.

Forgiveness is not easy. In some ways it is one of the hardest things God calls us to do. But what seems impossible for us is not difficult for God. You should be encouraged to know that the forgiving Jesus dwells in your inner man (heart) to give you all the strength you need. If you are unconvinced or "feel" like this is impossible for you to do, know that you're being deceived. The enemy of your soul will pull out all the stops to try and get you NOT to forgive, because he knows forgiveness clears your path to freedom. Nothing is impossible for God, and as you allow him to take over your heart, he will give you the power to do that which – by yourself and in your own strength – you could never do!

Truth Point

For to this end also I wrote that I might put you to the test, whether you are obedient in all things. But whom you forgive anything, I forgive also; for indeed what I have forgiven, if I have forgiven anything, I did it for your sakes in the presence of Christ, in order that no advantage be taken of us by Satan; for we are not ignorant of his schemes.

2 Corinthians 2:9-11 (NASB)

Application and Prayer

We are combining the two of these today. First, we have included a prayer for you to pray, inviting the Lord to reveal to your mind all the people that you need to forgive. After that prayer are some blanks for you to list the names that come to mind in response to your prayer. You will have the opportunity tomorrow to take those people and what they've done to you before the Lord and make the choice to forgive them from your heart.

Dear heavenly Father, I am reminded again that I was once like the man in the story from Matthew 18. Because of my sin against you, I had a debt that was impossible for me to pay. But you, being great in mercy, chose to wipe out my entire debt, forgiving me of all my sins – past, present and future. Thank you once again for doing that for me. I didn't deserve your forgiveness, but here I stand, your forgiven child. Too often I have been like that same man in Matthew 18 who, forgetting how great a debt I have been forgiven, have refused to extend mercy to those people who have hurt me. Instead I have felt justified in holding on to my anger, resentment and bitterness. I am genuinely sorry for doing that. Now, in your wisdom and complete knowledge, would you please show me the people that I need to forgive? Bring back to my mind all the painful memories that I have repressed, suppressed or tried to ignore. I trust in your grace to enable me to face my pain. In Jesus' name, I pray, amen.

List the people below that the Lord shows you that you need to forgive. Use additional paper if necessary.

_____

_____

_____

_____

DECLARATIONS

- Jesus Christ has forgiven me, therefore I can forgive others!

- Jesus Christ is my strength and my grace to empower me to forgive!

Identity Reminder:

I cannot be separated from the love of God.

Rom. 8:35-39

Hurt Yet Healed

The Heart of the Matter

I (Rich) will never forget one of the first times I saw someone go through the process of forgiveness as part of the *Steps to Freedom in Christ.* The dear lady who was there for counseling had been sexually abused by her father… numerous times. Despite how horrible that sin was and how terrible its effects on her life and personality were, I sat and watched in amazement as she forgave him. I could tell that it was coming straight from her heart.

What surprised me was how hard it was for the woman to forgive her mother. Her mother had not abused her. I would've thought forgiving her dad would have been the harder of the two, but it wasn't. Forgiving her mother was tougher because her mother had done nothing to stop the abuse. She had stood by passively and allowed it all to happen over and over again. Then she refused to talk about it afterwards, acting as if nothing had happened.

I still vividly remember the tears streaming down this woman's face as her voice became almost like a little girl's again. She said, "I forgive my mom for not coming to my rescue, even though mommies are supposed to protect their little girls." It broke my heart.

Facing that level of pain was something this woman was able to do because she felt safe with the man taking her through the "*Steps.*" And she felt safe in the presence of the God who knows that kind of pain and who promises to walk with us through it.

God in his faithfulness and kindness did exactly that for this woman on that day and joyful freedom was waiting for her on the other side of her courageous obedience. I saw it with my own eyes.

That joy and freedom awaits you as well.

Today and tomorrow we are going to give you an opportunity to face the pain in your life and begin the process of forgiving those who have hurt you. If you have already done a lot of work in forgiving others or if you have not been seriously wounded by other people, then you may not need a whole lot of time to work through forgiveness. You may be able to completely work through this exercise in a rather short amount of time.

On the other hand, if your wounds go deep, you will require more time. We encourage you, if at all possible, to find someone you trust to sit with you and pray for you as you work through the list of people you need to forgive. Take as much time as you need. It is well worth it.

We believe that there are a couple levels of forgiveness that you may need to visit. We'll look at the first level today and the second tomorrow. The first level involves forgiving people for the deed itself and its immediate effects on you. An illustration of praying through this level of forgiveness, from our story above, might go something like this:

"Dear heavenly Father, I forgive my mom for not coming to my rescue when my dad was sexually abusing me. I felt scared and helpless and confused, not knowing why she didn't stop it. I was so angry with my mom for acting like it never happened. I felt unbelievably alone and vulnerable. But Lord, as much as this hurts me, I choose to cancel the debt of her sin against me and leave this in your hands, Lord. Amen."

This first level of forgiveness deals with three primary issues:

- The perpetrator of the offense (who was involved).

- The nature of the offense (what was done by the perpetrator).

- The immediate emotional effects of the offense (how it made the offended one feel).

As you look down your list of people that you need to forgive (from yesterday's assignment), you may need to add "yourself" to that list. If you have been beating yourself up for past sins and past mistakes, you have been listening to the accuser of the brethren (the devil) who wants you to wallow in guilt and shame. God wants you to emerge from that trap and claim his forgiveness… *for you!*

The prophet Isaiah wrote:

"Come now, and let us reason together," says the LORD, "Though your sins are like scarlet, they shall be as white as snow; though they are red like crimson, they shall be as wool."

Isaiah 1:18 (NKJV)

Forgiving yourself is laying hold of God's forgiveness of you through Christ's shed blood on the cross and saying, "Thank you, Lord. It is done." Maybe you have felt like you were wearing a scarlet letter all these years, a bright crimson reminder to yourself and everyone around you of your sin.

God is saying, "Enough is enough! I died for that sin and in My Son, Jesus, it is gone." Think about a freshly fallen snow. The purity. The peacefulness. The beauty. That is you *in Christ*.

As you look at all the people you need to forgive, including yourself, you may have a good idea of what they did that you need to forgive them for. Some very significant memories, however, may be partially or completely buried. The following prayer is simply to give God permission to bring back to your mind anything and everything he wants you to deal with. We encourage you to pray it now.

Dear heavenly Father, some of the things that have been done to me and that I have done to hurt myself are very vivid memories. I remember them all too clearly. But I also acknowledge that there may be some pain that I have forgotten about, but it's still there and I need to exercise forgiveness. Please bring to my mind all the pain that I need to face so that I can thoroughly forgive those who have hurt me, including myself. In Jesus' name I pray, amen.

You may be fairly in touch with how their offense(s) made you feel; many people are. But not everyone can put their finger so quickly on their emotions. This part may not be easy for you if you have been raised in a home or church environment where emotions were made to seem unimportant or expressing strong emotions was frowned upon or seen as "sin." In that case, you may have buried your emotions out of fear of their getting out of control or the punishment to you that would have resulted. In order to "forgive your brother from the heart" as Jesus told us to do in *Matthew 18:35*, you have to allow your true feelings to come out. Why? Allowing damaged emotions to surface gives Jesus permission to touch you in those places and begin the healing process. Stuffing those painful feelings will short circuit Jesus' healing power in your life. The following prayer may be helpful for you:

Dear heavenly Father, you know that expressing emotions or even acknowledging that I have feelings about some things is very hard for me. You alone know what is buried in some "protective vault" deep down in my heart. In order for me to be free, I have to allow you to surface my true feelings. I hand you the keys to that "vault" and ask you to enable me to freely share how I feel as I move ahead in this process of forgiving others from my heart. Please take away my fear of being real or exposed or out of control and guide me by your hand. In Jesus' name, amen.

If naming or expressing your emotions is difficult for you, we have included below a list of "emotion words" that will help you get beyond generic terms like "mad" or "hurt." Circle any of the words below that accurately describe how others' sins or your own sins have made you feel:

confused	furious	worthless	helpless
stupid	heartbroken	incompetent	ripped apart
controlled	anxious	devastated	frustrated
betrayed	unlovable	unimportant	crazy
alone	manipulated	thrown away	trapped
ashamed	demoralized	disappointed	dirty
unloved	unlovable	fearful	disillusioned
terrified	abandoned	used	ganged up on
insecure	embarrassed	evil	exasperated
rejected	disrespected	condemned	vulnerable
"at fault"	foolish	not good enough	humiliated
full of dread	cut down	unwanted	forgotten

One of the most helpful exercises in forgiving others or yourself is to place an empty chair at a comfortable distance across from you in a room where you have the privacy to talk openly out loud. Take each one of the people on your list and imagine that they are sitting in that chair listening to you. This is a safe thing to do because Jesus is right there with you and obviously, the person is not really there and cannot harm you. If you feel more comfortable having someone actually sit with you in the room and pray while you express what you need to say, then by all means invite a trusted friend to sit beside you out of your direct line of vision.

Your goal is to be completely honest with those you are "inviting" to sit in the empty chair, telling them what they did that hurt you and expressing to them how you feel or felt. Then, after getting everything out that you need to say, bow your head and speak to God, telling him that you forgive them. In our *Wrapping Up* section there is a prayer you can use as an example (feel free to modify it to make it your own while keeping the basic components.) Be sure to express your choice to forgive that person (including yourself) of all he or she has done to you.

You cannot turn the clock back and undo what was done to you, but by the grace of God you can be free from the haunting, nagging, gut-wrenching pain of what was done to you. *Remember that freedom only comes through forgiveness.*

Truth Point

For you have been called for this purpose, since Christ also suffered for you, leaving you an example for you to follow in His steps, "who committed no sin, or was any deceit found in His mouth"; and while being reviled, He did not revile in return; while suffering, He uttered no threats, but kept entrusting Himself to Him who judges righteously;

1 Peter 2:21-23 (NASB)

Application

The application for today is to take the names of people you need to forgive that you wrote down yesterday (adding "yourself" if necessary as well as any other names that have since come to mind) and working through the forgiveness exercise described in today's *Winding Down* section. The use of the chair is optional. Many have found it to be helpful in getting started and being honest, but if that comes easily for you, you can simply talk to God about it all.

Remember the three components to this level of forgiveness. First you have to name names. Be specific in naming who hurt you. Second, be very specific in describing what he or she did to you. Avoid generic statements like, "Lord, I forgive my dad for the things he did and the ways he hurt me." Being specific in naming the offense will help you with the third component of this level of forgiveness: being very specific in expressing how the offense made you feel. If you feel some of that emotion bubbling to the surface, that is a good thing. Don't try and stop the flow of your feelings. Let them out and express them honestly. Then, once you have truly cleared the air and expressed your heart, you can pray using the prayer below (or something similar). There's nothing magic in the words, it's your heart that matters. (We'll skip the "Declarations" section today.)

Dear heavenly Father, as best I know how I have been honest and open about what *(name the person)* did to me and how it made me feel. Is there anything else, any other painful memories that I need to remember and talk about regarding this person? *[Take a few moments and see if anything else comes to mind.]* Father, I have expressed to you all the things in the "debit column" of what *(name the person)* did to me. I now make the choice to erase, cancel out the debt and forgive every one of these hurtful things that he/she did. I relinquish any right to extract my "pound of flesh" or seek revenge. It is all in your hands now and I thank you for taking it off my hands. I now invite you to work your healing in my heart in your way and in your time. If I am ever tempted to take up any of these offenses again, I ask you to remind me of this commitment to keep my hands off. In Jesus' name I gratefully pray, amen.

Identity Reminder:

I am established, anointed, sealed by God.

2 Cor. 1:21-22

Hurt Yet Healed

Going Deeper

WARMING UP

It is tragic to see how the sins of others can deeply affect us, especially when those sins occur in our childhood. The enemy of our souls lurks in the shadows of sin, just waiting to pounce on young, vulnerable hearts. He exploits those times of pain, when there are gaping wounds in our souls, and implants his lies there. Those lies can subconsciously chart the course of our daily lives for decades.

I (Rich) remember talking with a middle-aged woman. She had never been married but was preparing to do so and the Lord had some important surgery to do in her life to get her ready. The day before we met, God had brought to her mind several seemingly "everyday" events from her childhood. Some were more devastating than others, but all were hurtful. The result of those events had been the implantation of lies about herself that had stuck with her well into her 40s.

One event revolved around a holiday. She was at a relative's house when she spotted a new doll in a stroller. She hopefully asked, "Oh, is that for *me*?" The relative had harshly replied, "Of course not!" Even though the toys actually *were* for her, the Lord revealed that a lie had been planted at that time of childhood pain. The lie said, "Good things do not come to you."

Years later, her dad promised her a new bicycle if she made the Honor Roll. She did and was so excited about getting her new bike. Her dad, however, decided that what she really needed was a new watch and so he gave her that instead. Lie #2 was planted at that time, "Nobody cares about your heart, what you really want."

Taken together, along with other lies, a driving force in her life was forged – the heart decision and vow that "if I am ever going to get anything or get anywhere in life, I've got to do it myself." Along with that vow came the nagging thought, "…but I'll probably never be really happy in life."

The lies she had believed as a result of painful circumstances and the sins of others even caused her to seriously doubt the goodness of God. It took forgiveness and the renunciation of those lies to clear the way for freedom. Had it not been for this divine intervention, her marriage could very well have been a disaster.

Let's be quick to make a disclaimer here. We are not advocating a victim mentality. This is not the blame game. We cannot be absolved of our responsibility for making bad choices or wrong decisions in life because of the sins of others. We are not in any way making a case for people to wallow in self-pity or self-excusing based on the poor or even wicked behavior of others. That is a trap and a dead-end path on our journey to God's freedom.

Having said all that, however, it is also true that sin has consequences. Sin damages us and often predisposes us to certain behavior. The enemy uses those painful moments in life to inject his poisonous lies into our wounded places. Had we never been wounded by another's sin in that way, we would likely never have believed those particular lies in the first place. Our lives could very well have taken a different, better course. For example, a young boy who has easy access to pornography at home due to his careless, promiscuous father very likely will have a much more bitter struggle against sexual sin than a boy not raised in that environment. That is just a reality of life.

Today, we want to give you the opportunity to take forgiveness to a deeper level, if necessary. In some cases that won't be needed at all. Incidents that had no lasting impact beyond the immediate feelings of anger or hurt can be taken care of through the process described yesterday. For example, being unfairly yelled at once by your mom or dad after you got a "C" on an exam will likely need to be forgiven, but it's probably a "level one" forgiveness issue.

But if your parents told you every day of your life that you couldn't do anything right and that you would never amount to anything, that is another matter. That kind of behavior likely implanted "identity lies" about your value, acceptability, importance and competence.

This "level two" forgiveness then carries with it the following additional components:

- **Recognizing** the "identity lies" that took hold as a result of the sinful offense against you.

- **Renouncing** those lies and choosing the truth about your true identity in Christ.

- **Releasing** the offender of all guilt and blame for how their sin has affected your self-perception throughout your life.

Recognizing identity lies

Many times the very negative words that people have said to us function as a kind of "curse" on our lives. We come to believe what they said to us or about us and end up living our lives accordingly. Sometimes these lies come as a result of the enemy whispering them into our minds or by means of our own thought processes. However they take hold, their effects can be devastating.

The following prayer is an invitation to the Lord to begin to reveal those lies to you. Some may become clear to you today; others may be revealed over time. That's okay. The Lord has his timetable for helping you recognize and face them.

> Dear heavenly Father, your Son said that the truth would set me free, but I am not completely free. That means there are some areas in my life in which I am believing lies, especially about my identity—who I really am. I ask you to shine your light on my heart and mind and reveal to me the false conceptions and perceptions that I have of myself that have been born out of the pain in my life. I trust you to also reveal truth to me so that I might walk freely in that truth. In Jesus' name I pray, amen.

King David's prayer to God expresses the heart of what we are seeking God to do here. He wrote, **_"Surely you desire truth in the inner parts; you teach me wisdom in the inmost place" (Psalm 51:6 NIV)._**

Below we have listed some of the more common lies that we may have come to believe regarding our identity and value as a person. None of these things is true of a child of God, but they can _feel_ like they are true, especially if we have believed them for a long time. Circle any that have been part of your view of yourself. Write down any other lies that the Lord reveals to you in the blanks provided.

I can't do anything right

I am a mistake

I am stupid or ugly or evil or _____

I am alone in this world

Nobody really cares about me

I'll never be safe

I would be better off if I'd never been born

The world would be a better place if I were gone

I'll never amount to anything

My only value in this world is to provide sex for people

I am dirty and tainted

There's no hope for me

Even God has given up on me

This Christian life may work for others but I just can't get it

I've got to make life work myself because I can't count on anyone else

Good things come to others, but not to me

My feelings don't matter

_____

_____

_____

WINDING DOWN

We realize that it takes time to renew our minds, but that is the way we are transformed (**_Romans 12:2_**). A strong beginning point for renewing our minds with the truth is to renounce the lies that we have come to believe. To renounce means "to cut all ties with, to disavow any allegiance to, to reject." Once we renounce a lie, we are setting the stage for truth to begin to take hold (we encourage you to review truth about your identity in Christ from Week 2). The following exercise is most powerfully done out loud. It becomes more meaningful for you personally this way. It also amounts to drawing a line in the sand between you and the powers of darkness that have sought to keep you enslaved in these lies.

In the name and in the authority of the Lord Jesus Christ who is himself Truth, I right here and now renounce the lie that _(list any and all lies your circled or wrote in the blanks above)_. I am a child of God and no matter how long I have believed these lies and no matter how "true" they feel to me, I reject and disown them all and choose to believe the truth of God's word instead. I desire for that truth to make my mind new so that my life can be changed.

WRAPPING UP

PRAYER

Truth Point

At that point Peter got up the nerve to ask, "Master, how many times do I forgive a brother or sister who hurts me? Seven?" Jesus replied, "Seven! Hardly. Try seventy times seven."

Matthew 18:21,22 (MSG)

It is very normal for you to feel anger toward those who have contributed to your believing lies about yourself, especially if those lies have acted like evil winds blowing you off course all your life. Again, we are not saying that you are a helpless victim in this matter. You are still responsible for the choices you have made in life, regardless of how much you have been hurt. But you also need to acknowledge that the sin of others may have had serious consequences in your life, predisposing you to believe very damaging lies about yourself. For that negative contribution to your personal story, you need to forgive them.

In the *Truth Point* Jesus talked about forgiving people seventy times seven times. He wasn't suggesting we keep a scorecard. He was telling us to forgive no matter how many times we are sinned against. There are two ways to apply this Scripture. The most obvious way is to forgive someone even if they commit innumerable sins against you. The other way is to forgive someone no matter how many times their sin against you (especially the lies they said to you) comes back to haunt your mind.

The following prayer is designed to help you express to God your forgiveness toward those who have damaged your sense of identity and value. Feel free to use it "as is" or shape it to make it yours. There's nothing magic in the words. It is forgiving *from the heart* that frees us (**Matthew 18:35**).

Dear heavenly Father, this is deep stuff. I'm beginning to see that a large part of my life -- many of my decisions, ambitions, beliefs, struggles, fears and anxieties have been born out of lies I have believed. I thank you for revealing those lies and granting me grace to renounce them. I now choose to forgive *(name the people that lied to you or caused the pain out of which the lies you've believed were birthed)* for being used by the enemy to convince me that *(name the lies you have believed about yourself)*. There are so many ways that I have allowed those lies to dictate my life and behavior *(list them here)*. I choose to forgive these people for the fallout from those lies as well, and I accept my personal responsibility for my sinful choices. In Jesus' name I pray, amen.

Because of how important Days 17-19 are for your freedom, we want you to feel the complete freedom to take the next two days to continue to process this material if you need more time. We will have other material in Days 20 and 21 for those who are ready to move on, but the most important thing right now is to take unhurried time to work through forgiving others from your heart.

Space for Additional Notes:

_____

_____

_____

_____

_____

_____

_____

_____

_____

_____

_____

_____

_____

_____

_____

_____

_____

_____

_____

_____

_____

_____

Hurt Yet Healed

The Touch of Jesus

You are likely looking at this page and wondering where the *Warming Up* section is hiding. Don't worry, you haven't missed it. We just decided to shift gears for one day and put in a devotional that doesn't require any writing, just reading. You've just been through a very intense and important couple of days where we have looked at the area of *forgiveness.* By the way, you may still need more time to process through the forgiveness issues in your life. Feel free to take the time you need to do that.

We also decided to vary the format since today represents a bit of a milestone in our *Journey to Freedom* together. Congratulations, you've reached the halfway point! You've earned a little breather from writing, though we are convinced the content in today's devotional may be some of the most amazing and encouraging in the whole book!

So for today, we want you to just read and ponder some things about forgiveness and healing that we trust will be helpful for you. Most of today's devotional will be the first-hand story of a lady who has emerged from about as thick a shadow of darkness as you can imagine, into God's glorious light. We think you will be touched by her story.

But before we hear from her, I (Rich) wanted to give some introductory thoughts.

Just like you, I have had many things to forgive many people for over the years. In fact, hardly a day goes by that I have not had to express to the Lord my choice to forgive someone for something they said, did or didn't do.

I view this kind of forgiveness like basic common sense care of our bodies. If we eat a balanced diet with lots of fruits, vegetables and vitamins, get adequate rest, regular aerobic exercise and cast our stresses on the Lord, we will tend to be healthy people. We may have an occasional cold but our immune system will generally be strong and illnesses will be short-lived. It's the same way with forgiveness. Doing daily maintenance by keeping "short accounts" with God (by not allowing the sun to go down on our anger, but forgiving quickly) can save us from major headaches and heartaches later.

But sometimes we need more. Sometimes our bodies are struck by something much more serious than a cold. Sometimes we need antibiotics, radiation, chemotherapy or even surgery to get well. And often there is a long period of healing required after the treatment or operation because the disease has done such serious damage to our bodies.

So it is with our souls. Sometimes the traumatic nature of our pain is such that we need more than a couple days or even 40 to get well. In a short amount of time (like six weeks) we can make *some* significant progress toward spiritual healing, just as one could check into a hospital, have major surgery, and begin physical rehab during 40 days. But full healing of the body and soul often takes much longer. Sometimes the effects of our physical or spiritual trauma can last for the rest of our lives.

In one sense we are all "damaged goods." I like that expression because in Christ we *are* good – holy and clean before God. But because of life in a fallen world, we are all also damaged. The Bible calls these places of damage *weaknesses* or *infirmities*. They are factors in our lives that cause us to be physically, mentally, emotionally, socially or spiritually debilitated. We all have them.

One person may have a physical handicap such as dyslexia or diabetes. Another person may struggle with mental disabilities that hinder basic reading and writing skills and cause him or her to fall farther and farther behind others his or her age (as is the case with our adopted son, Luke.) Others may be socially backward due to growing up in an atmosphere of fear, having serious struggles making and keeping friendships. Still others may have suffered such physical, mental or sexual trauma and abuse early in life that they are now physically middle-aged but emotionally still children.

All of us need God's healing touch and the mystery of healing is that though God can and sometimes does heal instantaneously, many times it is a much longer process. Sometimes full healing does not come until we pass into eternity. But even when complete healing is distant, delayed or even denied on earth, there is an even deeper reality that we can experience.

We'll talk more about that reality in a moment, but for now we want you to hear from a true trophy of God's grace. She calls her story *Joy in the Desert*.

All of us have a "past," a pile of rubble that wants to intrude into our lives to keep us in a kind of rearview mirror bondage. Many of the rocks in my pile of rubble were giant-size, a few were just pebbles. I used to sit in elementary school and watch the other kids. I wondered what it would be like to live in a safe home, an alcohol-free home, an occult-free home. The other kids had time to do their homework. They weren't busy trying to stay alive physically and sane mentally.

One of the worst things about brutal abuse is that when you are consistently abused — some would later use

the word "Satanic ritual abuse" to describe my personal holocaust — you begin to believe that somehow you deserve it. Being treated like an animal begins to bring thoughts that perhaps you are less than human. Circling around in your mind are the beginnings of embedded lies, the kind of stuff that mental and emotional strongholds are built from.

My world had two parts, Part A and Part B, I concluded as a child. Part A had a façade of normalcy. We worked hard on the farm, went to Sunday school and to church, and took the bus to school on weekdays. I often wished that I could do some sort of mental gymnastics to convince myself that Part A was the only kind of life I lived.

But there was Part B. Generationally, our family had always made room for the spirit world. Their belief that anything supernatural was of god led my parents down the path of first using the psychic powers of spiritism, to finally embracing the hardcore worship of the god behind spiritism. On a regular basis my life as a little girl included physical abuse that would later be called torture, sexual abuse as my father prostituted me to his friends, and mental and emotional abuse that included words from my mother such as, "If you're still alive by the time you're twelve, I'll kill you myself!"

By the time I left home, I resembled the man of Gadara in Scripture. I had all the outward symptoms of mental illness and, like him, spiritual bondage as well. Powerful spirits which had been placed in my life by my family when I was only an infant, as well as demons that I had unknowingly invited into my life (they appeared to me when I was a little girl as beings that wanted to be my friends) worked to make me a very powerful witch and also worked to destroy me. Like the man of Gadara, I was sometimes driven to burn myself, gash my arms with razor blades or pursue desperate attempts at suicide. Somehow, with the level of inner anguish, these practices relieved the pain, at least for a brief moment.

I was left with physical scars inflicted by others as well. I have the imprint of a boot embedded in my side, the result of being viciously kicked. I have other deformities and infirmities from the torture I suffered.

Since wickedly distorted Scriptures are commonly used in occult rituals, I had hideous misperceptions of God. I believed that he wanted to kill me and that he would cruelly choke me when I died and appeared before him in heaven. My view of our heavenly Father was not kind. He was unpredictable, just like my earthly father. My belief that I was born to be wickedly used led me to a self-loathing that took years to cure.

"But God…" These two little words made all the difference for me. Even as a little seven-year-old, brand new Christian, I began a relationship with the Good Shepherd that has only grown in its sweetness over the years. In the midst of the weekly atrocities that were part of my world as a child, God granted me several incredible gifts.

One of God's gifts was an incredible ability to learn to live with the unexplained. He gave me a picture of an "unexplained box" and encouraged me to put into it those events and situations that, from my vantage point, made no sense. I could go on asking him to explain them to me, but not allow the enemy to keep me distant from him while I waited for the answers. One of the first things I put into my unexplained box was the question, "Where were you, Lord? Why didn't You stop them?"

Another priceless gift that brought me joy in my childhood desert experience was an incredible revelation of what he was really like. Once I was walking along the peak of our roof. I had just been reminded by the demonized people abusing me that I belonged to them and to their god. They had made a covenant for me even before I was born. I was walking along the ridge of the roof so I could jump off and end my life. At eleven years of age, I had already come to the conclusion that at least I could be in control of one thing in my life – when and where it ended.

As I walked I had an experience similar, I suppose, to that of Elijah when during his time of despair God intervened and spoke with him. God spoke to me. He asked me what I was doing. I told him that I didn't want to live anymore because I belonged to the darkness and they had made a covenant for me.

There up on that roof my incredible God revealed a powerful truth. "You did belong to them. They had made a covenant for you. But I made a new covenant. Now you belong to Me!" That blazing truth from the book of Hebrews penetrated the mind of that eleven-year-old on the roof, saved her life and drew her closer to her gracious God.

But he gave me still another present, the incredible gift of a rebuilt life. The freedom from spiritual bondage, the restoring of my soul, my emotions, the replacing of embedded lies with his truth and the incredible joy in the midst of the desert were all part of his work in my life. These things took time. They took courage on my part. They took the kind of endurance that can only come from the God of Endurance who filled me with all joy and peace in believing so that I could abound in hope by the power of the Holy Spirit. The psalmist said it well, "They will bubble over with his abundant goodness." That is the level of inner joy that he has placed within me.

We'll let this wonderful lady finish her story in a moment, but first we thought it would be helpful for you to know that she has spent her life in tremendous physical pain and suffering because of the damage done early in her life. Innumerable trips to the hospital, several brushes with death, constant chronic pain and humanly irreversible damage to her body have dogged her steps.

Yet I (Rich) doubt that I know a more joyful, light-hearted, fun person. That's no small feat, considering her ministry (which is worldwide in scope) is to those who have suffered oppression of the same variety as her own!

Let's pick up the rest of the story…

One week during the Bible study I was teaching, I requested prayer from the ladies in the group. I said that I needed prayer to help deal with the constant pain I was in due to my illnesses. They all enthusiastically promised to pray that the Lord would heal me of all my physical problems.

One night during the following week, as I lay awake because of intense pain, I said out loud in a moment of frustration, "Lord, I'd give anything to be without this pain for five minutes!"

"Would you?" He seemed to answer. "Would you give up what I have used this pain to accomplish in your life? Would you give up the preciousness of our relationship that has come out of your suffering?"

"No, Lord, I wouldn't trade that for anything!" I replied. Then what followed can only be called a "Hallelujah breakdown" as I spent several hours worshiping the Lord, my strength and my comforter.

Next week, the ladies returned to the Bible study feeling quite confident that the Lord had answered their prayers. "Did he heal you?" they asked with expectant looks on their faces.

"No," I said, "but…" and I began to tell them of my incredible encounter with the Creator of the universe, my compassionate Counselor. I watched as their faces went from expectation to disappointment. They were quiet for a brief moment and then added with a somewhat deflated hopefulness, "Well, we'll keep praying."

Their reaction told me that they, like I, often put "released from negative circumstances" at the top of their priority praise list. Things like "perseverance in the midst of…" "endurance in spite of…" or "trophy of his grace and comfort" were considered low priorities on their list. After all, isn't God's number one job description to give me an easy life?

My intimate, strengthening encounter with the Lord during that week meant nothing to them because they, in their concern for me, just wanted my suffering to be over. Were they wrong to pray for my healing? No. It was perfectly all right to pray for that. But when God chose to say "not yet" or "maybe never, until you see Me face to face", their limited theology about suffering and pain didn't allow them to rejoice with me over God's presence and communication to me in the midst of my suffering.

Like I (Rich) said before, I *know* this lady. She is the real deal. Though she has suffered far more than a vast majority of us ever will, there is not an ounce of bitterness, resentment or unforgiveness in her.

She is free, deep down inside where it really counts.

And beyond freedom, there is a constant, vibrant, pulsing reality that gives her daily grace to live. *She deeply knows the God of grace and that is enough.*

Her story is a testimony to me and you that **freedom is not the absence of suffering but the joyful walk of faith and patient enduring of pain in the midst of suffering.**

We all long for and pray for the healing touch of Jesus. When it comes, we rejoice and give him glory! But what about the *sustaining* touch of Jesus that enables us to endure with joy? Is that any less significant?

We invite you to pray as the Lord leads…

Hurt Yet Healed

What's It All About?

WARMING UP

Let's face it. Here in America we don't "do pain" very well. We are so used to getting exactly what we want, exactly when we want it that anything that disrupts our "paradise" makes us angry. In all honesty we're pretty spoiled.

For example, in a country such as ours where we have almost countless variations of soft drinks, coffee and alcoholic beverages to choose from, what would happen to us – God forbid! – if all we had to drink was water (and not "bottled water" either!)? I fear we'd collectively end up in the fetal position somewhere.

I (Rich) am no different. I think I'm suffering terribly if gas prices go up a dollar. I grumble and complain and go drink a grande latte mocha frappucino coffeemismo to drown my sorrows.

You'd think I would have accepted pain as an inevitable part of life by now. After all, for the past 30 years I have suffered from migraine headaches. Nasty things. They invariably start over my right eye then drill their way deeper into my brain. There are different parts of my head and neck that are particularly miserable during its assault. Almost any kind of light or noise is a killer. I pop pain killers in my mouth and plop ice bags on my head and receive some relief.

But unless I catch it really early, I know what's coming.

Almost like clockwork, the nausea comes. Then the violent vomiting. Then the collapsing back in bed, mercifully (maybe) dozing for a while until the headache or nausea wakes me up and the cycle repeats. Pounding head. Throwing up. Exhaustion. More pounding head…

Not fun.

Even though I discovered one of the main causes of the headaches is an allergic reaction to the flavor enhancer monosodium glutamate, there are still other triggers if I'm not careful.

I also am subject to painful lower back spasms… the kind that grab my muscles and twist them, like someone wringing out a washcloth, until the appropriate scream comes out of my mouth. They started over 20 years ago when I was nailed in the back by this little kid in a neighborhood football game. We were both going for a fumble. I got the ball, but then crawled off the field in agony. The rest is my history. I bet that kid has grown up and never had a backache in his life. He probably still plays football.

Once, maybe more than once, I've had the vomiting migraine and back spasms at the same time. I know I uttered words that are not found in the Bible.

That's just a snapshot of the physical pain. It doesn't include the harder, deeper, more gut-wrenching emotional suffering and grief of life.

What's the point of all this pain? Is there any redeeming value to it?

The troubling thing about pain is that the Bible makes it sound like it is a very "normal" part of life in an abnormal world. That's not good news to someone like me who's a product of a culture that views any kind of suffering as an insult.

As we finish up this week talking about all the pains in the neck— and the heart— that we experience, we've actually got some good news. God seems to think that something good, actually something *very* good, can come out of suffering. That is, if we are willing to let it happen. And though we would much prefer to experience freedom *from pain*, God wants us to know that we can experience freedom *in the midst of pain*.

Identity Reminder:

I am a citizen of heaven.

Phil. 3:20

Right up front, let us state something very important. We are not Christian fatalists. We do not believe we should simply lie down and accept all the misery this world can throw at us. If there's a treatment or remedy for a physical affliction, by all means pursue it. If you are engaged in a spiritual battle, fight! That's what week five is all about. If there is an avenue of justice to right a wrong that you are suffering, then go for it.

Scripture is filled with countless examples of God fighting for what is right and urging his followers to do likewise. Just one example:

> **Take your evil deeds out of my sight! Stop doing wrong, learn to do right! Seek justice, encourage the oppressed. Defend the cause of the fatherless, plead the case of the widow.**
>
> **Isaiah 1:16-17 (NIV)**

You ought to be encouraged to know that God is not the least bit passive but is a battler for good and justice in this wicked world. And so should we be.

But what happens when pain and suffering come our way and there is no remedy, no recourse and no removal? What does it take to walk in freedom then?

First of all, know that it is okay and very healthy to cry out to God for relief. The apostle Paul had some nameless affliction that was very hard to endure — and Paul was no whiner. He had endured hard labor, imprisonment, floggings, scourgings, beatings with rods, shipwrecks (three times!), hunger, thirst, nakedness, cold, sleeplessness, and danger everywhere from everyone. He was even once stoned and left for dead (see *2 Corinthians 11:23-29*). But whatever this thing was – this was a messenger from Satan sent to slap him around – it was *bad*. Here's Paul's testimony of how he handled it:

To keep me from becoming conceited because of these surpassingly great revelations, there was given me a thorn in my flesh, a messenger of Satan to torment me. Three times I pleaded with the Lord to take it away from me. But he said to me, 'My grace is sufficient for you, for my power is made perfect in weakness.' Therefore I will boast all the more gladly about my weaknesses, so that Christ's power may rest on me. That is why, for Christ's sake, I delight in weaknesses, in insults, in hardships, in persecutions, in difficulties. For when I am weak, then I am strong.

2 Corinthians 12:7-10 (NIV)

Paul pleaded with God to remove this thorn three times (probably taking his cues from Jesus who begged God three times to spare him from the cross, though each time surrendering to the Father's will). But God had a different… yes, a better plan… a plan even better than Paul's healing! It's almost unbelievable, but there it is.

By this "thorn" Paul was protected from pride that would have knocked him off God's ministry team. It kept him humble, dependent on God. It allowed Christ's power to pour in and through his life. And so Paul boasted gladly about his weaknesses, and even delighted in them! That is freedom!

How about you? Have you asked God repeatedly to take something painful from your life… some circumstance or condition that simply will not go away? (We're not talking about a sin in your life here!) Perhaps a family member or friend is very difficult to love. Maybe your job is putting great pressure on you. Possibly a physical affliction that neither prayer nor medication seems to change…

Can you see God's hand of humbling upon you through it? Can you thank him for it? We know this is tough stuff, but why not ask God to give you Paul's view of suffering? The blanks below are an ideal place for you to write out a prayer to God.

_____

_____

_____

_____

In addition to humbling us and protecting us from dangerous pride, the verses below give us other benefits of suffering. In the blanks provided after each verse, write down the benefit you see coming from pain.

Although he [Jesus] was a son, he learned obedience from what he suffered, and once made perfect, he became the source of eternal salvation for all who obey him.

Hebrews 5:8,9 (NIV)

_____

_____

_____

_____

Consider it pure joy, my brothers, whenever you face trials of many kinds, because you know that the testing of your faith develops perseverance. Perseverance must finish its work so that you may be mature and complete, not lacking anything.

James 1:2-4 (NIV)

_____

_____

_____

_____

Therefore, since Christ suffered in his body, arm yourselves also with the same attitude, because he who has suffered in his body is done with sin. As a result, he does not live the rest of his earthly life for evil human desires, but rather for the will of God.

1 Peter 4:1,2 (NIV)

_____

_____

_____

_____

Not only so, but we also rejoice in our sufferings, because we know that suffering produces perseverance; perseverance, character; and character, hope. And hope does not disappoint us, because God has poured out his love into our hearts by the Holy Spirit, whom he has given us.

Romans 5:3-5 (NIV)

_____

_____

_____

_____

Imagine for a moment someone said to you, "I have a surefire deal for you. By this thing you will learn to obey God, be set free from fleshly sin, become mature in Christ with deep, genuine Christ-like character, have hope and experience God's love in a fuller way." Wouldn't you jump at the chance to take that deal?

That's what suffering can do for us, if we let it. Your freedom and our freedom in this world of pain is… at least in part… going to be dependent on how we view the unavoidable suffering that comes our way.

Truth Point

Dear friends, do not be surprised at the painful trial you are suffering, as though something strange were happening to you. But rejoice that you participate in the sufferings of Christ, so that you may be overjoyed when his glory is revealed.

1 Peter 4:12, 13 (NIV)

Application

One of the most healing things that we can do is give thanks to God for the tough times that come our way. That same Paul, who "did pain" right, told us *"give thanks in all circumstances, for this is God's will for you in Christ Jesus" (1 Thessalonians 5:18 NIV)*. We *can* give thanks because *Romans 8:28,29 (NIV)* tells us, *"And we know that in all things God works for the good of those who love him, who have been called according to his purpose. For those God foreknew he also predestined to be conformed to the likeness of his Son…"* People without Christ have no such guarantee, but true followers of Christ can be assured that – though everything in our lives is certainly not good – God is able to bring good out of everything in our lives. And that "good" is to make us more and more like Jesus. *That* is worth saying, "Thank you, God." Below we have started a few statements with those very words, "Thank you, God." Will you, by faith, complete those statements with the circumstances in your life that have brought you pain and suffering?

Thank you, God _____

_____

Thank you, God _____

_____

Thank you, God _____

_____

Thank you, God _____

_____

PRAYER

DECLARATIONS

Dear heavenly Father, this all takes a lot of faith – maybe more than I feel like I have right now. But your word says that "faith comes by hearing and hearing by the word of Christ." So I ask that you increase my faith to truly receive what your word in this day's devotional says is true. I believe, Lord, but help my unbelief! Turn these trials into gold in my life. I choose to believe that you have a bigger purpose, a wiser plan, a better ending to my life and all its pain than simply hurting. I put my trust in you. Teach me how to live freely even while waiting for your healing… even if I have to wait until I see you face to face. In the name of Jesus who left me an example of how to suffer, amen.

- **God's word is more true than what my feelings tell me!**

- **I choose to believe the word of God.**

- **I accept the truth that God is turning and will turn every trial in my life for some kind of good in my life.**

- **I accept the truth that anything that makes me more like Christ is something I can thank God for!**

Broken Yet Chosen

Broken Yet Chosen
He is Gathering His Clay

Michael and I (Christi) have been married 20 years. It's amazing how old that can make you feel! Anyway, we are both quick to admit that our marriage has not been the easiest relationship in the world. In the first seven years, it is amazing that we both survived, let alone that we stayed in the marriage.

I am an extremely relational person. In fact, I once took a temperament test and was off the charts in my desire for deep, personal, meaningful relationships. Those words give me the "warm fuzzies" just writing them! Michael, on the other hand, went off the charts in the opposite direction. Give him an empty room, a radio and a "rest from relationships" and he will be one of the happiest guys around. You can imagine my frustration as a pastor's wife when he expended nearly all of his emotional energy on our church family.

About ten years ago, God began showing me that even if Michael were the most relational guy on the planet, it still wouldn't be enough for me. God showed me that he put those longings in my heart so that *he* could fulfill them! True, he would use Michael to meet *some* of my relational needs, but Michael is not responsible for meeting my *every* need. God is. And Michael is really relieved to know that!

Because of what God revealed at that time, I have taken a new outlook regarding my personal need for relationship. Since God made me the way I am, he is responsible for providing the "cake" (of my relational needs). And since Michael married me the way I am,

he is responsible for providing the "icing" of those relational needs. This works out pretty well for me because I love a big piece of cake with just a little bit of icing!

You may be wondering, in fact you may have wondered all your Christian life, "How can a God we cannot see, hear or touch richly meet our relational needs?" He can, you know, and he will if you let him.

We pray and hope this week – as well as the entire 40 days of this *Journey to Freedom* – will help renew your love relationship with the God who loves. He loves you passionately as a Groom loves his bride! We encourage you to continue walking in your new identity in Christ, and in the love of God, offering daily forgiveness toward those who have hurt or offended you. Since pain is an inevitable part of life, it is imperative that we allow God to teach us how to be forgiving people.

This week we are going to focus on a different kind of pain; a type of pain that we will refer to as *brokenness*. Brokenness occurs in us when God orchestrates circumstances – often difficult or painful – for the purpose of enabling us to grasp at a new level how incapable we are of making life work on our own. In order to become victorious through brokenness, our level of trust in God must *increase* and our level of self-reliance (on our own abilities and resources) must *decrease.* This is a large part of Christ's very intentional plan of romancing his bride... us!

Romance is something every female longs for. In counseling couples over the last few years, I (Christi) cannot count the times that women have sat in my office and pleaded for their husbands to "romance" them. In trying to articulate this concept to the left-brained, task oriented, type A individual, I have come up with a definition:

Romance is a passionate emotional attraction, attachment and involvement between two people that is characterized by a high level of transparency and devotion.

In short, romance could be described as *a love affair where both parties are heavily pursued, wanted and sought after.* Can we just get real here? Romance is *not* just a girl thing! Everybody wants *and needs* to be loved, accepted, and valued, wanted and sought after. It's just that most guys don't think it's cool to admit this. But Scripture makes it clear that God longs for a deep, passionate love relationship with all his children – both men and women – and so collectively we are called the bride of Christ.

You might ask, "How did we get here? What in the world does romance have to do with brokenness?" Hang with us; we're getting there. One of the most romantic stories in the Bible is found in Hosea 2. This story is a portrayal of Israel's unholy affair with idols (false gods) and how God's jealous passionate love won her back. Since we are all considered the bride of Christ, let's take a look at some of the highlights of this passage, trusting the Holy Spirit to reveal the truth about where we have placed our deepest affections. And maybe, if we listen closely, we will hear God's jealous heart pounding with intensity, longing to stir up and recapture the passion of our youth or the fervor we once had for him.

She [Israel] said, 'I'll run after other lovers and sell myself to them for food and drink, for clothing of wool and linen, and for olive oil.' "But I [God] will fence her in with thornbushes. I will block the road to make her lose her way. When she runs after her lovers, she won't be able to catch up with them. She will search for them but not find them. Then she will think, 'I might as well return to my husband because I was better off with him than I am now.' She doesn't realize that it was I who gave her everything she has—the grain, the wine, the olive oil. Even the gold and silver she used in worshiping the god Baal were gifts from me! "But now I will take back the wine and ripened grain I generously provided each harvest season. I will take away the linen and wool clothing I gave her to cover her nakedness. I will strip her naked in public, while all her lovers look on. No one will be able to rescue her from my hands. I will put an end to her annual festivals, her new moon celebrations, and her Sabbath days—all her appointed festivals. I will destroy her vineyards and orchards, things she claims her lovers gave her. I will let them grow into tangled thickets, where only wild animals will eat the fruit. I will punish her for all the time she deserted me, when she burned incense to her images of Baal, put on her earrings and jewels, and went out looking for her lovers," says the Lord.

Hosea 2:5b-13 (NIV)

You might be wondering, why would a loving God "induce" pain in the lives of his children? From the Scripture passage above, you might be tempted to view God as a "cosmic meanie" of some sort, the kind of god that delights in making our lives miserable and taking away all pleasure and joy. But you need to understand that not everything that *hurts* us, *harms* us. And when the path we are on is self-destructive and it takes the proverbial 2x4 over the head to get our attention, then God's judicious use of that 2x4 is an act of mercy.

God strongly desires to bring us to a place of *full surrender*, so that he will become Lord of our lives and thereby be glorified in and through us. With each area of our lives that is fully surrendered to his *Lordship* there is a release of his Spirit both inside and outside of our lives. This releasing of his Spirit in our lives is where we find true Christian vitality. The place of surrender is the place of healing, where we can experience God's love in a new, fresh and vital way.

As we continue with this passage from Hosea 2, you'll see that is what God is up to after all. See if you can catch the tender, romantic heart of God at work here:

"But then I will win her back once again. I will lead her out into the desert and speak tenderly to her there. I will return her vineyards to her and transform the Valley of Trouble into a gateway of hope. She will give herself to me there, as she did long ago when she was young, when I freed her from her captivity in Egypt. "In that coming day," says the Lord, "you will call me 'my husband' instead of 'my master.' O Israel, I will cause you to forget your images of Baal; even their names will no longer be spoken. At that time I will make a covenant with all the wild animals and the birds and the animals that scurry along the ground so that they will not harm you. I will remove all weapons of war from the land, all swords and bows, so you can live unafraid in peace and

safety. I will make you my wife forever, showing you righteousness and justice, unfailing love and compassion. I will be faithful to you and make you mine, and you will finally know me as Lord… I will show love to those I called 'Not loved.' And to those I called 'Not my people,' I will say, 'Now you are my people.' Then they will reply, 'You are our God!'"

Hosea 2:14-23 (NLT)

Israel had ventured off from the passion of her first love in this story. She had forgotten how God had rescued her from Egypt and he had provided for her every need. She became distracted and influenced by what everyone else was doing (worshiping other gods). Her heart had become hardened toward her first love through disobedience and she was finding herself empty and lost. We can see in this exposé, that her Lover, God, had something to say and do about all this. His jealous zeal caused him to block her at every pass until she finally realized his burning passion for her.

Has anyone ever loved you with this kind of love before? If this scenario had happened in these post modern times between most couples the spouse would have said, "Get lost… go have what you want!" But God's love for us is not threatened or conditional. His love is so deep that he will pursue us to the end of our days here on earth, no matter how far we run from him.

Thankfully, he does not stop with simply pursuing us or hoping that we return to his side; he continually obstructs our path with roadblocks so that we will realize that home is where we belong. This is where brokenness comes in; when we pursue the self-life and hit the wall, it hurts. In hitting these God-constructed walls, we eventually come to the understanding that life without Jesus as Lord is both unproductive and deeply empty. Then, by God's grace, we come running back into the arms of the One who loves us and showed it by giving up his very life for us.

So what affairs have you had on God? You might be thinking, "I haven't had an affair on God!" Well, why not honestly allow God to search your heart and see? King David wisely prayed, ***Search me, O God, and know my heart; test me and know my anxious thoughts. See if there is any offensive way in me, and lead me in the way everlasting (Psalm 139:23,24).*** If there is nothing offensive to God in your heart, there would be no reason to feel defensive.

An idol or *object of affection* is anything that your life is wrongly centered around. Therefore an idol could be any thing that you place at the core of your heart, mind and actions that you value more than your relationship with God. Why not take a first step into determining what your wrong objects of affection might be by asking yourself a few tough questions:

- What do I spend most of my time thinking about?

  _____
  _____

- What do I spend my extra money on?

  _____
  _____

- To whom do I give most of my attention or affection?

  _____
  _____

- To whom do I give my deepest respect?

  _____
  _____

- What are my dreams and desires based on?

  _____
  _____

Most people in the world today are serving other gods. As a nation, we in America have grown cold and indifferent to God's love. According to George Barna, American Christians have become increasingly apathetic and passively lukewarm in their faith and they do not even care. Check out this poignant observation from a recent survey:

> *"The fact that so few people have thought about how they could intentionally and strategically enhance their spiritual life reminds us that spiritual growth is not a priority to most people... Americans are generally satisfied with being average in their spiritual maturity. That betrays the fact that we do not serve an "average" God or one who is honored by people who are lukewarm about their faith."*

The excuse that "everybody's doing it" is not a legitimate excuse with God. After all, this is the lie that Israel served. God has called us and set us apart from the world, so that we will be different from everybody else. Our question today is, "Who is courageous enough to dive in to God's grace and swim against the tide of the world's average standard?" We believe that if we could get just one real glimpse of how deep, rich and satisfying the love of God is, we would stop our earthly pursuits and engage in an avid "seek and find" expedition after God and his will for our life.

Identity Reminder:

I am hidden with Christ in God.

Col. 3:3

Could we Americans be over-churched and under-changed? Have we heard of God's great love too many times without responding to it? The fastest way to get a hardened heart is to hear *"Jesus is Lord,"* and sing, *"I surrender all,"* every Sunday morning and not actually mean it or respond to it through obedience. When we hear God's word and do not respond to it through obedience, our hearts become hardened toward God. This can be very dangerous since we have an enemy who is prowling around seeking whom he may devour (see **1 Peter 5:8**)!

We need to have a meaningful encounter with the passionate love of God and we need to respond to this love by complete surrender. When the prophet Jeremiah spoke of Israel's coolness toward God he referred to Israel as being like a piece of pottery that was marred and in need of breaking and remaking. Could we need God to break and reshape us? Think about this for a moment:

> **But the jar he was making did not turn out as he had hoped, so the potter squashed the jar into a lump of clay and started again.**
>
> *Jeremiah 18:4 (NLT)*

God is gathering his clay; the wheel is turning and the kiln is hot at the Potter's house. He wants to take the old dried up, disfigured pots and grind them up, sift them, soak and soften them until they are the right consistency. Then he wants to mold the clay, shaping and smoothing out all the rough edges. Finally, he wants to make them into pots both beautiful and usable again by firing and glazing them.

God longs to hold you in his hands and shape your character into Christ's likeness. If he is not first place in your life, are you willing to return to him as your first love? He wants to be the Lord of your entire life. He cares for you intensely and longs to be the "leader of your life." He also wants to be Lord over every thought, feeling, desire and action. Does your passion need to be renewed? What affections in your life are robbing you of a wholehearted pursuit of your first love? Allow the Holy Spirit to reveal the areas where your affections have grown stronger than your passionate affection for God. Check the areas that God is dealing with you about.

☐ **Work / Goals / Ambitions**
☐ **Money / Possessions**
☐ **Information / Knowledge**
☐ **Ministry Involvement**
☐ **Fun / Pleasure**
☐ **Business / Activity / Accomplishments**
☐ **Relationships**
☐ **Academics**

☐ **Food / Substance**
☐ **Computer / Technology**
☐ **Media / TV / Movies / Music**
☐ **Sports / Physical fitness**
☐ **Image / Appearance**
☐ **Friends / Popularity**
☐ **Hobbies**
☐ **Others**

WRAPPING UP

Truth Point

Dear children, keep away from anything that might take God's place in your hearts.

1 John 5:21 (NLT)

Application

What is taking God's place in your heart? If you were on trial and your closest friends and family were the jury, could they find enough evidence in your life to find you "guilty" of *putting Christ first* in your life? Or would they find you "guilty" of *putting yourself first* in your life? Make a list of the evidence that you think they would find toward each case. Let the Holy Spirit lead you.

<table>
<tr><th>Evidence that proves
God is first</th><th>Evidence that proves
I am first</th></tr>
<tr><td>_____</td><td>_____</td></tr>
<tr><td>_____</td><td>_____</td></tr>
<tr><td>_____</td><td>_____</td></tr>
<tr><td>_____</td><td>_____</td></tr>
<tr><td>_____</td><td>_____</td></tr>
<tr><td>_____</td><td>_____</td></tr>
<tr><td>_____</td><td>_____</td></tr>
<tr><td>_____</td><td>_____</td></tr>
</table>

PRAYER

Father God, search my heart and know my ways. Show me the truth regarding our relationship. Am I really putting you first in my life? Do I really love you more that I love myself? I realize that having a personal relationship with you is not passive and will not just happen unless I make time for it to happen. I know that you are waiting for me to stop living my life for myself and start living it for you. I know that you are waiting for me to spend time communicating with you so that you can nurture me and cause me to bear fruit. I am sorry for the ways that I have put other things before you. I repent for *(list the ways that you have put yourself first from the list above).* I no longer want to live my life upside down; instead I want to live a life that is ordered by you. In Jesus Name. Amen.

DECLARATIONS

- **I admit the fact that I want to be both desired and desirable!**
- **I affirm the truth that God desires to be with me!**
- **I agree that many people around me are in pursuit of other gods!**
- **I announce that I will swim against the tide and begin pursuing God first!**
- **I declare that my passions toward God must be renewed day by day!**

Broken Yet Chosen

He is Grinding and Sifting

WARMING UP

After gathering his clay and all the dried pots that have been marred, the Potter then begins grinding and sifting. Ah, the grinding and sifting process! Or should we say **ouch!** When I (Christi) think of the word *grind* I automatically think of sitting in the dentist's chair, and being at his mercy. A couple of months ago Michael needed to have a wisdom tooth pulled. The dentist said it would be no problem, so off he went for his appointment. But when the dentist got in there around the tooth he ran into some difficulties; the tooth wasn't coming out. So the dentist had to break it up with a pair of pliers and then dig it out one piece at a time. Michael said at times the dentist was leaning over him and digging with all of his weight. **Ouch!**

I (Christi) can clearly recall many times in my life when God has deemed it necessary and in my best interest to take hold of my clay pot and smash it to smithereens *(some of us need this more than others)*. I struggle with control, pride and selfishness at times and God is determined that these attitudes are going to be broken out of my life. So he continues to grind and sift.

Several years ago, during our tenure at the district office, the Lord opened up the door for me to be the interim youth pastor at a nearby church. After several months of bonding with the youth, discipling them and taking them out witnessing on Friday nights, I began to realize that I was falling in love with shepherding this group of teens. We had a special bond that was both enjoyable and spiritually inspiring.

From the first day that I started working with them, the senior pastor was candid with me regarding his intentions to hire someone to fill this position. But as time went on, my bond with the kids grew and I began to feel like he would not actually replace me. I was pretty sure that he would notice how great things were going with the youth and offer me the job. God continued filling my heart with vision for the group so I took this as God's approval of me for the job. The parents of the youth often told me "one on one" that their kids were growing and they hoped that I would get the job. With all of these affirmations taking place, I really believed that this "changing of the guard" would not take place.

I believed this all the way up until the very day that the senior pastor came in my office and told me to pack up my things because he had hired a youth pastor who would be arriving soon. My heart felt like it was crushed into a million pieces that day. But I had to realize that if God really wanted me to be there, he could have made it happen. He chose *not* to allow me to be their youth pastor and I had to deal with it and accept it… and continue going to this church because it was our home church while we served at the district office. **Ouch!**

The artist always knows *best* what his artwork will become. ***Isaiah 64:8*** says, ***Lord, you are our Father. We are the clay, and you are the potter.*** Sometimes things happen that we don't understand, but we have to remember who we are. We are the clay and he is the Potter. This means that if we are going to surrender to him as Potter and Lord, then we have to relinquish our right to control our lives and our circumstances. The job of the clay is to be first found and then surrendered. If we know Christ, then we have already been found, so our next assignment is to surrender. James challenges us in the first part of *James 4:7* to submit ourselves to God. The New Living Translation says *humble* ourselves before God. *The Message* says to *let God work his will in you.* In other words, we are to give God *all of what we are* and trust him as the Potter to make our lives (and us) what he wants us to become.

Identity Reminder:

I can find grace and mercy in time of need.

Heb. 4:16

During the time that this painful event was taking place in my (Christi's) life, I allowed several lies to take root in my thought process. Soon after that, I developed some deeply ingrained thought patterns (strongholds) and before I knew it I had adopted a negative attitude toward God, others, and myself.

Satan is privy to our pain. You can be assured that when you are hurting, he will be there with his pack of lies. I lost my peace, my joy and even my enthusiasm because I allowed his lies to control my thoughts and feelings rather than trusting in God as my Potter and Lord.

Let's take a look at some lies that Satan tries to use to torment us when we are in pain. Have you ever found yourself in a painful situation that you did not understand? Which of these lies did the enemy tempt you to believe? Feel free to circle the accusations that you believed about either yourself or God.

Accusations against yourself	Accusations against God
No one loves me	God doesn't care
I can't do anything right	The Christian life does not work for me
I am a failure	God has forgotten me
I don't fit in	God loves others more than me
I am alone	God is not there
I cannot trust anyone	God is not trustworthy
I am worthless	God is not satisfied with me
I am trapped	God will not help me

I believed that God was not trustworthy; after all, he put those passions and visions (to lead the youth group) in my heart! Can you see where Satan played right into my pain? I also bought into the lie that I was not good enough; that must be why the senior pastor felt the need to hire someone else.

Once we fall into this trap of believing Satan's lies, we weave them into our faulty belief system and over time a stronghold is formed. Here's a very simple layman's definition of strongholds:

Strongholds are hiding places that hurting people run to in order to find protection.

These "hiding places" can certainly be geographic places or even other people, but our main concern in this devotion has to do with our *internal* hiding places – the places in our hearts where we go when we're scared, anxious or confused.

The Bible talks about strongholds, both good and bad. Numerous times in the Psalms, God is the writer's stronghold. Here's just one example:

The LORD is a refuge for the oppressed, a stronghold in times of trouble. Those who know your name will trust in you, for you, LORD, have never forsaken those who seek you.

Psalm 9:9,10 (NIV)

Proverbs conveys that same idea of God being a safe place where we can go when times get tough:

The name of the LORD is a strong tower; the righteous run to it and are safe.

Proverbs 18:10 (NIV)

Unfortunately, we can also construct our own strongholds of self-protection (rather than God-protection) and these "inner fortresses" of fleshly self-will and self-sufficiency are deadly to intimacy with God. They cannot be repainted, repaired, remodeled or renovated. They must be removed. They must be destroyed. God's word powerfully teaches that truth.

For though we live in the world, we do not wage war as the world does. The weapons we fight with are not the weapons of the world. On the contrary, they have divine power to demolish strongholds. We demolish arguments and every pretension that sets itself up against the knowledge of God, and we take captive every thought to make it obedient to Christ.

2 Corinthians 10:3-5 (NIV)

It is so easy to allow Satan to persuade us to hide behind false protection and defense. It feels so safe there. But that is the deception. The only safe place is securely surrendered in the arms of our Savior.

In order for us to be able to call out to God to demolish the fleshly strongholds in our lives, we need to know what they are. Some of the more common areas of false protection and defense are:

Strongholds

Control	Defensiveness	Blame
Trying harder	Putting on masks	Lying
Intimidation	Sarcasm	Critical spirit
Withdrawal	Nonchalance ("Whatever…")	People pleasing
Self-medicating		Escaping

Soon after I (Christi) started believing the lies that I couldn't trust God and that I was not good enough, people at the church began asking me questions and sharing their opinions. "Why do you think you didn't get the job?" "I think you should have got the job." And there I was hurting and confused by lies and having to come up with an answer to their questions.

I'm ashamed to admit it, but I hid behind several strongholds. I tried to pretend like it didn't bother me and I blamed the senior pastor for not hearing God. Oh the tangled web we weave!

There are many unhealthy thinking patterns that we are tempted to fall into once we start believing lies. A few of them are:

personalizing – *receiving the words of others as personal rejection or attacks when they are not.*

magnifying – *blowing situations out of proportion / unnecessarily amplifying problems or becoming overly dramatic.*

minimizing – *believing or saying "it doesn't matter" when it really does.*

generalizing – *allowing past pain to cause too broad or stereotypical a viewpoint (e.g. all men are evil).*

emotional reasoning – *decisions and choices based solely on one's feelings, rather than upon an objective standard of truth.*

polarizing – *seeing everything naively as either "black" or "white" and even seeing other Christians as either "good guys" or "bad guys".*

Satan's plan is to get us so tangled up in these wrong ways of thinking that we can't even see the light of the truth. In the long run you'll find it is so much easier to surrender to God right away when tough things happen, rather than going through God's painful breaking process later. If we delay, it can become quite difficult to dig out of a mess of strongholds and lies.

I even had to go to counseling over the mess I had gotten myself in. Unfortunately, the counselor's opinions only made matters worse. It has only been recently that I have realized (through other painful events that have transpired in my life) that the truth God wanted me to learn is that I can trust his wisdom and will no matter what happens.

Often these issues in our lives are not a matter of who is right and who is wrong, but rather a matter of trust. When I finally surrendered to this truth: *God is sovereign and he has the right to order my life as he wishes,* both my peace and my joy returned.

All of us need to learn to "take captive every thought to make it obedient to Christ." If we do that, we will experience peace and joy. If we don't, our emotions can easily spiral out of control and we may find ourselves wallowing in the miry clay of frustration, confusion, depression or despair.

Identity Reminder:

I am the salt and light of the earth.

Matt. 5:13-14

What events in your life has God used to break you from self-sufficiency and increase your trust in him? Broken health? Broken careers? Broken dreams? Broken relationships? Broken finances? A broken reputation? God is waiting for us to stop grumbling about the pain and GIVE UP on ourselves and accept his will for our lives. To do this we can:

> **G**rasp God's greatness
>
> **I**dentify and admit our personal inadequacy.
>
> **V**iew our inadequacy in the light of God's sovereignty.
>
> **E**mbrace our need for God.
>
> **U**nderstand how much God has helped us by giving us our new identity.
>
> **P**re-determine in our heart to relinquish all control and follow God!

Maybe you have been broken and surrendered before, but have allowed accusations, strongholds and wrong attitudes to blemish your pot again. You can trust God. ***Proverbs 3:5*** encourages us to ***trust in the Lord with all of our heart; and not to depend on our own understanding.*** So many times we get caught up in trying to figure out the why's and how's when we should be spending our time trusting and surrendering. God loves you and this is why he takes the time to work with your pot. He doesn't want you to be a blemished pot sitting on a shelf somewhere. He wants you to be perfected and usable; he has your best interest at heart! He wants to make you into a beautiful vessel that he will later use for his glory.

Truth Point

Don't copy the behavior and customs of this world, but let God transform you into a new person by changing the way you think. Then you will know what God wants you to do, and you will know how good and pleasing and perfect his will really is.

Romans 12:2 (NLT)

Application

List the events in your life that God has used in attempting to break you of self-sufficiency and increase your trust in him.

_____

_____

_____

_____

_____

_____

_____

_____

_____

_____

_____

_____

_____

_____

Have these painful events made you bitter or better? Circle the characteristics that describe your attitude when you think back to those painful circumstances.

Bitter	Better
Controlling	Surrendered
Independent	Dependant
Stubborn	Repentant
Prideful	Humble
Selfish	Selfless
Rebellious	Submissive
Apathetic	Passionate
Self-Pitying	Joyful
Defensive	Vulnerable
Blaming	Responsible
Lying	Honest

PRAYER

DECLARATIONS

Dear loving, wise Potter, thank you for loving me enough to break me. I repent for the times that I have responded to the pain of the breaking process with false accusations against myself and against you. I am sorry for allowing strongholds to become a part of my thought process and belief system and I regret having been controlled by wrong attitudes because of not surrendering my will to you. Father God, you know the breaking process can be difficult and I need you to give me the strength and courage to simply let go of myself and cooperate with your Spirit. I'm learning to appreciate all that you are doing in my life to break me. In Jesus Name. Amen.

- **I admit that being broken can be painful!**

- **I agree that I need to be broken to move into deeper levels of trust in God!**

- **I declare that I do not need to accuse or hide when I am hurting!**

- **I announce that I need to face the pain and take on the mind of Christ!**

- **I choose to lay down my wrong attitudes and take on the heart of Christ!**

Broken Yet Chosen

He is Soaking and Softening

During one summer Michael and I (Christi) had a lot of fun watching Michael's dad, Bill, work magic with his vegetable garden. Bill really knows what he's doing when it comes to gardens. He is also a very generous person and loves raising a healthy garden so he can treat his friends and family to all the vegetables they could ever want! Because of his example, Michael and I decided that we would try our hand at raising a small garden in the spring.

On a beautiful fall day we took advantage of the good weather by turning the ground in our wannabe garden with a pitchfork. Apparently this was a tough job because the guys wouldn't even let me try it! Bill explained to me that the ground would need further tilling and softening before it would be ready for planting in the spring. He assured me that raising a garden was a big job that would take plenty of time, energy and patience. The funny thing is if you were to compliment Bill on the amount of hard work and effort that he puts into his garden, his response would always be the same. "What do you mean hard work? God does ninety percent of the work himself."

Bill knows who is responsible for producing his crop. According to Scripture, having fertile soil plays a large role in reaping a bumper crop.

But some seeds fell on fertile soil and produced a crop that was thirty, sixty, and even a hundred times as much as had been planted.

Matthew 13:8 (NLT)

I believe Bill's garden is so plentiful because he takes so much time working with his soil. God wants to work with the soil of our hearts so that it will be fertile and softened and ready to produce to its fullest potential.

I can remember a time in my life when it felt like God stuck a big pitchfork in my heart and turned over a lump of hardened soil. As a teenager, I had strong morals and high values and was determined to live a good, clean life before God. Sometimes other kids made fun of me, but I didn't care.

I loved being acknowledged as different. Looking back now, I would have to say that I had a problem with legalism, spiritual pride and haughtiness. I guess my parents were glad I was "into" legalism rather than believing I had a license to sin. What I really needed was the grace of God, and a load of it!

During my seventh grade year I had a couple of friends that we'll call Jackie and Jill. Jackie and Jill both liked me, but they despised each other. They were jealous of each other and were always trying to cut each other down.

One day Jackie convinced me that Jill was not a good friend and that she had a bad reputation and that we needed to write her a nasty anonymous note (cutting her character to shreds) and put it in her locker. Jackie didn't want the note to be written in her handwriting so she told me that I needed to do the writing and that she would tell me what to write.

I am not sure what came over me, but I sat down and started writing the most horrible things about Jill, just the way Jackie dictated. When the note was finished (and believe me it was bad), I put it in my book bag, where it would rest safely while awaiting delivery.

Little did I know that this terrible note's first delivery would be into the hands of my father and mother. Keep in mind that the words written on this paper were so nasty that they had never come out of my mouth before. My parents could not believe that I had taken part in such slander. When mom and dad looked into my face holding my handwritten note that day, I thought I was going to melt under the heat of both their and God's conviction. I am convinced that God exposed that sin to humble my heart and bring me to a place of true, godly sorrow.

I believe that he wanted my tears to land on my heart and soften the soil that had hardened there due to my pride and haughtiness.

There is a story in Isaiah that records a melt down conviction experience far worse than the one I had.

In the year that King Uzziah died, I saw the Master sitting on a throne--high, exalted!-and the train of his robes filled the Temple. Angel-seraphs hovered above him, each with six wings. With two wings they covered their faces, with two their feet, and with two they flew." And they called back and forth one to the other, Holy, Holy, Holy is GOD-of-the-Angel-Armies. His bright glory fills the whole earth. The foundations trembled at the sound of the angel voices, and then the whole house filled with smoke. I said, "Doom! It's Doomsday! I'm as good as dead! Every word I've ever spoken is tainted -- blasphemous even! And the people I live with talk the same way, using words that corrupt and desecrate. And here I've looked God in the face! The King! GOD-of-the-Angel-Armies!" Then one of the angel-seraphs flew to me. He held a live coal that he had taken with tongs from the altar. He touched my mouth with the coal and said, "Look. This coal has touched your lips. Gone your guilt, your sins wiped out."

Isaiah 6:1-8 (MSG)

Can you picture this? Isaiah stood in the presence of our holy, Almighty God, and suddenly he realized that his sins were totally exposed, out in the open for all of heaven to see. In humiliation, shame and despair, he cried out before God. Then an angel swooped down and touched his lips and declared that his guilt was gone and that his sins had been forgiven!

This is a wonderful symbolic picture of the atoning power of the blood of Jesus. Once our sins are exposed and we cry out in repentance, Jesus' blood is applied. Immediately, our guilt is gone and sins are forgiven! Wouldn't it be great if we could forgive ourselves as quickly and completely as God forgives us? God wants us to.

It is interesting to note that Isaiah's name means *"The salvation of Jehovah."* Isaiah certainly experienced the fulfillment of his name at that time! But God was not finished with Isaiah in just cleansing him from sin; he also wanted Isaiah to be his holy mouthpiece, his prophet to Israel. Listen to the next thing Isaiah heard directly after this powerful cleansing experience in *Isaiah 6:8: And then I heard the voice of the Master: "Whom shall I send? Who will go for us?"*

Isaiah humbly spoke up after this miraculous cleansing episode *(v.8): "I'll go. Send me!"*

Do you want to become more usable to God than you are now? Maybe you have lost your tenderness toward his conviction of your sin. Maybe you have grown comfortable with the excuse that other people's sin is worse than yours. Or maybe you just don't like the idea of saying from the heart, "I'm sorry. You are right, God, and I am wrong."

Whatever your thoughts, God recognizes what you need in order to be fully usable by him. He knows that we need to be gathered, ground, softened and fired before we will be ready and usable. He also knows exactly what it will take to bring each of us "to" and "through" the softening process. We can trust him.

When we have lived life for a while on the "couch" of complacency and self-satisfaction, it is easy to just go on living that way – especially when life seems to be going along just fine. But life is Christ and he is calling us to something much better, more rewarding and fulfilling.

At least twice in Scripture, God exhorts and warns his people that it is time to pull out the pitchfork and hoe and whack away at the places in our hearts that have become dangerously dry and hard.

> *This is what the LORD says… "Break up your unplowed ground and do not sow among thorns.*
>
> *Jeremiah 4:3 (NIV)*

And then again in Hosea:

> *Sow for yourselves righteousness, reap the fruit of unfailing love, and break up your unplowed ground; for it is time to seek the LORD, until he comes and showers righteousness on you.*
>
> *Hosea 10:12 (NIV)*

Since true sorrow and repentance are the substances that God uses in the course of softening our hearts, we would like to invite you to take the time to engage in some heart-felt repentance today. Would you like to have your heart softened by God? Anything worth having takes time to obtain. In examining your heart, you might find that you are in need of a serious spring-cleaning of the soul. Don't be discouraged, be encouraged because God is standing near, ready to do the job. No sin is too big for God!

To help you along in the process of repentance, we have listed some sins of omission below (these are things that we should have done, but didn't do). We urge you first to prayerfully invite the Holy Spirit to shine a light on any sinful ways in your life. Then we encourage you to express true sorrow for your sin. As Isaiah did, cry out to God in agreement that you need a cleansing. Finally, get ready for your guilt to be gone and your sins forgiven; great healing follows repentance! God promises us this:

> *Then if my people who are called by my name will humble themselves and pray and seek my face and turn from their wicked ways, I will hear from heaven and will forgive their sins and heal their land.*
>
> *2 Chronicles 7:14 (NLT)*

Before you start, remember that you are totally loved and accepted by God. It is the kindness of God that leads us to repentance (*Romans 2:4*). Allow God to bring *godly sorrow* to your heart; this is when he gently points out areas that need to be changed. Respond to that godly sorrow with *confession (agreeing with God that you sinned),* expressing godly sorrow for that sin. After God points out these areas, he will then begin to guide you to *repentance (changing your mind about your sin)* leading to the knowledge of the truth.

Second Timothy 2:25,26 expresses our prayer and hope for all working through this devotion *"that God will grant them repentance leading them to a knowledge of the truth, and that they will come to their senses and escape from the trap of the devil, who has taken them captive to do his will."*

While working through the exercise below, if you feel condemned (hopelessly wrong), then stop and take authority over those discouraging thoughts and feelings with the truth. God's word clearly states in **Romans 8:1** that, *There is therefore now no condemnation to those who are in Christ Jesus!*

Before you begin, we would like to give you one more verse to encourage you. The apostle Paul, writing to the believers from the city of Corinth wrote:

God can use sorrow in our lives to help us turn away from sin and seek salvation. We will never regret that kind of sorrow. But sorrow without repentance is the kind that results in death. Just see what this godly sorrow produced in you!

- *Such earnestness,*
- *Such concern to clear yourselves,*
- *Such indignation,*
- *Such alarm,*
- *Such longing to see me,*
- *Such zeal,*
- *And such a readiness to punish the wrongdoer.*
- *You showed that you have done everything you could to make things right.*

2 Corinthians 7:10,11 (NLT)

This is a soul-searching exercise and we encourage you not to take it lightly. Though it may be a bit painful to take the pitchfork and hoe to these areas of your life, any pain is well worth it, for you are helping prepare the soil for God to plant a harvest of good things in your life far beyond what you can imagine!

As you prayerfully and thoughtfully look over each of the following areas, immediately express to God your sorrow for any sins that he reveals to you. Tell him that you want to and need to change and ask him to transform your heart with his power and love.

We trust that you are now ready to begin making things right, so instead of hitting the ground running, let's hit the ground kneeling in repentance!

Sins of Omission

Ingratitude:

Tell God specifically any ways in which you have taken him for granted. God's goodness to us has never stopped. He has saved his people from hell. As you express your sincere sorrow for any ingratitude he shows you is there, God will begin to give you a thankful heart.

Lack of love for God:

Think of how grieved you would be if you discovered that the one you love most was focusing their affections on someone else. God hurts when we love other things above him. This is spiritual adultery *(see James 4:4)* and very serious sin. Repent specifically for offending him by your indifference and misplaced priorities.

Neglect of His Word:

Has reading God's word become more a duty than a delight? Repent for the times you have ignored or avoided God's written or spoken word altogether. God's word was meant to be a lamp for your feet and a light for your path. Express to God your sorrow for allowing your feelings, your own thoughts or the advice of others to become more of a guide to you than the Bible.

Unbelief:

Repent for all the times that you implicitly accused God of being a liar, by living in anxiety and fear as though his promises were not true.

Neglect of Prayer:

Repent for all the times that you have neglected personal prayer, family prayer, or prayer meetings believing that it was not worth the time or effort.

Neglected Grace:

God's love for you in Christ is unconditional. Repent for the times that you have pursued duties and activities in an attempt to gain God's approval, rejecting the truth that his gifts are 100% free, and that his acceptance is based on Christ's perfect life, not yours.

Lack of love and concern for the salvation of those without Christ:

Think about those around you who don't know Christ – family, friends, neighbors and others. Perhaps you have not cared enough to tell them the truth. Have you stood by unmoved by whether they are lost and without Christ, facing eternity in hell? How many days or years have passed without your offering even one fervent prayer for their salvation? Have you separated yourself relationally from the lost to the point that you have ceased to influence unbelievers for Christ?

Neglect of family:

Have you neglected to feed your family spiritually? Have you been gone so much physically and emotionally that you have caused their hearts to grieve? Have you made "providing for" them financially a higher priority than just being there for them? What specific efforts do you need to start making to nurture and strengthen your loved ones in their personal spiritual growth and emotional health?

Neglect of your own life:

How little we sometimes care about the state of our own souls. Has your heart become cold or hard or just perhaps indifferent (lukewarm) to the things of God? Is it time to break up this fallow ground?

Neglect of your brothers in Christ:

Repent for any times where you have watched your brother or sister fall into sin and not taken the time to pray and seek to gently restore him or her. Have you been afraid of "offending" them and possibly losing their friendship and so have not been willing to speak the truth in love?

Neglect of giving to the Lord and to the poor:

In America we are guilty of loving money more than God. Have you been unwilling to inconvenience yourself financially for the sake of loving others? Have you been afraid to deny yourself some of the luxuries of life in order to meet the needs of the poor? Repent of giving only out of your surplus wealth rather than sacrificially. The poor woman, who put in her mite, demonstrated more self-denial than all of us. (See *Luke 21:2*)

Be sensitive to the Lord's leading. There could possibly be other areas of selfishness, self consciousness and self-absorption that have turned your heart away from experiencing the love of God and expressing that love toward others. Confess any other sin that he may bring to your mind in the hours or days ahead knowing that *"if we claim to be without sin, we deceive ourselves and the truth is not in us. If we confess our sins, he is faithful and just to forgive us our sins and purify us from all unrighteousness"*

1 John 1:8,9 (NIV)

We trust that through godly sorrow, the soil of your heart is being soaked and softened. In order to maintain a soft heart before the Lord we encourage you to make repentance a normal occurrence in your life. It should never become dull and routine, but should become as natural to you as breathing – responding to the gentle, loving convicting work of the Holy Spirit. This will keep the clay of your heart pliable and soft in the Potter's hands, just the way he likes it!

Truth Point

The sacrifice you want is a broken spirit. A broken and repentant heart, O God, you will not despise.

Psalm 51:17 (NLT)

Application

What truths did God reveal to you today that broke through the hardness of your heart?

_____

_____

_____

_____

_____

_____

_____

_____

_____

_____

Father God, thank you so much for all you are doing in me! Now that my heart is beginning to soften, I feel your love in a richer way than before. Intimacy with you is so wonderful. Your grace and mercies are new every morning. I want to keep my heart tender toward you by learning to live in a state of repentance. I invite your Holy Spirit to nudge me as often as you desire; and when he does I will stop and repent. I know that my heart is becoming more workable in your hands each day as I surrender more of myself. I need you more every day. I was so wrong for thinking I could live life on my own. I can exist on my own, but real life only comes from you! I love my new life in you! In Jesus name I pray, amen.

- **I believe that God is softening my heart!**
- **I choose to live my life in an attitude of repentance!**
- **I insist on remaining open and malleable before the Lord!**

Broken Yet Chosen
He Molds and Shapes His Vessel

WARMING UP

Just three months after Shirley and I (Rich) got married, we received the letter. My first reaction was to throw it in the trash; my wife's response was to cry. It wasn't a nasty letter at all; it actually contained a great opportunity. I just wasn't interested in moving so soon after the wedding. My Georgia-born wife thought the cultural adjustments of moving to the Philadelphia area from the South were daunting enough. The Philippines was just too much. After all, she sadly exclaimed, "I just got my drapes up!"

The ministry we were a part of was asking us to consider moving to Manila, Philippines to start a city-wide high school ministry. I knew this could not be God's will. I'd already been there (10 years earlier) and it seemed like I had sweated half my body weight away at that time. I didn't like the tropical heat and humidity and God knew that. He's the One that made my body prefer Iceland to Sweatland anyway. We concluded that God was calling someone else to go.

Eight months later we said our tearful good-byes to family and friends and boarded the plane for Manila. I had protested to no avail, telling our ministry's leadership that my heart passion was to see revival come to America. Unknown to me, the Lord had some major heart surgery to perform in my life and his operating table happened to be in the Philippines.

Once launched into the ministry there, we hit the ground running. After a huge summer outreach we were left with 52,000 comment cards of students wanting more information about Christ. I moved from ministry *director* to ministry *dictator*. Driving my staff

hard and myself harder, we sent out follow-up material by mail (hand addressed!) to all 52,000. We also revisited many of the high schools and began ministries in a few strategic ones.

Of course I was clueless as to how angry I was making those around me. I was too busy marveling at the openness of the dear Filipino people to the gospel! Shirley reminded me of my commitment to pray for half a day each week. "We don't have time to pray!" I snarled. I'm sure God was taking notes.

Somewhere in the midst of my ministry frenzy, I heard a Christian song on the radio where the chorus kept repeating, "Lord, have mercy! Lord, have mercy!" over and over again. I thought the song was cheesy and made fun of it.

Strange thing. Within a week I was in the hospital with the Filipino version of Montezuma's revenge. While in the hospital I contracted double pneumonia (both lungs). On top of that I developed an undiagnosed case of asthma.

One night around 2 am I could barely breathe. Nothing I did helped. I was afraid it was all over. Lying on the floor, gasping for air, I found myself desperately crying, "Lord, have mercy!" over and over again.

Fortunately he did and I'm still here. That cry for mercy became a cry of repentance as the Lord began to soften my heart. With that softening came a new freedom to be led by the Spirit rather than being driven by the flesh and its selfish agenda. I learned to relax and enjoy relationships more. I think my wife was very relieved.

God our Father is the perfect Parent. He knows exactly what he's doing. He knows what he wants to accomplish to make us more like Jesus (see **Romans 8:29**) and he knows exactly how to chisel away the stuff in our lives that doesn't look like Jesus. The process is called *discipline* and is clearly explained in Hebrews:

> *My son, do not regard lightly the discipline of the Lord, nor faint when you are reproved by Him; for those whom the Lord loves He disciplines, and He scourges every son whom He receives. It is for discipline that you endure, God deals with you as sons… Furthermore we had earthly fathers to discipline us, and we respected them; shall we not much rather be subject to the Father of spirits, and live? For they disciplined us for a short time as seemed best to them, but He disciplines us for our good, that we may share His holiness. All discipline for the moment seems not to be joyful, but sorrowful, yet to those who have been trained by it, afterwards it yields the peaceful fruit of righteousness.*

> *Hebrews 12:5-11 (NASB)*

Here are some key points to keep in mind from that Scripture:

- God's discipline is an expression of his love, not his anger. This is of primary importance to remember.

- Don't take it too hard or treat it too lightly when God disciplines you. It's not the end of the world but neither is it a trivial matter.

- Discipline hurts. It has to hurt to break us of depending on our own self-centered way of living (flesh).

- Discipline really is for our own good… that we might be holy like God.

- Discipline is never fun; it is not something you *enjoy*; it's something you *endure*.

- If you let discipline have its way, you'll be changed for the better and God's peace will come.

What happens if you (assuming you are truly a child of God) refuse to submit to God's disciplining work? What does God do when you persist in following your own ways?

He turns up the heat.

When you play "hard to get" God plays hard ball… but it's still in love. Tough love. God makes this point straightforwardly:

> *Therefore strengthen the hands that are weak and the knees that are feeble, and make straight paths for your feet, so that the limb which is lame may not be put out of joint, but rather be healed.*

> *Hebrews 12:12,13 (NASB)*

And that's always God's plan… to heal, not to harm. We hope and pray you will make the decision now – whether this is a time of God's loving chiseling in your life or not – to cooperate with him. God's discipline of his child *will* come. That is inevitable. How tough it has to get depends on you.

So, if God is so interested in breaking us of dependence upon our flesh, what exactly is flesh and how do you recognize its operation?

Flesh is – at its core – **selfishness**. Write a short definition of each of the following terms even as you ask the Lord to show you if any of them are problem areas for you.

Self-centered _____

_____

Self-conscious _____

_____

Self-protective _____

_____

Self-sufficient _____

_____

Self-empowered _____

_____

Flesh is everything that you choose to rely on instead of depending on Christ – your talents, your gifts, your intelligence, your personality, your physical prowess, your family name, your financial know-how, your problem-solving ability, your sense of humor, your degrees, your accomplishments, and so on. You'll notice that these things we just listed are not necessarily evil; in fact many are God-given abilities. But when we choose to lean on our own understanding and refuse to trust in the Lord and acknowledge him in our ways, sin *always* results.

Then what we end up doing, no matter how noble our intentions, is to actually oppose the work of God's Spirit. That's serious business. God word reveals that truth:

> ***But I say, walk by the Spirit, and you will not carry out the desires of the flesh. For the flesh sets its desire against the Spirit, and the Spirit against the flesh; for these are in opposition to one another, so that you may not do the things that you please.***
>
> ***Galatians 5:16-19 (NASB)***

There it is, the potential for outright war inside the believer in Christ, in whom the Spirit of God lives. It is civil war of the soul. Peter urged the believers to "abstain from fleshly lusts which wage war against the soul" (*1 Peter 2:11 NASB*). What *are* these fleshly lusts anyway? You've seen them in action on TV, in movies, in the newspaper as well as, to some degree, in your own home and heart. According to *Galatians 5:19-21 (NIV)*, they are as follows. Some have definitions; others have been left blank for you to fill in yours.

sexual immorality _sexual intercourse outside of marriage_

impurity _morally unclean thoughts, words, deeds_

debauchery _living without any moral restraint; excess_

idolatry _____

witchcraft _sorcery; dark magic, often accompanied by drugs, spells, etc._

hatred _____

discord _quarreling; unresolved conflicts between people_

jealousy _an unhealthy, possessive, controlling spirit_

fits of rage _____

selfish ambition _seeking one's own advancement with little or no regard for others_

dissensions _cutting oneself off from others; creating divisions_

factions _complete separations based on doctrinal preferences and heresies_

envy _____

drunkenness _____

orgies _riotous parties and carousings usually with drunkenness_

Walking according to the flesh happens naturally if we don't consciously walk by the Spirit. It looks something like this: we just cruise through life and allow our thoughts, feelings and choices to be unabated and unrestrained. We do what pleases us, not what pleases God. This act of natural passivity is called living in an unholy manner or walking according to the flesh.

God's plan is that we learn to walk (live) by his Spirit and leave our selfish ways behind. Because Christ's Spirit lives within us, there is a new way of living, the way of freedom. It is the way of life, peace, hope and joy. It is God's way of beginning to mold and shape us into the image of Christ.

We will explain more of what it means to walk by the Spirit in Day 28. For now, an important step is to come to grips honestly with the specific ways you have allowed your flesh to be in charge. Be honest with God and yourself as you walk through the *Wrapping Up* exercises. God opposes the proud, but gives great grace to the humble (*James 4:7*)!

Truth Point

As obedient children, let yourselves be pulled into a way of life shaped by God's life, a life energetic and blazing with holiness. God said, "I am holy; you be holy."

1 Peter 1:15-16 (MSG)

Application

Look back at the descriptions of "selfishness" and the definitions of "the flesh" from this lesson. Ask the Lord to show you any areas that are true of your life and list them below.

_____

_____

_____

_____

_____

_____

_____

_____

_____

_____

_____

_____

_____

_____

_____

_____

_____

_____

_____

Father God, I want to become all that you want me to become. I know that there are patterns of selfish and fleshly living that are evident in my life… especially to your holy eyes. Open my eyes, Lord, to see these things as you see them. I now confess and repent of *(list areas of "self" and "flesh")* I am sorry that I have often not represented you the way that I should have. You are real and good and you really change lives, so I am asking you to change me. Thank you for forgiving me for my sins through Christ's shed blood on the cross for me. In Jesus' holy name I pray, amen.

- I recognize that all I do apart from dependence on Christ is flesh and sin!

- I repudiate the flesh and all its selfish manifestations in my life!

- I receive God the Father's loving discipline in my life.

- I will cooperate with God's process of breaking me.

Identity Reminder:

I am confident that the good work God has begun in me will be perfected.

Phil. 1:6

Broken Yet Chosen

He Bisque-Fires His Vessel

The Lord has given Michael and me (Christi) the opportunity to invest some time and love into the lives of a few younger aspiring ministers we know. Our heart goes out to them in their new endeavors because we can easily remember those first few years of ministry when we felt like we were being baptized with fire.

In encouraging these young pastors-to-be to become solid in their walk with God, the scenario generally plays out predictably. After receiving encouragement and counsel, they are zealous to begin and jump headfirst into ministering. It never fails. As the "kiln" heats up in their world or life in ministry gets tough, they often (not surprisingly) show up at our doorstep shocked and overwhelmed by the trials they are experiencing.

God is bringing them to a place where we call "the rubber meets the road." We believe it is at these places of testing for all of us that the wheat gets separated from the chaff in our lives. The heat will either make us or break us.

Do I ever remember the first time the heat got turned up in my world! I was 18 years old, right out of high school, and zealous to give my entire life to Jesus, serving him in full-time vocational ministry. I married a young evangelist and off we went together on a quest to tell the whole world about Jesus. Truthfully, I had no clue about my identity in Christ and had received no inner healing from my past. Nor did I really understand what it meant to walk by the Spirit.

Nevertheless, there I was, an evangelist's wife who (in my mind) was required to be perfect in every way, able to sing like a bird, play the piano like a pro… all while smiling continuously! But night after night something kept happening to me that was threatening my "inner smile." Everywhere we went in ministry, people would ask me cynically, "So how old are you anyway?" The more this happened, the more I became annoyed… and threatened. I became bitter about it all in my heart.

But God kept turning up the heat. We realized that the $10,000 motor home for which we had given up nearly everything and which was our only real home, was a piece of junk. Our only option was to park it and travel in Michael's old van. Life in motels got old fast, especially in the ones we were forced to stay in.

Then God turned the heat up even more. One week we had to scrape together all the change we could find just to eat. I clearly remember walking into the grocery store and buying 12 packs of Top Ramen® noodles for a dollar. I then ran hot tap water over them and we crunched on them for dinner. This was the same week that we had to keep flushing the toilet to get a warm shower! It was also the same week that we couldn't sleep together because the twin beds in our motel room were separated by a dresser that was bolted to the floor. We can laugh about it now but worn out mustard-colored carpet and a Coke® bottle filled with dirty, plastic flowers is not our idea of attractive décor!

Most of that year, I was physically ill with a variety of infections. I can't imagine why! When I wasn't on stage performing I was sitting in a motel room somewhere crying and sulking over the decisions I had made to get married and go into ministry.

But God still wasn't through turning up the heat. Michael had to cancel a revival halfway through due to the fact that I was having a serious allergic reaction to some antibiotics, even to the point of hallucinations.

By that time I was fed up with ministry and was prepared to pretend it had never happened. I wanted to go back home to my parents and finish growing up. But my mom wisely said, "No way! You made your bed. Now you're going to have to sleep in it!" That wasn't what I wanted to hear.

I felt like Shadrach, Meshach and Abednego, only the flames were burning my rear and I was pretty certain that they were going to consume me. Nowhere in the fire could I see anything that resembled the Son of God (though to be perfectly honest, I wasn't looking for him very hard). Plus, to top it all off, I was quite sure that I had married King Nebuchadnezzar!

That was 20 years ago, and let me tell you what I think now. I can honestly say that I would not trade what happened for all the fame and fortune in the world. I absolutely love serving Jesus in full-time vocational ministry, and I certainly did not marry Nebuchadnezzar. Michael is much more like Boaz (see the book of Ruth)! And, I guess I'm learning how to make s'mores by the heat of the fires the Lord brings into my life.

WALKING ON

Before you jump the gun and conclude this day's devotional doesn't apply to you (if you're not in "the ministry") think again. If you are a Christian, then you are called into ministry. It may not be full-time vocational ministry, but your calling *is* full-time. Every believer is both called to reach unbelievers (see **Mark 16:15**) and to serve other believers (see **1 Peter 4:10**) and that is what ministry is.

Is your pot ready for use? In other words, has the Lord brought you through trial's fires to strengthen your character and deepen your surrender to him?

After the potter gathers, grinds, softens and shapes his pot into his desired form, he then puts it into the kiln for bisque firing. Bisque firing is a process that reduces the fragility of the pot and removes any undesirable matter from the clay.

Malachi describes two similar processes:
But who can endure the day of his coming? And who can stand when he appears? For he is like a refiner's fire and like fuller's soap. He will sit as a refiner and a purifier of silver; he will purify the sons of Levi, and purge them as gold and silver, that they may offer to the Lord an offering of righteousness.

Malachi 3:2,3 (NKJV)

God wants to place us as pots into a kiln that will slowly be heated over a long period of time so that we can become more durable. God's bisque firing occurs at a temperature just hot enough to burn off the undesirable matter in our lives and to make us stronger, while ensuring that the furnace is not so hot that we as pots crack or explode (though at times we may feel that way!)

In going through this bisque firing, God wants to test us and purify us by removing doubts, fears, uncertainties, hesitations, reservations and disbelief. He wants to reduce our feebleness and increase our spiritual and emotional durability by instilling in us greater faith, trust, confidence, perseverance, patience, devotion and loyalty. This is what God's heat does in our lives if we let it.

There were times during my first year of ministry that I fought the fire tooth and nail. But in retrospect, those hard times began to teach me how much I could really trust God. He taught us one day that he would always provide for us when I was able to find enough change in our van to eat for a week! He taught me that he is my shield when I am criticized or questioned. And he began to build in us a contentment that enables us to live with little or with much.

Perhaps most important of all, God taught me how to be married… to hang in there and grow up where he'd placed me and not try and run and hide from my problems. Too many times we have seen people buck God's heat and turn away from him. Pressure will do that, you know. It will either push you closer to God or drive you farther away from him. That is why it is critical we keep things honest and open between us and the Lord and other people so that we always move toward him.

Abraham needed to learn to walk by faith, just like us. He went through some pretty tough bisque firing when he was first called by the Lord (*Genesis 12*). God told him to leave his home country and go to a land that he would show him. God also promised to make him a great nation. All this took great faith, but Abraham obeyed and went as the Lord instructed him, not knowing where he was going.

Then God turned up the heat. According to *Genesis 12:10*, a famine struck the land, right where God had called him to go. This was Abraham's time of bisque firing and he came out of God's kiln stronger and more holy, because he unquestioningly obeyed God's leading.

How did Abraham pass the test? By faith! *Hebrews 11:8 (NIV)* says, *"By faith Abraham, when called to go to a place he would later receive as his inheritance, obeyed and went, even though he did not know where he was going."*

Trials and times of testing… whether great or small… will come to all of us, no matter what age, season of life or maturity in Christ. When they come we should not be surprised or shocked because God has already told us in his word that we should expect them.

Dear friends, do not be surprised at the painful trial that you are suffering, as though something strange were happening to you. But rejoice that you participate in the sufferings of Christ, so that you may be overjoyed when his glory is revealed.

1 Peter 4:12, 13 (NIV)

Instead of being caught off guard as the enemy would like us to be, we should rejoice for having the opportunity to share in Christ's sufferings. When we share in Christ's sufferings we also get the privilege of sharing in his glory (*Romans 8:17*), and this brings us great joy.

What are you going through right now that is difficult or painful? _____

_____

_____

How are you handling it? _____

_____

_____

Can you see God's bisque firing at work? What impurities do you see him trying to remove from you? In what ways can you tell he is trying to make you stronger?

_____

_____

_____

_____

Times of testing give us opportunities to learn how to endure and persevere; that is, if we don't wiggle our way out of God's kiln!

You know that under pressure, your faith-life is forced into the open and shows its true colors. So don't try to get out of anything prematurely. Let it do its work so you become mature and well-developed, not deficient in any way.

James 1:3-4 (MSG)

There have been plenty of times when God has turned up the heat in my life and I have chosen to escape from the kiln rather than to endure. Even now I am learning to stay the course no matter how hot it gets. There are glorious spiritual rewards that come to us both here and in eternity for patiently sticking in there. *Hebrews 10:35,36 (NASB)* has been a rock for us.

Therefore, do not throw away your confidence, which has a great reward. For you have need of endurance, so that when you have done the will of God, you may receive what was promised.

If we really trust that God is in control, and that he is working things together for our good… the good of becoming more like Christ (see *Romans 8:28,29*)… then we can make it through the fire without being burned.

He indeed is in the fire with us, for he is with us always whether we are aware of him or not.

WINDING DOWN

If we remain faithful to God and hang in there during the firing process, we will become a beautiful pot which is useful for the Master, for his glory. There were once three young men who were bent on serving God no matter how hot the fire got. Check out how the Lord was glorified through their act of obedience:

Nebuchadnezzar was so furious with Shadrach, Meschach, and Abednego [for not bowing down and worshipping his golden statue] *that his face became distorted with rage. He commanded that the furnace be heated seven times hotter than usual. Then he ordered some of the strongest men of his army to bind Shadrach, Meschach, and Abednego and throw them into the blazing furnace. So they tied them up and threw them into the furnace, fully clothed. And because the king, in his anger, had demanded such a hot fire in the furnace, the flames leaped out and killed the soldiers as they threw the three men in! So*

Shadrach, Meshach, and Abednego, securely tied, fell down into the roaring flames. But suddenly, as he was watching, Nebuchadnezzar jumped up in amazement and exclaimed to his advisers, "Didn't we tie up three men and throw them into the furnace?" "Yes," they said, "we did indeed, Your Majesty." "Look!" Nebuchadnezzar shouted. "I see four men, unbound, walking around in the fire. They aren't even hurt by the flames! And the fourth looks like a divine being!" Then Nebuchadnezzar came as close as he could to the door of the flaming furnace and shouted: "Shadrach, Meshach, and Abednego, servants of the Most High God, come out! Come here!" So Shadrach, Meshach, and Abednego stepped out of the fire. Then the princes, prefects, governors, and advisers crowded around them and saw that the fire had not touched them. Not a hair on their heads was singed, and their clothing was not scorched. They didn't even smell of smoke!

Daniel 3:19-30 (NLT)

[bracketed statements ours]

Truth Point

When you pass through the waters, I will be with you; and when you pass through the rivers, they will not sweep over you. When you walk through the fire, you will not be burned; the flames will not set you ablaze.

Isaiah 43:2 (NIV)

Application

Earlier in this devotional, we had you look at the difficult or painful things going on in your life right now. Now obviously, any sin on your part that has brought about the difficulty or pain must be confessed and repented of. And you most likely will have to endure any natural consequences of your sin even though you have confessed it and repented of it. For example, if you lose your driver's license for DUI, then you'll have to live without driving a car for awhile. *2 Timothy 2:20,21 (NASB)* reminds us, *"Now in a large house there are not only gold and silver vessels, but also vessels of wood and of earthenware, and some to honor and some to dishonor. Therefore, if a man cleanses himself from these things, he will be a vessel for honor, sanctified, useful to the Master, prepared for every good work."*

Is there anything you need to confess to the Lord today?

Secondly, if the trials we are going through result from life in a fallen world, the sins of others, or the sovereign hand of Almighty God putting us through the bisque fire, we must simply endure. The following Scripture verses, if practiced by faith, will help keep your heart strong during this time.

Rejoice always, pray without ceasing, in everything give thanks, for this is the will of God in Christ Jesus for you.

1 Thessalonians 5:16-18 (NKJV)

Take a few minutes and apply those three liberating verses to your current trials.

Identity Reminder:

I have not been given a spirit of fear, but of power, love and a sound mind.

2 Tim. 1:7

PRAYER

Father God, I thank you for being with me and protecting me from being overwhelmed by my difficult circumstances. I realize that some of my difficult circumstances are because of my own sins and I thank you for your forgiveness of those failings. I realize, too, that some of these difficulties are times of testing which are prompted by you. As you set our clay pots in the kiln for firing, I trust you to adjust the temperature to be hot enough to burn off undesirable matter and to make me more durable. I also trust you to protect me so that these pots don't crack or explode. Reduce my feebleness and increase my faith, trust, confidence, perseverance, patience, devotion and loyalty. I thank you for producing these fruits in my life. May they bring much glory, honor and joy to you. In Jesus' name I pray, amen.

DECLARATIONS

- **I affirm that God is removing my doubts, fears and uncertainties!**
- **I affirm that he is removing my hesitations, reservations and disbelief!**
- **I announce that God is instilling in me more faith, trust and confidence!**
- **I announce that he is instilling in me more perseverance, patience and loyalty!**

Broken Yet Chosen

He Glaze-Fires His Vessel

Day 27

WARMING UP

Life was treating us (Michael and Christi) great. We had been married for about ten years at the time, and had a five-year-old daughter. It seemed like our lives had calmed down considerably on all levels. The testing fires that came with life as a traveling evangelist's wife were over and I had survived without leaving the ministry or killing Michael. Now we were serving as youth pastors in a wonderful little town that was voted into the top 10 places to live in America.

We had sold the dilapidated motor home and purchased a cozy little house that was less cramped and much more livable. Being a trained hairdresser, I decided to open up a beauty shop in our basement, and before long I had established a nice little business and had lots of wonderful customers. We also had established some meaningful relationships at the church and were having a blast working with youth.

Life couldn't have been better for us. Then one day in March, 1995, Michael received a visit from Dave, the district youth director. Dave told Michael of his plans to resign his position and wanted Michael to consider running in the next month's election to replace him.

When Michael got home that day, he told me of his conversation with Dave. For about five minutes I felt honored, but then I realized what all this might mean. My world began to crumble around me *again*, or at least that's how it felt.

Our senior pastor was nearing retirement and we had all talked about the possibility of Michael stepping into that position in the future. In our minds, we had

finally reached our Promised Land and had no plans of leaving anytime soon. Now with another option in front of us, we had to pray and hear from God.

Days went by and our prayers seemed to go unanswered. Perhaps this was because we weren't listening very well or maybe it was because we weren't really interested in what God had to say! I was afraid because I knew what I wanted and was worried that God had other plans.

After praying through my fear and surrendering all my wants to the Lord, he began to direct me to several Scripture passages. In those passages was his answer to our question. God began challenging me about whether I would travel *my way* in this life or *his way*. He let me know that it was time for me to grow deeper in my level of trust in him and commitment to him through obedience. It was at this point that I made the hard choice to prefer God's ways over my own. I knew we were headed for a move to West Virginia. Soon Michael knew that we were going there as well.

One of the hardest days of my life was leaving my customers and friends at the church where we were youth pastors. I can remember Michael standing in front of the church to tell them we were leaving. I could not control the tears or pain that seemed to be slicing my heart in two. Many of our friends could not understand why God would call us to do something we really didn't want to do. It was hard to explain to them, but we knew in our hearts that we had to trust and obey God.

WALKING ON

There was an Old Testament hero of faith who faced a time of testing when God asked him to do something he didn't want to do. Only his test was much harder than ours! Let's visit the story, starting in *Genesis 15:5*. We'll be looking at the *New International Version* throughout this day's devotional.

God made a covenant with Abraham. He took him outside and said:

"Look up at the heavens and count the stars – if indeed you can count them." Then he said to him, "So shall your offspring be."

Then in *Genesis 17:2-8* God said:

"I will confirm my covenant between me and you and will greatly increase your numbers."

(v.2)

Though God had promised Abraham and Sarah descendants, both of them had grown very old and there was no sign of his promise coming true. But finally after years of waiting, Abraham and Sarah received their long-promised son, Isaac, when Abraham was 100 years old.

Abraham and Sarah had finally reached their "Promised Land" and no doubt, they had settled into a nice comfortable place of enjoying their life and watching their precious son grow up.

Then God decided to test Abraham's faith and obedience.

"Abraham!" God called. "Yes," he replied. "Here I am."

"Take your son, your only son – yes, Isaac, whom you love so much – and go to the land of Moriah. Sacrifice him there as a burnt offering on one of the mountains, which I will point out to you."

Genesis 22:1,2 (NLT)

Can you imagine how Abraham must have felt, not to mention Sarah? After making it through a 25 year bisque-firing experience of waiting and waiting and waiting for a son, watching their bodies grow older and older…. and now this? Finally enjoying the birth of Isaac and his growth into a young man, soon to be old enough to have children of his own, and God was putting an end to it all? What about his promise?

But Abraham stepped obediently into the kiln again, though this one probably felt seven times hotter than the earlier one. You see, the glaze firing occurs at a much higher temperature than bisque firing. Glaze firing fuses the glaze and clay together and has a dramatic effect on the final appearance of the vessel.

Let's pick up the story again:

The next morning Abraham got up early. He saddled his donkey and took two of his servants with him, along with his son, Isaac. Then he chopped wood to build a fire for a burnt offering and set out for the place where God had told him to go… Abraham placed the wood for the burnt offering on Isaac's shoulders, while he himself carried the knife and the fire. As the two of them went on together,…

Genesis 22:3,6 (NLT)

When presented with God's question (in essence), "Who do you love more, me or Isaac?" Abraham unreservedly chose God. His choice was clear, even in the face of the heart-breaking question from his son:

Isaac said, "Father?" "Yes, my son," Abraham replied. "We have the wood and the fire," said the boy, "but where is the lamb for the sacrifice?" "God will provide a lamb, my son," Abraham answered. And they both went on together.

Genesis 22:7,8 (NLT)

You may be wondering, "Why would a loving God do this to Abraham?" Was God going back on his promise? Is he a God who delights in playing with our emotions? Does he take sadistic pleasure in giving us something that delights our hearts simply to yank it away at a later time? No. God wanted to deepen Abraham's capacity to both trust and obey him. He had no intention of breaking his promise. Watch what happens:

When they arrived at the place where God had told Abraham to go, he built an altar and placed the wood on it. Then he tied Isaac up and laid him on the altar over the wood. And Abraham took the knife and lifted it up to kill his son as a sacrifice to the Lord. At that moment the angel of the Lord shouted to him from heaven, "Abraham! Abraham!" "Yes," he answered. "I'm listening." "Lay down the knife," the angel said. "Do not hurt the boy in any way, for now I know that you truly fear God. You have not withheld even your beloved son from me."

Genesis 22:9-12 (NLT)

God had placed Abraham in the fiercely-heated kiln, and when he came out, his will had been fused to the will of God. Abraham had learned to truly fear

and love God by not withholding anything from him. What had been Abraham's heart desire – to be God's man through and through – was tested and proven and forged in the glazing fire. And God responded by not withholding anything from his servant either. Read on:

Then Abraham looked up and saw a ram caught by its horns in a bush. So he took the ram and sacrificed it as a burnt offering on the altar in place of his son. Abraham named the place "The Lord Will Provide." This name has now become a proverb: "On the mountain of the Lord it will be provided."

Genesis 22:13,14 (NLT)

Though Abraham was not required to actually kill Isaac that day, he did have to sacrifice him in his heart by being willing to kill him. He had to come to the place of doing whatever God required of him. By walking Isaac up that mountain, it became clear that Abraham loved God more than he loved Isaac. By looking into Isaac's terrified, confused, trusting eyes and yet still raising the knife to slay him, he passed the test of tests. He chose God and God gave him Isaac back and much, much more.

Today is a very important day in our *Journey to Freedom.* We will be traveling up the mountain of *full surrender* today, and we'd like you to join us. It's your choice of course. Journeys like these are always voluntary. Just thinking about embarking on this journey will likely set off a major struggle in your heart. Why? Because at the top of the mountain is an altar, an altar where you will have opportunity to sacrifice your "Isaacs" – the things most precious to you in your life. At the altar you have the opportunity to let go of them and give them to God knowing

he has the right and power to take them away if he chooses.

It should not surprise us that God will eventually ask us to make this journey. After all, Jesus made it and we are his followers. Jesus' journey was to a garden rather than a mountain, the Garden of Gethsemane. Faced with the horror of becoming sin and being stripped of fellowship with the Father (which he had enjoyed uninterrupted for all eternity past), he sweat great drops of blood but still prayed,

"Father, if you are willing, please take this cup of suffering away from me. Yet I want your will, not mine"

Luke 22:42 (NIV)

Jesus Christ was required by God to lay his life down for us, so that we might live. What would have happened if he had refused?

Likewise, God is telling us to also lay down our lives, to fully surrender to his will. What will we miss out on if *we* refuse?

Before we head up the mountain, we want you to know: This Jesus is no longer in the grave. He has risen and he is eagerly anticipating journeying with us to the top of the mountain.

At the top, the kiln is hot and the Potter is prepared to fuse our will to his.

Truth Point

I urge you therefore, brethren, by the mercies of God, to present your bodies a living and holy sacrifice, acceptable to God, which is your spiritual service of worship. And do not be conformed to this world, but be transformed by the renewing of your mind, that you may prove what the will of God is, that which is good and acceptable and perfect.

Romans 12:1,2 (NASB)

Application

What are *your* Isaac's? What are the things that you have been holding too tightly… the things the Lord wants you to release into his hands? Below is a list of some possible Isaac's in your life. Beyond this list, however, ask the Lord through his Spirit to reveal what they might be for you… today.

- **Relationships with loved ones** – parents, spouse, children, brothers and sisters, grandchildren, or other extended family members. Have you been trying to control their lives or a part of their lives? Have you been holding on too tightly for fear of losing them? Have you intruded into their lives in ways that reflect your own insecurities?

- **Friends** – Have you been possessive, controlling, smothering or dependent upon them in unhealthy ways?

- **Career** – Have either present demands or ambitions for the future taken too high a priority in your life? Have they taken too high a toll on your family? Your health?

- **Possessions** – Sometimes our "dream" house or car or our clothing, jewelry, furniture, family heirlooms, memorabilia, etc. can consume too much of our time and attention either admiring it or protecting it.

- **Portfolio** – Have you placed your trust in your net worth? Have you been preoccupied with the accumulation of money? Are you guilty of hoarding? Do you love money?

- **"Rights"** – Many of the good things we have in life can subtly become our gods. We can feel like they are what we deserve. We can subconsciously exist clinging to the "right" to: self-rule; self-protection; physical strength and health; long life; circumstantial happiness; reputation and image; popularity; career success; the pursuit and attainment of dreams and ambitions; power and influence; material comfort; ease or prosperity;

stress-free relationships; a nice home; nearness to family or friends; church "the way you like it"; to be married; to have children; to have children that cause no pain; job security; being loved, accepted, respected and understood by people.

There are many other possible "Isaac's" in life. As the Holy Spirit guides you, write what you have been holding on to in the space below. Even if your "Isaac" was listed above, you may need to get more specific here.

My Isaac's are:

_____

_____

_____

_____

_____

_____

_____

Father God, my Potter, here we are together on this mountain, at the place where you provide all that I need. I have come here to lay down my Isaac's. I have come here to worship you alone. I declare today that I love you more than anyone and anything else that I might be holding on to. Because I love you more, I choose to lay down *(list your Isaac's)*. I lay down all my relationships with family and friends. I lay down my career with all its possibilities and potentials. I lay down all my money and possessions. They belong to you anyway. And I lay down all my so-called "rights" and acknowledge I really only have one right – the right to be called your child (***John 1:12***). If I cling to that "right", then I know you will truly be for me ***"The Lord Will Provide."*** I also lay down all anguish and trust you for peace. I lay down all anger and trust you for love and patience. I lay down all fear and trust you for faith. I lay down all guilt for you have forgiven me. I give all that I am, including all my gifts, talents, abilities, plans, ambitions and dreams. I lay before you all that I am and all that I am not, including all my weaknesses. As I completely surrender all to you, I ask that you would be glorified through me. Entering into the kiln, I trust you to forge and fuse my will to your will. I trust that this glaze firing will have a dramatic effect on the final appearance of my life. In spite of not knowing all or much of what you have planned for me, I declare that ***"No eye has seen, no ear has heard, and no mind has imagined what God has prepared for those who love him" (1 Corinthians 2:9 NIV)***. I pray all this knowing your will is good, acceptable and perfect for me.

Father God, you are like the perfect goldsmith who has looked into my heart as a melting pot with boiling gold. You are removing from within me, ladle after ladle of dross (imperfections) that rise to the top in your furnace. Lord God, your fire's power is tremendous, but you have kept the heat on because you are looking for something more. As the gold of my faith becomes purified and the dross diminishes, no longer disturbing the surface, you are looking to see the reflection of your Son, Jesus, in my life. I know that only in eternity will that be perfectly true of me. Until that time, may he become clearer and clearer in and through me each day. In his name, amen.

DECLARATIONS

- I have been to the mountain where God provides.
- I have sacrificed my Isaac(s) there.
- By making this sacrifice, it is clear that I love God more than all.
- My will has been fused with the will of my heavenly Father!

Identity Reminder:

I am born of God; the evil one
cannot touch me.

1 Jn. 5:18

Broken Yet Chosen

He is Glorified Through His Vessel

Off we (Michael and Christi) went to the district office, which meant – for me – learning to live on the mountain of sacrifice… in the hot kiln.

When we moved I left all my friends, and now was virtually alone, sitting in a house watching my husband fulfill his role as district youth director. I felt like my world had come crashing to a halt, with my main duties reduced to mowing the grass in the summer and watching it snow in the winter. Mainly I was just trying to be content.

Sitting around really grated against my basic temperament. I am an activist, but during this period of time, God wanted me to slow down. Unfortunately, I didn't take to that "prescription" very well. I ended up spending several years in the back yard trying to dig up all the Isaac's I had sacrificed. I wanted to have a great big pity party. Looking back, I was clearly tangled in deception again as I had begun to question God and blame him for moving us to West Virginia and dumping me off!

After wrestling with God for a couple years, it finally began to dawn on me that God had not dumped me off. Instead he had stopped my world in order to give me the greatest gift I have ever received – an understanding of what he had done for me in Christ, the gift of freedom! I realized that he had taken me all the way to the mountains of West Virginia to do heart surgery on me.

And so I let him.

When I did, he opened me up and truly exchanged my heart of pain and misery for a heart that was free in Christ! During this time in my life, God began pouring into me truth about my new identity in Christ. He began setting me free from the bondage of my past, and began teaching me what it really means to walk by the Spirit. I also learned to be content just being his child, nothing more and nothing less.

Several years after soaking in freedom and being tested in it, God made it clear that it was time to move again. The assignment? To pastor Heritage Church in Dublin, VA, where we remain even now. When he called us to make that move, God impressed on my heart these words: *I am sending you to reap the harvest!* I was thrilled to the bone but also greatly humbled. I couldn't believe that God would entrust us with the wonderful job of reaping a harvest for his kingdom, after all we had been through! But by his grace, this vessel had come out of the fire and was ready to be used again… this time for his glory!

Here in Virginia we are still busy loving God and people. Many have already come to know the Lord. Many others have also begun to experience their freedom in Christ. There is an excitement, a sense of anticipation in the air since we have become vessels used for his glory. We never know from day to day what he will do through us, but whatever he wants with our lives is fine with us. For now, the doors keep flying open!

Sometimes we put limits on God by thinking that God can only do certain things *in* our lives and *through* our lives. But God is infinitely creative and ingenious and he is able to do exceeding abundantly beyond all that we can ask or even imagine. And he wants to do so through his church (that's us!) for his glory! (*Ephesians 3:20, 21*).

So don't ever limit God in any way!

If we are willing to walk with God, he will amaze and astound us by leading us into the good works he has prepared for us to do (*Ephesians 2:10*). We hope you noticed something in that last sentence. It is not *our* works, created and carried out by our own energy that God is interested in. It is *his* works, created by him and carried out through us by the power of the Holy Spirit that brings him glory.

That's the way Jesus lived and is the way we were intended to live as well. Jesus said:

> *I assure you, the Son can do nothing by himself. He does only what he sees the Father doing. Whatever the Father does, the Son also does.*
>
> *John 5:19 (NIV)*

Like Jesus, you and I were chosen to serve God. Unlike Jesus, you and I have to be broken of our own self-sufficiency and self-will in order to become usable to the Master. That's what this whole week has been about. He chose you so that you would follow him and in the process lose your confidence in the *flesh* and gain increasing confidence in the *Spirit*. When we walk with Christ in the power of the Holy Spirit, we glorify our Father in heaven by the fruit (good results from good works) we bear in him. Jesus put it this way:

> *I am the vine; you are the branches. The one who remains in me – and I in him – bears much fruit, because apart from me you can accomplish nothing… If you remain in me and my words remain in you, ask whatever you want, and it will be done for you. My Father is honored by this, that you bear much fruit and show that you are my disciples.*
>
> *John 15:5, 7, 8 (NET)*

What are some synonyms for "remain in"? _____

_____

_____

_____

The picture created by this word is to *reside, continue in, abide in* or *dwell in.* In a sense, it is like living in a house. The longer you live in a house, the more at home you feel. You feel comfortable there. Though sadly not always true in a fallen world, a home is designed to be a sanctuary, a refuge, a place of security, a place of warmth, a place of love. It is where you *live.* When people ask you where you live, you give them the address of your house, your "abode," the place where you dwell. That is how our relationship with Jesus is to be. He is our home and we are to make our home *in him.*

God wants us to find our home in Jesus, to stay close to him, living in intimate relationship with him as you would with a loved one in your home. In fact, *Ephesians 5:22-32* paints a picture of our relationship to Christ as a wife to a husband! Now that's intimate!

In *John 15* Jesus used grape vines as his picture because there is another element to "remaining" or "abiding" that he wanted us to understand. The branch must remain attached to the vine in order to bear fruit.

In a healthy branch-vine "relationship", all that the branch needs to bear fruit courses through the vine and into the branch. A branch cut off from a vine is fruitless, and so are our lives.

Therefore, Jesus is not only our home where we are to dwell, but he is also our *life*. We are to continually live with his life coursing into us by his Spirit in union with our spirit and through us (our soul and body) to the world around us. When we abide in Christ that way, we bear spiritual fruit.

From your understanding of the Bible, what "fruit" is Jesus talking about our bearing?

_____

_____

_____

_____

_____

_____

If you're stumped, take a look at the continuation of Jesus' words:

Just as the Father has loved me, I have also loved you; remain in my love. If you obey my commandments you will remain in my love, just as I have obeyed my Father's commandments and remain in his love. I have told you these things so that my joy may be in you, and your joy may be complete. My commandment is this – to love one another just as I have loved you. No one has greater love than this – that one lays down his life for his friends.

John 15:9-13 (NET)

Let's sum up what Jesus was teaching here:

- Jesus loves us as much as the Father loves Jesus! Wow! That's enough to keep you going for a few centuries!

- God doesn't stop loving us if we mess up, but in order to fully experience the Father's love, we must live a life of obedience. Jesus is our example of that kind of life.

- Jesus wasn't trying to make our lives miserable by this teaching, not at all. He was instructing us because he wanted to share his joy with us so that we could experience joy to the fullest!

- What is the main thing on Jesus' mind for us to do? To sacrificially lay down our lives for others in love.

- Therefore, the main fruit of abiding in Jesus is love.

Now, ***Galatians 5:22, 23*** unpacks what God's love looks like – it is joyful, peaceful, patient, kind, good, faithful, gentle, self-controlled – but those are like facets of the gem. The gem is love! In conclusion...

- God's good works for us always involve a self-sacrificing, life-laying down **love**.

- God's love expressed through us only comes through the life of Christ flowing in and through us in the power of the Holy Spirit, as we abide in Christ.

- God's love at work through us in the lives of others **is** bearing fruit!

- God is glorified when we bear fruit!

WINDING DOWN

When God was breaking me (Christi) of my fleshly self-confidence, I mentioned that he began teaching me what it really means to walk by his Spirit. God wants that for all his children. He wants that for you!

And do not be drunk with wine, in which is dissipation; but be filled with the Spirit, speaking to one another in psalms and hymns and spiritual songs, singing and making melody in your heart to the Lord, giving thanks always for all things to God the Father in the name of our Lord Jesus Christ, submitting to one another in the fear of God.

Ephesians 5:18-21 (NKJV)

Galatians clearly shows the contrast and the battle between fleshly living and Spirit-filled living:

But I say, walk by the Spirit, and you will not carry out the desire of the flesh. For the flesh sets its desire against the Spirit, and the Spirit against the flesh; for these are in opposition to one another, so that you may not do the things that you please. But if you are led by the Spirit, you are not under the Law.

Galatians 5:16-18 (NASB)

Being filled with the Spirit is the only way to fully experience and express God's love.

Being filled with the Spirit is the only way to love others with God's love.

Being filled with the Spirit is the only way to bear fruit that glorifies God.

Being filled with the Spirit is the only way to walk in freedom!

What does it mean to be filled with the Spirit?

Being filled with the Spirit means that rather than your listening to and obeying the flesh and its impulses (*Galatians 5:19-21*), you are allowing the Spirit of God through the word of God to lead you, direct you and give you power to overcome sin in your life and express God's love to others.

What does it take to be filled with the Spirit?

- First, it requires a longing to walk with God and be used by him for his glory.

- Second, it requires a cleansing from sin in one's life; we encourage you to take advantage of going through the *Steps to Freedom in Christ* either in a group setting through your church, individually or with a trusted friend. Copies of the "*Steps*" can be ordered through Freedom in Christ Ministries toll-free at 1-866-462-4747. The *Steps to Freedom in Christ* are a tool designed to allow the Holy Spirit to shine the searchlight on your life so that you can repent of sin and renounce lies that have kept you in bondage.

- Third, it requires a surrendering of the controls of your life over to God, letting him "do the driving," so to speak.

- Fourth, it requires faith to believe that he will fill you with the Spirit as you invite Christ to take his role as "vine" and you as a "branch" in submission to and in dependence upon him.

WRAPPING UP

Truth Point

"Not by might nor by power, but by My Spirit,"
says the Lord of hosts.

Zechariah 4:6b (NASB)

Application

Being filled with the Holy Spirit is like replacing a couple of AA batteries with a jet engine in your heart! No matter how strong physically you might be, the flesh is weak (*Matthew 26:41*). No matter how weak physically you might be, the Spirit of God, who raised Christ Jesus from the dead lives in you – if you are a child of God! (*Romans 8:11*) That means the very power of the resurrection is in you!

Knowing the kind of mighty power that is inside of you, which is available through the filling with the Spirit, changes everything. Problems that seemed insurmountable suddenly are conquerable in the power and wisdom of God. Relationships that seemed irreconcilable are infused with new hope and love. Areas of bondage in your life that once appeared invincible crumble, demolished through the power of the Spirit of liberty.

Below is some space for you to write down the obstacles in your life that have defied all human (fleshly) power or logic to change. After that is a prayer where you have opportunity to present them to the "Mighty God, Wonderful Counselor, Prince of Peace", Jesus Christ, for him to act for his glory.

A large part of living by the fullness and power of the Holy Spirit is prayer, asking God to powerfully act – through you to accomplish his plans!

If you remain in me and my words remain in you, ask whatever you want, and it will be done for you.

-- Jesus in John 15:7 (NET)

_____

_____

_____

_____

_____

_____

_____

_____

_____

_____

Identity Reminder:

I am a branch of the true vine, a channel of His life.

Jn. 15:1,5

PRAYER

Dear heavenly Father, all my life – including these last four weeks – you have been drawing me away from life lived by myself, for myself and through myself. You have been chiseling and firing, molding and breaking flesh dependency so that I can learn to be filled with and walk by the Spirit and therefore glorify your name. These current problems that I am going through are just more reminders that I can't do it. I can't make life work on my own and by my own strength and resources. I surrender (name the obstacles written above) to you. I ask you to act to glorify your holy name. I renounce trying to fix these problems or anything else in my life by my own human abilities. I ask you to cleanse me from all my sin and fill me with the Holy Spirit so that I can be led, guided, directed and empowered by him. In the name of Jesus who made the way for the Spirit to come by his perfect life, death, resurrection and ascension I pray, amen.

DECLARATIONS

- **I declare that the flesh is weak and profits nothing!**

- **I admit that apart from Christ I can do nothing to bear lasting fruit!**

- **I agree that I need my heart purified and cleansed so that I can be filled with the Holy Spirit!**

- **I welcome the Spirit's work to bring to light all sin in my life!**

- **I choose to be filled with the Holy Spirit as that cleansing takes place!**

Tested Yet Triumphant

Tested Yet Triumphant

Welcome to the War!

WARMING UP

Things were not going well on the summer mission project. A group of youth ministers, including myself (Rich), were living with a group of Christian high school students, teaching them how to follow Christ and share their faith. Great concept. Wrong kids… at least some of them.

Among the guys there was a lot of anger and rebellion. They had packed that emotional baggage and brought it along to the beach resort where we were living. The mission project simply provided the pressure cooker environment to bring it out. One kid was caught shoplifting; I'm not even sure he was a believer. It was all very bad.

Needless to say, our "witness" in the community could have been better.

During the peak of the chaos, I woke up in the middle of the night from a sound sleep. I know I was not dreaming.

As I opened my eyes, there in front of me was an ugly, laughing, leering face. And it wasn't one of the teenage boys either! Now whether this face was actually suspended in the air above me or was projected into my mind, I'm not sure. But it was very real.

At that time I was in my twenties and at the peak of my strength and virility. I'd been a child of God for at least six or seven years, walking with God somewhat consistently for at least three. I was a spiritual man as well as a red-blooded American citizen. So I did what

any other red-blooded American man would do at that hour of the night.

I yelled and pulled the sheets over my head, hoping and praying that whatever it was would be gone by morning!

I have no doubt in my mind that what I saw was a demon. By the way, I never saw one before and haven't seen one since. I have, however, felt their presence and heard them speak numerous times. The effects of their work are everywhere.

That middle of the night wake-up call served to accomplish a couple of things. First, it woke us youth ministers up to our need for concerted prayer. The result was a wonderful movement of repentance among us all and in the end God was greatly glorified on that mission project. Second, it awakened me to the reality of what has been called "the invisible war" – what most people call *spiritual battle*.

From the moment of your conception (and even before!) to the moment you pass into eternity, you are part of a cosmic war of immense proportions. The casualties in this war are staggering; the stakes astronomically high. Everyone is in this war, and that means *you!* If you're not a true follower of Christ, you're currently on the losing side, but there's still time to defect. If you are a true follower of Christ, you're a soldier in this battle. You may be AWOL or a POW or even MIA, but you're a soldier. No exceptions.

As former Green Beret captain Stu Webber, says, "Welcome to the war."

I hope we didn't make you choke on your morning cup of coffee just now. We just wanted to get your attention.

This devotional was designed to do on a Sunday, but it may not be Sunday for you today. You may be doing this day's devotion before you go to work or head off to class. You might be taking a break during a busy-but-fairly-routine day at home. Maybe it's a day off. Or maybe you're just grabbing a few minutes to read over lunch break. Wherever you are and whatever you've been up do today, you may not *think* you are in a war. It very well might not *feel* like a war or *look* like a war around you. After all, there are no bombs exploding, no blood flowing, no people moaning… at least not where you are.

Nevertheless, the Bible says we're very much in a war, whether we believe it or not, whether we like it or not. Our intention this week is to further equip you to wage spiritual war and even more importantly to *win*! Your freedom depends on it.

Welcome to the war, soldier.

Although Bible details are sketchy, the war apparently started before God created the world. It may have happened sort of like this… A high level angel, likely very powerful, very beautiful and very glorious, looked into a mirror in heaven one day and asked, *Mirror, mirror on the wall, who's the fairest of them all?* The right answer was *God.* The angel got the wrong answer and decided it was himself. At that moment he decided to duke it out with the Almighty and he and about one third of the angels got thrashed. Kicked out of heaven, they had nowhere to hang out until God created earth. Suddenly planet earth became a battlefield, a deadly stage with its own set of villains – Satan (the instigator of the rebellion) and his army (which the Bible calls demons).

The outcome of this epic drama is not in question. We win because Jesus already won the conclusive battle on the cross. Rejoice in the truth of the Scriptures below and then write out your own declaration of Christ's victory in the blanks afterwards.

Since the children are made of flesh and blood, it's logical that the Savior took on flesh and blood in order to rescue them by his death. By embracing death, taking it into himself, he destroyed the Devil's hold on death and freed all who cower through life, scared to death of death.

Hebrews 2:14,15 (MSG)

And even though you were dead in your transgressions and in the uncircumcision of your flesh, he nevertheless made you alive with him, having forgiven all your transgressions. He has destroyed what was against us, a certificate of indebtedness expressed in decrees opposed to us. He has taken it away by nailing it to the cross. Disarming the rulers and authorities [demonic powers], *he has made a public disgrace of them, triumphing over them by the cross.*

Colossians 2:13-15 (NET)

[bracketed statement ours]

He who does what is sinful is of the devil, because the devil has been sinning from the beginning. The reason the Son of God appeared was to destroy the devil's work.

1 John 3:8 (NIV)

_____

_____

_____

_____

_____

_____

_____

_____

The devil's weapons of sin and death were snatched from his hand by Christ at the cross. Jesus took all of humanity's sins upon his body and paid the full penalty of death for mankind. And all who put their faith in Christ as the sacrifice for *their* sins are released from the devil's chains! The believer's *"Emancipation Proclamation"* is:

There is therefore now no condemnation for those who are in Christ Jesus. For the law of the life-giving Spirit in Christ Jesus has set you free from the law of sin and death. For God achieved what the law could not do because it was weakened through the flesh. By sending his own Son in the likeness of sinful flesh and concerning sin, he condemned sin in the flesh, so that the righteous requirements of the law may be fulfilled in us, who do not walk according to the flesh but according to the Spirit.

Romans 8:1-4 (NET)

In simple courtroom terms, here's what happened. We, the defendants, had broken the law of God. Guilty as charged! The devil, acting as prosecuting attorney, accused us, threatened us and demanded that we die. His case was airtight… almost. Then Counsel for the defense, Jesus Christ, made his brilliant, closing argument: he died in our place and rose from the dead. With furious fists pounding and voice screaming, the devil cried, "Objection!" "Overruled!" the Father-Judge roared. "The defendants are declared NOT GUILTY! They shall not die, but live." The Spirit of God swept over our chains and they fell off. We… *you…* walked out of that courtroom free!

Life now becomes about living out that freedom, that victory – day by day moment by moment. The devil still seeks to win the daily skirmishes, though he knows he has lost the war.

So, we find ourselves still waging war as soldiers in the "mopping up" operations until Christ returns to make all victories final.

In the days ahead we want to expose the enemy's schemes designed to take you out. The apostle Paul wrote that *"we are not unaware of his* [the devil's] *schemes"* (*2 Corinthians 2:11 NIV*). If the truth be known, many of us *are* unaware of Satan's schemes. And, in this case, ignorance is NOT bliss. It is fatal.

For now we want to list some of the names and descriptions that the Bible gives to our enemy. The list will not be exhaustive but will give you a pretty good idea of the kind of being we're dealing with. We will compare and contrast them with Christ, though Jesus and the devil are not opposites. Jesus is the Creator God and always will be. The devil is a created being and never will be anything different. But the devil is a forger, counterfeiter and pretender and so it is helpful to expose his true colors. Knowing who he is will help us in the coming days to unmask what he does and how he does it in opposing Christ.

The Lord Jesus Christ	The Enemy
Advocate (our defense attorney) 1 Jn 2:1	*Satan (means "adversary") 1 Peter 5:8*
Author & finisher of faith (builds up) Heb 12:2	*Devil (means "slanderer") 1 John 3:8*
Holy, blameless and pure Heb. 7:26	*Tempter 1 Thessalonians 3:5*
Redeemer Ephesians 1:7	*Accuser Revelation 12:10*
Truth John 14:6	*Liar, Deceiver John 8:44*
Resurrection & Life John 11:25	*Murderer John 8:44*
The Light of the World John 8:12	*Disguises self as angel of light 2 Cor. 11:14*
King of kings and Lord of lords Rev. 19:16	*Prince of the power of the air Eph. 2:2*
Lamb of God who takes away the sin of the world John 1:29 and ... *Who is a victorious warrior! Zephaniah 3:17*	*The great dragon Revelation 12:9*

Satan and his demonic forces are not all-powerful though they are more powerful than people and very dangerous for those apart from Christ to tangle with. (see *Acts 19:13-16*) They are not all-knowing though they are very intelligent, cunning and subtle. Nor are they able to be everywhere at once, though their network of communication and activity is highly sophisticated.

The good news is that *"the one who is in you [Christ] is greater than the one that is in the world [the devil]" (1 John 4:4 NIV)*. Though we are told to be on the alert in regard to the enemy's attacks (*1 Peter 5:8*), believers in Christ are never told to fear the devil. Christ is Victor and in him you can be victorious, too. Your freedom depends on it.

Truth Point

Be of sober spirit, be on the alert. Your adversary, the devil, prowls about like a roaring lion, seeking someone to devour. But resist him, firm in your faith, knowing that the same experiences of suffering are being accomplished by your brethren who are in the world.

1 Peter 5:8, 9 (NASB)

Application

Here are two questions for reflection. Jot down your thoughts in the blanks provided.

First, what evidence do you see in your life, home, work, church, and neighborhood that there really is a spiritual battle going on?

_____

_____

_____

_____

_____

Second, which of the names/descriptions of the evil one best depicts his primary tactic(s) in your life right now?

_____

_____

_____

_____

_____

Dear heavenly Father, in some sense I feel like someone who was drafted into the military while asleep and then woke up to find himself in a barracks bunk bed with bombs exploding all around. There's a part of me that wants to run to the battle and there's another part that would prefer the life of a civilian, thank you very much! I need you to train me, Father, in how to be a good soldier. How do I fight an enemy I can't see? Grant me the eyes of faith to understand what is going on in the unseen world, even beyond what I can observe in this material world. I thank you, Father, for allowing your Son, the Conquering Warrior, to live in me and empower me. In his name, Jesus, I pray, amen.

- **I admit that I am in a spiritual battle and will be until I die.**

- **I declare that he Lord Jesus Christ has already won the war so I can win the battles!**

- **I proclaim that greater is he who is in me than he that is in the world!**

Tested But Triumphant

It's All in Your Head

WARMING UP

When I (Rich) first became a Christian, the concept of spiritual warfare or demonic activity seemed very foreign to me. I was raised in a culture that had largely embraced science as "the way, the truth and the life" and I had been a scientific-minded, skeptical, evolutionary agnostic as a nonbeliever. That mental programming dies hard.

So when I would read Scriptures that depicted Jesus doing battle with the forces of darkness, it seemed like good drama but not relevant for today. After all, I reasoned, we're much more sophisticated now. I figured much of that stuff in the Bible about the devil was merely superstition.

But then I started to hear stories from the mission field about encounters that intelligent, educated missionaries were having with the enemy. I could no longer hide in my pseudo-academic shell thinking "that stuff maybe happened *back then*." So I found another shell. This one was labeled "that stuff maybe happens *over there*… but certainly not in America!"

To my amazement and fascination, however, I discovered that I was certainly wrong! Reading books from American pastors and counselors who were wrestling with dark angels opened my eyes to the fact that encounters with the powers of darkness not only happened in this country… they happened in our churches. People whose salvation was not in question were struggling with obsessive thoughts… even voices in their heads… compulsive or self-destructive behaviors, etc. and they were being set free through Christ, who is the Truth.

As the Lord was enabling me to "get a clue" about the reality of spiritual battle, my eyes needed to be opened even more. I needed to see that the battle was not just *back then* nor was it only *over there* nor was it limited to *out there* (with some church people). I had to come to terms with the unsettling reality that it is also *in here*, right between my own ears.

It is a battle for the mind… *our minds*. Yes, it's all in our heads. But make no mistake about it… it is very, very real.

Identity Reminder:

I have been chosen and appointed to bear fruit.

Jn. 15:16

Below we have listed a variety of symptoms, conditions, beliefs and practices. Circle any that you think could possibly have a demonic component to them:

violent behavior	rebellion	depression
lustful thoughts	anxiety	cult beliefs
religious pride	nagging thoughts	shame
occult practices	slander	eating disorders
illegal drugs	pornography	unforgiveness
fear	prejudice	anger
rage	legalism	unbelief
lustful actions	lying	dark moods
witchcraft	bitterness	war

The key words in the directions to the exercise above are *could possibly have.* The answer is "all of the above." Every one of those items could have a component to them that is from the enemy, because every one of them involves a battle for the mind at some level.

Hear us out here. We are *not* taking a "the devil made me do it" stance. Not at all. We are all individually responsible for the choices we make. Nobody can make us sin, including the devil.

However, the instigation of a sinful course of action with a tempting thought or the insistence on a particular behavior with a penetrating, persistent pressure of thought is right in line with the enemy's job description. Let's take a look at an example from Scripture. First we'll set the stage:

It was early in the life of the First Christian Church of Jerusalem. Jesus' resurrection was fresh on everyone's minds. The apostles were performing amazing miracles. Thousands of people had joined the congregation and everyone was excited. Because some of the new believers were poor, men and women led by the Holy Spirit were actually selling property and homes in order to give the proceeds to the poor. It was "church" like church was meant to be.

Then along came a spider…

Let's pick up the story.

But a man named Ananias – his wife, Sapphira, conniving in this with him – sold a piece of land, secretly kept part of the price for himself, and then brought the rest to the apostles and made an offering of it. Peter said, "Ananias, how did Satan get you to lie to the Holy Spirit and secretly keep back part of the price of the field? Before you sold it, it was all yours, and after you sold it, the money was yours to do with as you wished. So what got into you to pull a trick like this? You didn't lie to men but to God."

Acts 5:1-4 (MSG)

Peter asked two very poignant questions in that passage of Scripture. What were they? Fill in your answers in the blanks below.

_____

_____

_____

_____

_____

_____

_____

_____

How *indeed* did Satan get Ananias to lie? What *did* get into him?

Do you think the devil appeared in a red suit, complete with pitchfork and horns and announced to Ananias and Sapphira, "Hi guys, I'm the devil and I've got a really cool idea for you…" Of course not.

What "got into him" was a *thought.* Here's maybe how it happened. Ananias and Sapphira were having coffee one morning and Annie put down his newspaper and looked at Sapphire (who was no gem of a wife!)

A:	*Hey Sapphire, that was pretty amazing at church yesterday, wasn't it?*

S:	*What are you talking about?*

A:	*You know, when Barnabbas came waltzing in with $75,000 from selling that riverfront property of his. I mean, everybody oohed and ahhed and patted him on the back and all…*

S:	*Yeah, the apostles were real buddy-buddy with him after that. I bet Barney and his wife, Betty – that hussy – are going to be part of the inner circle now. I can just see her parading around like she's something special…*

A:	*Y'know honey, I've been thinking…*

S:	*Really? This oughtta be good…*

A:	*No, seriously. I mean, why can't we get in on the action, too?*

S:	*I'm listening…*

A:	*Well, what if we sold our land, too, but instead of giving all the profits away, we keep half… just to supplement our retirement… and present the rest to the apostles as if it were the whole kit and caboodle?*

S:	*That's a drop dead awesome idea!*

And so it was… drop dead, that is. Peter, through the Holy Spirit, sniffed out their plot and both hubby and wife fell dead on the spot.

Their crime? Lying. That's it. You see, it wasn't as if God demanded "dues" of all the church members or that all proceeds from property sales were required to be donated. As Peter said, the property and the money from its sale were at Ananias' and Sapphira's discretion to do with as they chose. What they did was lie and pretend, and their attempt to deceive God himself was met with swift judgment.

Somewhere in their foolish and fatal thought processes was the voice of the enemy. They allowed the devil to bait them with a suggestion (appealing to their greed and likely desire for popularity) and they took the bait. Problem is, they didn't see the hook.

Let's go back to the list of items at the beginning of the *Walking On* section. Knowing that Satan and his demons are liars (***John 8:44***) and that they use falsehood, deception and misleading thoughts in order to gain the upper hand in our thinking, what might be an example of an *impression, suggestion, insinuation* or *falsehood* that could initiate or exacerbate each of these conditions? We'd like you to give this a shot. We've filled in some of them to jump start you in the right direction.

There is one very important point we need to make here. The thoughts implanted into our minds from the enemy are very often expressed in the "first person singular." That is, they are presented to us with words like "I", "me" and "my" in order to dupe us into believing the thought originated from us. You'll see that expressed below.

violent behavior	*That person needs to pay for what they did to me.*
lustful thoughts	*I wonder what it would be like to…*
religious pride	*Our church (denomination) is the most biblical…*
dark moods	*Nobody listens to me, nobody notices me, nobody cares.*
bitterness	*If he/she hadn't done that to me, I would still be…*
rebellion	
anxiety	
nagging thoughts	*I can't do anything right; I'm a screw-up (**repeated**).*
occult practices	*Finally. A way to get what I want and control my life…*
pornography	*This is the only time I feel really alive and excited…*
depression	*There's just no way out for me…*
cult beliefs	*These people are more sold-out than the Christians I know.*
shame	
slander	*I can cut this person down to size; that'll show them!*
war	*We must destroy or we'll be destroyed!*
fear	
rage	
lustful actions	*I deserve this; besides everybody's doing it!*
eating disorders	*I don't deserve to eat; I am evil.*
unforgiveness	*What they did to me hurts too much; I can't forgive them!*
prejudice	*The world would be better without those people…*
legalism	*I've just got to do better; I so much want God to be pleased*
anger	
unbelief	*I just wish I could believe this, but I can't.*
lying	
witchcraft	*It is good to be able to tap into such ancient wisdom…*
illegal drugs	*Let's party and have some real fun!*

Never underestimate the power of a lie. It was just such a lie… *the lie*…that instigated the fall of the human race. "You shall be like God" was (and still is) the most powerful lie ever spoken and the rest is history… the history of fallen sinful mankind.

Our minds can be bombarded by lies from the world system around us, the flesh within us that gravitates toward self-sufficiency, and the devil and his cohorts. This is a daily battle for the control of our soul. And the battleground is our mind!

It would be easy to feel overwhelmed right now, so we'll conclude this section with one very powerful statement to encourage you.

The power of truth is always greater than the power of the lie.

Hang onto that. We'll spend the rest of the week equipping you to defeat lies with truth.

Identity Reminder:

I am a personal
witness of Christ's.

Acts 1:8

Truth Point

He couldn't stand the truth because there wasn't a shred of truth in him. When the Liar speaks, he makes it up out of his lying nature and fills the world with lies.

John 8:44 (MSG)

Application

In the exercise above we looked at 27 issues that could, to some degree, be initiated or magnified by the devil's lies. Pick out one that you tend to struggle with most. Ask the Lord to show you any lies that you have believed that are adding "fuel to the fire" of this condition. List it/them below.

_____

_____

_____

_____

_____

_____

_____

_____

_____

_____

_____

_____

_____

PRAYER

Dear heavenly Father, lies are most effective when they are concealed, when we don't even realize they are lies. Open my eyes to any of the lies that I have unconsciously been believing. Shine the light of truth on my mind and expose any deception, falsehood or counterfeits that have attached themselves to my belief system. I admit to you that I have believed the lie(s) that *(name any lies that you listed above)*. Thank you for forgiving me for believing such untruth. Please fill my mind now with truth in the areas where I have wallowed in the lies of the world, flesh or devil. I trust you to do this on a continual basis as you set me free. In the name of Jesus the Truth I pray, amen.

Identity Reminder:

I am God's temple.

1 Cor. 3:16

DECLARATIONS

- **I recognize that spiritual battle is primarily a battle for my mind.**

- **I understand that lies fuel sinful and destructive behavior.**

- **I declare that the truth is always more powerful than a lie!**

Tested Yet Triumphant

The Invincible Place of Humility

Humility is the one quality that once you think you've got it, you've lost it! Though we all fall far short of the Lord Jesus' example, humility and submission to authority are areas we must be growing in if we are to win on the spiritual battlefield. Humility is truly non-negotiable in the world of warfare.

Pride and rebellion are primary characteristics of the devil's character, and he would love for people – especially God's people – to be conformed to his image. In addition, he knows that when we move out of humility and submission to God's authority and enter into his arena of pride and rebellion, we have moved onto his playing field and he always has the "home field advantage" there.

It's always a bit risky (for the reason stated above) to share an example of humility from one's own life, so I'll take the opposite approach. I'll talk about a time where I (Rich) did not exercise that godly virtue and how it messed up my witness for Christ and could have gotten me into bigger trouble. Maybe my "bad example" will help you avoid yours! It was a late Friday afternoon, around 5 pm, and I was sitting in my car in the shopping center parking lot where my son, Brian, was inside taking his taekwondo class. I was trying to relax and get some reading done… important reading, I'm sure. The problem was that a furniture and appliance store a few doors down from where Brian was training was blasting country music into the parking lot from their sound system.

I hate country music to begin with, plus it was disturbing my very important reading. I decided to take definitive action.

I marched indignantly into the store and demanded that they turn down their music. I told the lady behind the counter that it was obnoxious and insensitive to people like me who were trying to get their crucial reading done out there in the parking lot. The poor lady was shocked and immediately turned the music down. I marched back triumphantly to my car and then drove to an available parking space closer to the taekwondo studio.

Settling back into my world-changing reading, I was alarmed when I heard the music suddenly turned up to a volume twice as loud as it had been originally! Now the very angry proprietor of the store was striding down the sidewalk to the taekwondo studio. At that moment my son's taekwondo instructor came curiously out of the studio wondering why the music was blaring. Not wanting the store owner to get to him first, I jumped out of my car and hurried over to him.

You can imagine the rest. Angry words. Accusations. Threats. Tensed muscles. Bulging eyes. Fortunately the taekwondo instructor kept his cool. As I realized the store owner was about 20 years younger and much more muscled than I was, I became quite grateful that the fourth-degree black belt instructor was standing between us!

Boy did I feel stupid. All the kids inside the taekwondo school were staring at us in our heated argument. I can imagine them saying, "Hey, isn't that your dad, Brian? The minister guy?" My angry pride began shriveling up in my shame of messing up a witness for Christ, not to mention embarrassing my son.

Well, the epilogue is that I apologized to the store owner after we'd both cooled off and he told me that I had a lot of guts for doing that. Guts actually had little to do with it. Relief was more like it as the Spirit of God was not about to let me off the hook on this one without thoroughly cleaning up my mess.

No, this wasn't a spiritual war on the level of traveling into a remote tribal area as part of a mission trip. But this was a spiritual battle nonetheless, a battle "middle-class American style."

Spiritual battle occurs in and around us any time we are faced with a temptation or a test of our faith. I blew it because of my angry pride and lack of submission to God as well as to another person.

Your battle with angry or self-reliant pride and submission may not be over country music, but it will be over something. Tragically far too many friendships, marriages, families, businesses and churches are spiritual wrecks because humility is so rare. We trust this lesson will help you in your battles and in your growth toward Christ-like humility.

Taking a look at the beginning of the section on spiritual warfare in Ephesians 6, you should be able to see immediately why I lost that battle described above.

Finally, be strong in the Lord, and in the strength of His might.

Ephesians 6:10 (NASB)

There are really only two options in life when it comes to strength. Either it is self-generated or it comes from the Lord. It is very simple.

In the first half of **_Ephesians 6:10_** we are exhorted to **_"be strong in the Lord"_** (emphasis ours). What does this mean? Since the book of Ephesians is to be taken as a "whole" letter, you cannot understand **_Ephesians 6_** without first understanding **_Ephesians 1._**

In the first chapter of Ephesians, we are told who we are _in the Lord._ We are blessed with every spiritual blessing _in Christ._ We are chosen _in him._ We are adopted, forgiven, loved, redeemed, granted the Holy Spirit, and so on… _in Christ_ or _in the Lord._

In the flesh (apart from Christ) we may be smart or not so smart, strong or not so strong, wealthy or not so wealthy, aggressive or… you get the picture. But _in Christ_ we have every spiritual blessing and resource we could possibly need.

Now, when I found myself irritated by the country music and my anger started to rise, I was very aware of who I was _in the flesh._ I saw myself as an American citizen and patron of that shopping center who, doggone it, has rights. I saw myself as a noble defender of all the other patrons of that shopping center who had rights, too. I saw myself as a hater of country music who shouldn't have to be subjected to such abuse! And on and on. I was strong in the flesh

– in my fleshly identity – but I was not strong *in the Lord* (who I was/am in Christ).

I was already defeated.

In the second half of the verse we are urged to *"[be strong]* **in the strength of his might."** **Ephesians 1** talks about the power that raised Jesus from the dead and seated him at God's right hand (***vv. 19-23***). What incredible power! In **Ephesians 3:16 (NASB)** the apostle Paul prays that we would be **"strengthened with power through his Spirit in the inner man."** And at the end of that prayer he worships God for being able to do far beyond what we can ask or imagine through his power working with us (***v. 20***)!

Clearly there is no power shortage with God nor is there a shortage *in us!* Amazing as it may seem, the same power that raised Jesus from the dead is able to also give life to our bodies through his Spirit! (***Romans 8:11***)

My problem was that I was not filled with the Holy Spirit during my angry incident. I was walking according to the flesh, and therefore relied on my own fleshly strengths – loudness of voice, anger, indignation, force of personality, facial intensity, ability to argue, quickness of tongue, skill at using someone's words against them, etc. – in order to "win."

I lost – maybe not on a human level – but certainly on a spiritual one.

Can you see this in your own life? Do you see the ways you tend to fall back on fleshly weapons of warfare, such as being strong in some fleshly (not Christian) perception of who you are (identity) in order to win life's battles? In the blanks below there are some spaces for you to write down the fleshy fighting techniques you use with friends, enemies, family, co-workers, etc.

(Some examples would be: arguing, yelling, screaming, withdrawing, threatening, and so on.)

_____

_____

_____

_____

_____

Hang on to those for now. You'll need them later.

Why is this area of humility, submission and surrender to God so important? In essence life in the universe was designed to run on humble submission. The Son did nothing except what he saw the Father doing (***John 5:19***). The Spirit does not speak on his own initiative but only what he hears from the Father; he glorifies Christ (***John 16:13,14***). The authority stops with the Father, for he is the ultimate Head. But notice that the Son and the Spirit, though co-equal in nature with the Father, are not in it for themselves. Never do we find them acting independently of the Father. Humility and submission is in perfect harmony with the operation of God himself! And so it is to be the way we live and wage spiritual war.

James put it this way:

"But he gives a greater grace. Therefore it says, "God is opposed to the proud, but gives grace to the humble." Submit therefore to God. Resist the devil and he will flee from you"

James 4:6, 7 (NASB)

God opposes proud people because pride is the opposite of God. He gives grace, however – his providing, protecting, powerful presence – to those who are humble.

When we humble ourselves under God's authority and submit to his kind, just, good rule in our lives, we can beat the devil. When we resist him – strong *in the Lord* and in the strength of *his might* – we win. The devil flees. He *has* to.

Spiritual *authority* always flows from spiritual *identity*, lived out in humble submission to God. Spiritual authority against the powers of darkness is at absolute zero for those who are proud and non-submissive to the Lord's loving rule. A proud, non-submissive person can try to resist the devil until he's blue in the face, but the enemy won't go.

This story from Luke should drive this critical point home. Here's the story:

After Jesus had finished teaching all this to the people, he entered Capernaum. A centurion there had a slave, who was highly regarded, but who was sick and at the point of death. When the centurion heard about Jesus, he sent some Jewish elders to him, asking him to come and heal his slave. When they came to Jesus, they urged him earnestly, "He is worthy to have you do this for him, because he loves our nation and even built our synagogue." So Jesus went with them. When he was not far from the house, the centurion sent friends to say to him: "Lord, do not trouble yourself, for I am not worthy to have you come under my roof. That is why I did not presume to come to you. Instead, say the word, and my servant must be healed. For I too am a man set under authority, with soldiers under me. I say to this one, 'Go,' and he goes; and to another, 'Come,' and he comes, and to my slave, 'Do this,' and he does it." When Jesus heard this he was amazed at him. He turned and said to the crowd that followed him, "I tell you, not even in Israel have I found such faith." So when those who had been sent returned to the house, they found the slave well.

Luke 7:1-10 (NET)

Why do you think that Jesus was so impressed with the centurion's faith? Write your answer in the blanks following. _____

_____

_____

_____

The first thing that stands out is that the centurion had faith to believe that Jesus didn't have to be physically near the sick one to perform healing. He knew Jesus' word was powerful enough to heal his slave, even if that slave were a thousand miles away. That's some pretty impressive faith!

But there's something more. Notice what the centurion said: "For I too am a man set *under* authority" (emphasis ours). Do you see that? That's really an amazing insight for a man who likely never even met Jesus!

The centurion did not say, "For I too am a man *with* authority." That's probably what we would have said, had we been in that man's sandals. But the centurion didn't say that. Instead, he identified himself with Jesus as being a man *under* authority.

Somehow, perhaps by supernatural revelation, this centurion put his finger exactly on how Jesus operated in the spiritual realm of authority and how we are to operate as well. The principle is clear:

You cannot exercise spiritual authority unless you are <u>under</u> spiritual authority.

That's why Paul prefaced the description of the armor of God (*Ephesians 6:14-17*) with the words, *"Finally, be strong in the Lord, and in the strength of his might." (v. 10)* Trying to put on God's armor without being in humble submission to God simply won't work. Period.

That's why James wrote,

Submit therefore to God. Resist the devil and he will flee from you.

James 4:7 (NIV)

You cannot resist the devil without first submitting to God. Period.

That's why Peter wrote:

You younger men, likewise, be subject to your elders, and all of you, clothe yourselves with humility toward one another, for God is opposed to the proud, but gives grace to the humble.

Humble yourselves, therefore, under the mighty hand of God, that He may exalt you at the proper time, casting all your anxiety upon Him, because He cares for you. Be of sober spirit, be on the alert. Your adversary, the devil, prowls about like a roaring lion, seeking someone to devour. But resist him, firm in your faith...

1 Peter 5:5-9a (NASB)

You absolutely cannot keep your adversary from sinking his nasty teeth into your life unless you humble yourself, cast your anxiety onto God and resist him firm in your faith.

One final note on my country music fiasco: If I had remembered this, I would have done much better:

For our struggle is not against flesh and blood, but against the rulers, against the powers, against the world forces of this darkness, against the spiritual forces of wickedness in the heavenly places.

Ephesians 6:12 (NASB)

People are not the enemy. They may be victims of the enemy and even tools of the enemy, but the real invisible enemy operates behind the scenes. The devil delights when we fight our battles against people, because then we don't have the time, energy or insight to fight the *real* battle against him. In that scenario, the real villain gets off scot-free.

I wonder how many friendships, marriages, families and even churches would be saved from division and destruction if we'd just learn this one principle!

Truth Point

He who dwells in the shelter of the Most High will abide in the shadow of the Almighty. I will say to the LORD, "My refuge and my fortress, my God in whom I trust!

Psalm 91:1, 2 (NASB)

Application

Earlier we had you list any fleshly fighting strategies that you tend to use rather than humbly trusting in God. We'll give you a chance to talk to the Lord about those in a moment in the *Prayer* section. For now, we'd like you to jot down in the space below any areas in which the Spirit of God has shown you that you're still not surrendering to the Lord.

In these devotions we've tried to paint a picture of how immeasurably better it is to submit to God than it is to fight him. It is the path to fellowship and friendship with God, which is what we were created for. It is the way to experience the.deepest love, greatest satisfaction, most unshakeable peace, purest joy and most comforting hope on the planet. It is the beginning of a journey to freedom and the road to the fulfillment of God's eternally brilliant ambitions for your life.

In this devotion we've added another reason to turn your life fully over to God. It is the only place of safety on this fallen planet with an invisible killer on the loose. Kind of a scary thought, we know. But the scarier thought is trying to live life here on earth apart from being in the sheltering shadow of the Almighty.

Is there anything at all that you are withholding from the Lord today? If so, write it below.

_____

_____

_____

_____

_____

_____

_____

_____

Dear heavenly Father, it's kind of embarrassing and sobering to look back at all the times I viewed people as a threat or enemy and defended myself selfishly in order to "win." As I look back, to have risked relationships with people that I love and for whom you died, in order to feed my ego was so wrong. I am sorry for fighting the wrong battles and using the wrong weapons. I confess that I have *(list any fleshly weapons you have utilized)* and sinned against you and against people. Thank you for your wonderful forgiveness and cleansing that is mine in Christ. I also admit that I have not always surrendered every area of my life to your Lordship. I now give to you *(list the areas that you have been withholding from the Lord)* and I thank you that you will take these areas and through your powerful presence protect me and provide for me all I need. I thank you for your peace, in Jesus' name, amen.

- I declare that my strength is in who I am in Christ and not in any fleshly identity!

- I also declare that my strength is found in Christ's mighty power and not in my own fleshly defenses!

- I will surrender my life fully to Christ and dwell and abide in the shelter and shadow of Almighty God!

- I proclaim the truth that as I humbly submit to God and resist the devil, he will flee from me!

Identity Reminder:

I am a minister of reconciliation for God.

2 Cor. 5:17-21

Tested Yet Triumphant

Stop! Who Goes There?

Early in our marriage, my wife Shirley and I (Rich) moved from Philadelphia to the Philippines. We were missionaries sent out to develop ongoing ministries in public high schools in Metro Manila. Life in the city was draining but we were very fortunate to be able to house-sit for other missionaries who were on furlough in the States. Relaxing in the evening in our air conditioned bedroom was a Godsend after all day in the grueling heat, humidity, traffic, air pollution and noise of Manila.

One night I was in bed waiting for my wife to get ready for bed. She was in the bathroom getting cleaned up and I was anticipating her arrival! All of a sudden a thought came into my mind – a lustful thought – and it was not about my wife. Now, I hadn't been looking at pornography or even suggestive scenes on TV. It came totally out of the blue.

Realizing quickly that the enemy was trying to sabotage intimacy with Shirley, I said out loud – though not too loud, since she was in the bathroom nearby! – In the name and authority of the Lord Jesus Christ, I reject this thought! Then I quoted a Scripture, *Philippians 4:8.* I said something like, "For it is written, *"Whatever is true, whatever is honorable, whatever is right, whatever is pure, whatever is lovely… I choose to set my mind on these things!"*

And the thought was gone.

A short while later I was lying in bed still waiting for Shirley to come out of the bathroom. Another thought struck my brain. It was an impression, something like, "I'm not a very good Christian…" Huh? Where did that come from?

Immediately I was reminded that a couple weeks earlier I had developed this prayer journal and I had committed myself to praying through it each day. I realized that it had been at least seven days since I had opened the thing up. That was the context for the thought about being a no-good Christian.

For a moment I started to get down on myself. I was starting to agree with the thought when I realized what was going on. It was another enemy attack on my mind; it just happened to be in a totally different area than the first.

So again, out loud but not too loud, I said, "In the name and authority of the Lord Jesus Christ, get out of here Satan." Then I quoted *Romans 8:1, "There is therefore now no condemnation for those who are in Christ Jesus."* And that thought was gone, too.

How did I know that this thought was from the enemy and not a convicting work of the Holy Spirit? I knew it wasn't God simply because the thought was condemning, and God doesn't condemn his children. The Bible says so.

What was I doing? I was exercising my authority in Christ, resisting the devil by "taking every thought captive in obedience to Christ." It is an essential element in winning spiritual battles and will be our topic for today.

Words, information, data and ideas are swirling around us constantly. It is impossible to protect our minds from every negative, ungodly and potentially damaging message. After all, we live in a real world that is really fallen and fatally infected by sin. Some of it can be tuned out (e.g. by "muting" TV commercials) but some stuff is going to get through. That's unavoidable. Much of what gets through can simply be ignored; it has no power over us. But not everything. Some stuff pushes our buttons and can infiltrate our minds and corrupt our beliefs about God, ourselves and others. In those cases, a more aggressive, active approach must be taken. Scripture warns us that this is going to be necessary.

> *Finally, be strengthened in the Lord and in the strength of his power. Clothe yourselves with the full armor of God so that you may be able to stand against the schemes of the devil. For our struggle is not against flesh and blood, but against the rulers, against the powers, against the world-rulers of this darkness, against the spiritual forces of evil in the heavens. For this reason, take up the full armor of God so that you may be able to stand your ground on the evil day, and having done everything, to stand.*
>
> *Ephesians 6:10-13 (NET)*

> *Therefore, prepare your minds for action; be self-controlled; set your hope fully on the grace to be given you when Jesus Christ is revealed.*
>
> *1 Peter 1:13 (NIV)*

What are the words used in the verses above to indicate that this is an active not a passive war? List them in the spaces below:

_____

_____

_____

_____

_____

_____

Okay. Having set the stage by showing that it is going to take effort and energy (through the Holy Spirit) to stand firm and resist the enemy, let's take a look at a key Scripture that instructs us how to do that.

> *For though we live in the world, we do not wage war as the world does. The weapons we fight with are not the weapons of the world. On the contrary, they have divine power to demolish strongholds. We demolish arguments and every pretension that sets itself up against the knowledge of God, and we take captive every thought to make it obedient to Christ.*
>
> *2 Corinthians 10:3-5 (NIV)*

If there was still any doubt in your mind regarding the location of the spiritual battle, these verses should convince you! We are battling *arguments* (sometimes translated "speculations") and *pretensions* that are raised up against the *knowledge* of God. And we are taking captive *thoughts.* Clearly the battle *is* for our minds.

You might be wondering what a "stronghold" is. Think of a fortress, a protected area in our minds, a well-defended area, a place we retreat to when we feel threatened. Several places in the psalms indicate that *God* wants to be our place of refuge, our stronghold (see **Psalm 18:1, 2** for instance). But in the case of **2 Corinthians 10,** the fortress or "stronghold" is a bad thing. It is raised up against the knowledge of God, that is, it keeps us from knowing him as our defender, robbing us of intimacy with God.

Every one of us develops ways of coping with problems and trying to make life work apart from Christ. We develop deeply ingrained patterns of how we think, how we feel and what we do. These self-protective strategies for living are "strongholds." They can develop slowly over time or quickly as the result of traumatic experiences. There are many, many strongholds operative in humanity. A few would be: *insecurity, self-pity, homosexuality, alcoholism, people-pleasing, workaholism, materialism, controlling behavior fear* and so on.. As you can see, some strongholds are socially acceptable and, at times, viewed as very positive. Others are not.

To the outside observer, it may seem irrational for someone to find "refuge" in an ungodly stronghold. It doesn't make sense. But to the person in bondage, that fortress is familiar and seems safe. It often gives the person the sensation of power, of being in control even though they are not. So you can see, there is a very strong element of deception at work in a stronghold. However, when someone begins to see the destructiveness of the stronghold and sees that he or she is trapped and wants out, then there is hope for freedom.

The good news is that God's weapons can *demolish* these strongholds and free us to experience God and his love on a whole new level.

Special Note: One of the tools God has given his people to tear down strongholds is called the *Steps to Freedom in Christ.* This guide, based on the truth of God's word, is part of the *"40 Days of Freedom"* strategy. Consult your church about when you will have the opportunity to pray through the *Steps to Freedom in Christ.* It could be one of the most liberating things you have ever done!

The Bible says that a spiritual war requires spiritual weapons, not weapons used by the world (apart from Christ.) Listed next are a whole series of weapons. See if you can identify which are worldly weapons and which are spiritual weapons. Circle the ones below that you believe are "spiritual" rather than "worldly" weapons.

violence	prayer
persuasiveness	God's word
worship	shouting
optimism	faith
stubbornness	hope
gifts of the Spirit	logic
human reasoning	fasting
physical strength	truth
argumentation	love
perseverance	grace

Anything that comes out of sheer human determination, human logic, reasoning, physical prowess or power is worthless in spiritual warfare. As *Zechariah 4:6 (NASB)* says, *"Not by might nor by power, but by My Spirit, says the Lord of hosts."* We defeat *arguments, speculations, vain imaginations, pretensions* and *false or negative thoughts* by spiritually empowered weapons.

So what does it mean to "take captive every thought to make it obedient to Christ" and how do you do it?

- First, pray and ask the Lord to help you identify whether the thoughts coming into your mind are "friend" or "foe".

- If those thoughts are friends, they will be aligned with truth; if they are enemies they will be lies designed to distract, defeat or discourage you.

- If the thoughts line up with the truth of God's word, they are friends; welcome them!

- If the thoughts are not true, then reject them and focus on the truth instead. We'll discuss more about how to do that tomorrow.

This is warfare! In order to protect your mind, which is like the strategic center where the generals are located, you have to station "sentries" around your brain. Take an active, aggressive stance when a thought comes in. Take it captive! Say to it, in essence, "Stop! Who goes there?"

You may be shocked at what you've been letting in!

One of the things that we've discovered is that it is a whole lot easier to "take captive" our thoughts, once negative strongholds are torn down. Here's a case in point: If you have a stronghold of bitter unforgiveness toward someone, you will likely be barraged by negative thoughts about that person. You can capture those thoughts and try your best to think positively about that person, but until you forgive them you are fighting a losing battle. It is like there is a factory of anger, bitterness and negativity inside you that is pumping out critical thoughts about them 24/7. But once the stronghold is demolished (the factory is destroyed) random critical thoughts about that individual can be dismissed with a simple, "I'm not going there. I've forgiven them in Jesus' name" and let that thought go.

So our encouragement is to take advantage of the next opportunity to go through the *Steps to Freedom in Christ!* It is a God-given tool to demolish strongholds!

Truth Point

Keep watching and praying, that you may not enter into temptation; the spirit is willing, but the flesh is weak.

Matthew 26:41 (NASB)

Application

One of the ways that we can defeat the negative, lying thoughts from the enemy is by demolishing arguments, speculations and vain imaginations. Very often we violate the Scriptural admonition to ***"judge not lest you be judged"*** (see ***Matthew 7:1***). We *speculate* as to why someone has done something to us. We come up with *vain imaginations* about their motivations and in so doing we *judge* their hearts and often their character. This is very wrong. Below is a prayer to pray, asking God to reveal any judgmental speculations that you may have been engaged in. Sometimes we even do that with God! After that prayer is another prayer, part of which will give you opportunity to confess anything necessary.

Identity Reminder:

I am God's co-worker.

(1 Cor. 3:9)

2 Cor. 6:1

Dear heavenly Father, I know that it is wrong to speculate and come up with vain imaginations about why people do what they do, especially in relation to me. Please reveal to my mind all the ways that I have judged other people's hearts, motivations and character. And if I have done that with you, please show me that as well. I want to be free from this form of attack on my mind. In Jesus' name I pray, amen.

Dear Father in heaven, I acknowledge that I have not been aggressive, vigilant and diligent to protect my mind from the lies of the world, flesh and devil. Part of that sin is that I have judged others. I confess that I have judged *(name the person)* by *(be specific in describing the judgment)*. Thank you for your forgiveness. I choose not to act as judge, jury and executioner of people any longer. And I ask you to continue your work of demolishing the strongholds in my life so that I can effectively take captive every thought and make it obedient to Christ. It's in his name I pray, amen.

- **God's weapons will demolish strongholds!**
- **I will be diligent to protect my mind from negative, damaging input!**
- **I will ask God to empower me to take my thoughts captive to the obedience of Christ!**

Identity Reminder:

I am seated with Christ in the heavenly realm.

Eph. 2:6

Tested Yet Triumphant

The Devil Can't Make You Do It

WARMING UP

Comedian Flip Wilson once made the line *"The devil made me do it!"* a household word. For a period of time, his sassy delivery of the excuse cracked up a whole nation. What was funny in a comedy act, however, is serious business in life, because the truth is that the devil can't *make* you do *anything*. He can and will, however, tempt, pressure, lie, nag, harass, and seek to persuade, manipulate and control us, but he cannot succeed unless we give in and let him.

The temptations from the enemy can be as flagrant as inciting someone to commit murder or as subtle as luring a person to use just slightly unethical means to accomplish a noble end. No matter how "sold out" someone may be for Christ and his kingdom, the devil is able to tailor-make a temptation for that individual.

When I (Rich) got to my junior year in college, I caught fire for Jesus. The months of fleshly living and compromise had turned bitter in my mouth and I had developed a holy hatred of sin. Some Christian buddies and I had started a fellowship among meteorology students at Penn State and we were making Christ's presence strongly known in that field. We shared Christ with almost anything that moved and took a stand for righteousness wherever we could. It was that zeal which the enemy sought to turn for his purposes.

One of our meteorology professors had written a paper. In it he raised a question about whether some of the events described in the Bible could have possibly been optical illusions. He was mainly referring to the parting of the Red Sea and Jesus' walking on the water.

By the way, there *is* at least one case in the Bible where God *did* use an optical illusion to accomplish his purposes. You can read about it in *2 Kings 3:20-25.* The point is, however, that God made no attempt to deceive the *reader* about what happened in that incident. As for the parting of the Red Sea and Jesus' walking on the water, if those were optical illusions, then the Scriptures would be guilty of deception, since those events are portrayed as having actually occurred. This professor's cautious allegations were serious accusations to me.

My zeal for God's glory and the honor of his word was offended, deeply. I wanted to be totally ready to refute the professor's arguments and put him "in his place." My anxiety came from the fact that there was only one copy of that paper around that I was aware of and nobody knew where it was. I figured (and logically so) that before I developed my rebuttal, I needed to read the original work.

The lecture was coming up within the hour and I still hadn't laid my hands on that copy. Then I saw it. I "happened" to be in the office of some graduate assistants when I saw the paper lying on one of their desks. The problem was that he wasn't around to grant me permission to read it. So, concluding that I was only "borrowing" it and would soon return it and that this was, after all, for a "good cause," I took it with me to read. This is called rationalization!

As I was walking out of the office, one of my Christian friends "happened" to come by and I excitedly told him about my find. He got this strange look on his face and asked me where I'd found it. I told him and he proceeded to read me the riot act on why I could not take it. I protested and argued but he was adamant.

To take something that didn't belong to me, even for a short period of time and even for a "good cause" was not right. I could not justify it.

I believe that the Lord sent him there at that time so that I would be delivered from such a subtle temptation. I put it back. When I did, he was relieved, and much to my surprise, so was I.

The epilogue to that incident is that as the professor spoke, the Lord gave us such wisdom in how to refute his statements that by the end of the lecture he was so apologetic and timid that we felt sorry for him. In the end we were able to speak very compassionately and, I believe, pointed him to Christ (which was God's design all along!).

Had I been disobedient and succumbed to the subtle pressure to use unethical means to accomplish God's work, I believe our efforts would have been fruitless. We would either have been refuted ourselves or even more likely, I would have been so scathing in my remarks that the cause of Christ would have been discredited.

The moral of the story? Nobody, no matter how sold out to Jesus, is immune from temptation.

Identity Reminder:

I am God's workmanship.

Eph 2:10

Before we give our definition of temptation, write yours in the spaces below. By the way, don't give into the temptation to look at our definition before writing yours!

_____

_____

_____

_____

Here are some synonyms of "temptation": *appeal, enticement, lure, persuasion, pull, attraction, inducement, seduction.*

Temptation is the enticement to do that which is contrary to the character or will of God.

It can be very overt and obvious or very covert and subtle (as in the example above). It can be a blatant appeal to do that which is clearly wrong, or it can be an allure to do something only slightly unethical, seeking to make "the ends" justify the "the means." In the former case it is a bold, brash attempt to entice us to sin openly. In the latter it is only the first move in a long chess game designed to "check mate" us into some disastrous and tragic compromise with evil. In some cases, temptation may manifest as simply a matter of taking action before God's appointed timing. Any time we are anxious, hurried, worried, restless or impatient, we are prime targets for temptation.

The temptation of the Lord Jesus in the wilderness by the devil provides great instruction for us in how to fight and win our battles against temptation. Listed below are the three temptations thrown at him after fasting for 40 days and nights. Notice the means by which Jesus refutes each temptation:

The Devil's Temptation	Jesus' Scriptural Response
If you are the Son of God, command that these stones become bread.	It is written, "Man shall not live on bread alone, but on every word that proceeds out of the mouth of God."
If you are the Son of God throw yourself down; for it is written, "He will give his angels charge concerning you"; and "On their hands they will bear you up, lest you strike your foot against a stone."	On the other hand, it is written, "You shall not put the Lord your God to the test."
All these things [the kingdoms of the world] will I give you, if you fall down and worship me.	Begone, Satan, for it is written, "You shall worship the Lord your God and serve him only."

Let's take a look briefly at the first temptation, and we encourage you to study the other two on your own. Why would it have been wrong for Jesus to turn that rock into a loaf of sourdough? After all, he was hungry and he had the power to do it, right? Sure he did. It would not have been a temptation unless Jesus had the capacity to do it. That's why this particular temptation has probably never been a problem for you and me! But the general principle lying behind the temptation *has* been a temptation … we guarantee it!

You see, the devil was basically telling Jesus to let his body do the talking, to be the dictator of what he should do. You're hungry, so eat. Do you see how this is a battle for all of us? We are hungry and so we eat and eat and overeat. We see food that looks good so we eat it even if it's not good for us and even if we're not hungry. (Or in some eating disorder cases, we see food we should eat, but we are tempted to *not* eat it and we give in to that temptation.)

We see clothes and like the way they look and so we buy them even though we are already well-clothed. We see someone sexually attractive to us (besides our spouse) and our body says to have intercourse and so we do or at least fantasize about it.

Jesus' response to the devil's temptation is hugely instructive for us:

- First, he did not engage in discussion or debate with the devil, trying to logically refute his assertions.

- Second, Jesus did not succumb to the temptation to prove himself to the devil. Satan had said, "If you are the Son of God…" Jesus knew who he was and who mattered (the Father), so he did not care if the devil believed it or not.

- Third, Jesus did not let his body be his guide. The Word of God the Father was his guide and the Father's 40 day red light to eating had not changed yet. Jesus would eat when the Father said to eat, not on the devil's timetable.

- Jesus knew that the truth of God's word was his weapon, and so he pulled out the sword of the Spirit (see *Ephesians 6:17*), the Word of God and struck a blow that wiped out the devil's temptation. He quoted from the book of Deuteronomy.

If there's nothing you glean from this lesson but the following statements, then that would be okay. Please file these deeply in your heart:

Jesus came to earth as a man and lived as a man in total submission to the Father and his will, empowered by the Holy Spirit. He did nothing on his own initiative, but only what he saw the Father doing (see *John 5:19, 20*) We are to live the same way – in total submission to the Father, empowered by the Holy

Spirit. Every temptation that overtakes us is an attempt to get us to disavow this calling – to make choices apart from the Father's will and apart from the Holy Spirit's power.

Take a moment and think about the areas where you are being currently or consistently tempted. In the table below, write the temptation and then write the biblical guidance that temptation violates. An example is given.

Temptation	Biblical Guidance
Indulge the desires of the eyes and body by checking out pornography on the Internet; nobody will know and it won't hurt you	*"Beloved, I urge you as aliens and strangers to abstain from fleshly lusts which wage war against the soul."* *1 Peter 2:11 (NASB)*

Of course, there are numerous Scriptures that could be used in the example above. Ask the Lord to direct you to the ones that deal the most definitive death blow to the way temptation strikes you.

Before concluding with some important summary principles for battling temptation, we need to let you know that not all temptation is from the devil directly. He is the "god of this world" (**2 Corinthians 4:4**), meaning he is the ruler of the corrupt values that pervade every culture. Therefore, he has already set in place many things around us (often through the media) to appeal to our flesh. James lets us know, however, that our flesh is a powerful tempting force within us, whether the devil is involved or not:

Let no one say when he is tempted, "I am being tempted by God"; for God cannot be tempted by evil, and he himself does not tempt anyone. But

each one is tempted when he is carried away and enticed by his own lust *[lust is any strong, out-of-control desire, not just sexual].* ***Then when lust has conceived, it gives birth to sin; and when sin is accomplished, it brings forth death. Do not be deceived, my beloved brethren.***

James 1:13-16 (NASB)

[bracketed statements ours]

Principles for Stopping Sin in Midair
- **Be strong in the Lord and in the strength of his might!** (**Eph. 6:10**). Meditate and learn who you are in Christ and his mighty resurrection power at work in you. You are not a skin-wrapped bag of salivary glands and sex drives! You are a child of God, a saint in whom the Holy Spirit dwells!

- **Recognize that you are dead to sin and alive to God in Christ Jesus!** (*Rom. 6:11*). Sin's power to control you and enslave you was broken at the Cross. When you came to know Christ, sin ceased to be your master. No matter how many times you may have failed in the past, you do have a choice. By the grace of God and the power of the Holy Spirit in you, you can say "No!" to sin and "Yes!" to righteousness (see *Titus 2:11-14 NIV; Gal. 5:16-18*). Never believe the lie that your situation is hopeless!

- **Fix your eyes on Jesus!** (*Heb. 12:2; Col 3:1-3*). The best defense against sin is a good offense. As you seek Jesus and fall more deeply in love with him, the lure of sin begins to lessen. Why would you forfeit fellowship with One so caring, so good, so faithful, so strong?

- **Present your body and its parts to God for righteousness** (*Rom. 6:12, 13*). Have you already given parts of your body over to sin? Then confess those sins and present your body and its parts back to God as weapons of war against sin! He will cleanse your body and receive its parts for his army of righteousness! (See the *Application* and *Prayer* sections for further guidance in how to do this.)

As you already know, temptation is an unfortunate part of life on planet earth. But temptation always has a way out. Paul wrote,

"Therefore let him who thinks he stands take heed lest he fall. No temptation has overtaken you but such as is common to man; and God is faithful, who will not allow you to be tempted beyond what you are able, but with the temptation will provide the way of escape also, that you may be able to endure it."

1 Corinthians 10:12, 13 (NASB)

That "way of escape" is always to run to Jesus for strength,

"for since he himself was tempted in that which he has suffered, he is able to come to the aid of those who are tempted."

Hebrews 2:18 (NASB)

At the moment temptation hits, run to Jesus for escape! The longer you wait, the tougher it will be to resist.

Truth Point

Since then we have a great high priest who has passed through the heavens, Jesus the Son of God, let us hold fast our confession. For we do not have a high priest who cannot sympathize with our weaknesses, but one who has been tempted in all things as we are, yet without sin. Let us therefore draw near with confidence to the throne of grace, that we may receive mercy and find grace to help in time of need.

Hebrews 4:14-16 (NASB)

Application

Ask the Lord to show you the ways you have allowed the parts of your body to be used by sin for sin. It is simply impossible to sin without using your body in some way, even if it is just your brain. Write those parts of your body below that need to be re-surrendered to the Lord. As you do so, confess any ways of using the parts of your body as instruments of unrighteousness that the Lord brings to mind. You'll be praying a prayer of surrender in a moment.

_____

_____

Identity Reminder:

I may approach God with freedom and confidence.

Eph 3:12

Dear heavenly Father, many times I have given in to temptations because I didn't think I really had a choice, the pressure and persuasion were so strong. Now I realize that was a lie. I thank you that I really am dead to sin and alive to God in Christ! Temptation and sin were defeated at the Cross! I choose to enter into the full power of the crucifixion of my old sin-loving self and my resurrection to newness of life in Jesus! Lead me, Lord, into such a deep love relationship with you and a powerful knowledge of your word that when temptation comes I would want to and be able to flee from it immediately. I recognize that I have allowed my body to be used by and for sin and I confess using _(name the parts of your body used for sin)_ as instruments of unrighteousness. I now surrender those parts of my body, _(name the same parts of your body)_ to you as weapons of righteous warfare and I give all my body to you for your use and glory. In the name of my forgiving, cleansing and empowering Lord Jesus, amen.

- **I declare that I will flee youthful lusts and pursue righteousness, faith, love and peace with those who call on the Lord from a pure heart!**

- **I choose to walk by the Spirit and not obey the desires of the flesh!**

- **I surrender my will to the Lord's and choose, by the power of the Spirit, to obey his word!**

- **I present every part of my body to God as an instrument of righteousness, knowing that I belong to God and my body is his temple!**

Tested Yet Triumphant

The Prosecution Loses

WARMING UP

My (Rich's) former pastor from Georgia served as a missionary to Mexico early in his ministry career. He loved the people and acclimated well to the culture. There was one problem, however, which caused him and the other Americans a lot of headaches.

Some of the police officers in Mexico City were not always law abiding citizens themselves. Traffic cops in particular liked to pull over drivers, especially rich Americans, on fraudulent charges in order to extort cerveza (beer) money from them.

One day my pastor friend was riding with another American in a powder-blue minivan. They might as well have hung an American flag from the van's antenna! While traveling down a street in Mexico City, they came to an intersection where the traffic light was stuck on red. A police officer on the other side of the intersection waved them on through, so they crossed.

Then as soon as they crossed to the other side the policeman pulled them over for running a red light!

They couldn't believe it. It was another classic case of a cerveza-thirsty cop taking advantage of some "rich" gringos.

Understandably, my friend was sick and tired of this kind of treatment, and he mentioned it to a Mexican acquaintance who happened to be a fellow believer in Christ. The man was in charge of all media in Mexico and was feared as being the director of espionage for that nation. The man chuckled at my pastor friend's dilemma and gave him his business card.

"The next time a police officer pulls you over for no reason, pull out this card and show it to him. Tell him I told you to. Then watch what happens."

My friend could hardly wait for the next time, and he didn't have to wait long. Soon he was pulled over for another bogus reason. When the police officer came to the driver-side window, my friend flashed the business card and told the officer that his friend had given him the card and had told him to show it. The policeman's face turned pale and he quickly, nervously waved the American vehicle back out into traffic. Problem solved!

There is a vivid spiritual application to this story. The first part illustrates how the devil operates. The conclusion portrays how we defeat him.

The first Mexican policeman was demonstrating what we in spiritual battle call "the double whammy." When he beckoned the unsuspecting American van driver to go through the red light, it was temptation – yesterday's topic. The officer was luring them into a trap, assuring them that it was "okay" to break the law, so to speak.

Then, once they had taken the bait and crossed the intersection against the red light, the trap was sprung and the "friendly" welcoming officer became an ugly accuser. That "face" of Satan – as the accuser of the brethren (**Revelation 12:10**) – is our focus for today's devotional.

WALKING ON

How many times has this scenario been played out in your life? First you are tempted and have thoughts like:

- Oh come on, it's not a big deal. Nobody will know.

- Compared to a lot of stuff I could be doing, this is nothing.

- Once won't matter. I can always confess it later anyway.

- Everybody's doing it.

- You're missing out. You know it. You've always wondered what it would be like. Well, here's your chance.

- This Christian life isn't all it's cracked up to be. It's time I had a little fun.

And so on. You get the picture. Too often you (and we!) take the bait, give into the temptation and sin. Then what happens? The beckoning cop becomes the prosecuting attorney! It sounds like:

- Look what you've done!

- Oh my G_d, I've done it now. I'm in trouble. People are going to find out…

- I can't believe what a hypocrite I am.

- I've committed the unpardonable sin.

- God has turned his back on me. I'm such a sinner.

- That's it. I've committed that sin one time too often…

- You're hopeless!

Can you see the devil's strategy? Before we sin he tries to *minimize* sin's consequences. That's temptation. That's what he succeeded in doing with Eve in the Garden of Eden. "You surely shall not die," the devil lied, persuading Eve that God was forbidding something that was actually quite good (*Genesis 3:4*).

Then after we sin, he *magnifies* the consequences of sin so that we become overwhelmed with guilt and shame. That's accusation.

Maybe you can relate. If you don't know how to deal with the devil's accusations, you can be hounded, haunted and harassed by guilt and shame for a long time. Many of God's people have suffered torment this way for years!

The writer of *Psalm 44:15, 16 (NIV)* captured this awful misery:

> *My disgrace is before me all day long, and my face is covered with shame at the taunts of those who reproach and revile me, because of the enemy, who is bent on revenge.*
>
> *Psalm 44:15, 16 (NIV)*

Accusation is the attempt of the devil and his demons to convince us that the good, encouraging truths God says about us in Christ are not true.

God says we're forgiven. The devil wants us to drown in guilt and shame.

God says we're saints. The devil wants us to see ourselves as dirty, no-good, lousy sinners.

God says we are accepted in Christ. The devil wants us to believe we are only lovable when we're "good", if at all.

One of the devil's primary strategies is to portray God as an angry, finger-pointing cop in the sky. We need to see him as he truly is or the devil, our overly sensitive conscience, or both will make our lives miserable.

Below we have placed a chart that provides a helpful contrast between the condemnation of the devil and the conviction of the Holy Spirit. The Bible says that *"Therefore, there is now no condemnation for those who are in Christ Jesus" (Romans 8:1)*. God in no way condemns his children. But the devil tries to accuse and condemn us and in the process he attempts to make us believe God is the one doing the condemning. Read the chart over thoroughly and then write down in the blanks provided afterwards the ways you tend to come under the enemy's accusing attacks.

Conviction of the Holy Spirit	**Condemnation of the devil**
Tone of voice. Gentle, loving voice of the Father imploring, beseeching and urging our return to him.	**Tone of voice**. Accusing, nagging, mocking voice, generating fear, causing confusion, projecting a sense of rejection, inciting doubt about what God has said.
Specific. The Spirit says, "Deal with this matter and you will be free." He commands you to take specific action, to make a choice of the will. Conviction is specific to the sin. The Spirit defends you against an oversensitive conscience.	**Vague and general**. Satan brings a blanketing, choking sense of general guilt, as though everything is wrong and there is no one action you can really take to overcome. Often a sense of complete hopelessness and weakness prevails.
Encouragement is God's message. He encourages you to rely on God's power, not on your own strength or righteousness.	**Discouragement**. Satan centers his attack on you as a person. Cuts your self-image to ribbons. Tells you that you are weak, unloved, worthless, rejected, etc.
Deal with sin and then forget the past. That's the Spirit speaking. The Holy Spirit reminds you that your sin is forgiven, forgotten, cleansed, removed and put away, never to be held against you. (*Jn. 1:29; Ps. 103:12; 1 Jn. 1:7; Ps. 51:7; Mic. 7:19; Heb. 10:17*)	**You can never be free from the past.** That's Satan speaking. He replays the videotapes of past memories of sin, guilt and shame. He draws up accounts of your past sins, failures and offenses that are under the blood and makes you feel like they will haunt you forever.
Attraction to God. There is a wooing back to God. He generates in you an expectancy of kindness, love, forgiveness, a new beginning with God's help. Holy Spirit speaks of your permanent relationship as a child of the Father. (*John 20:17*)	**Rejection as though by the holiness of God.** Satan disguises himself as an agent of holiness. He produces the feeling that God the Father has rejected you as unworthy and unholy. Satan speaks of God as your judge …and that you are a miserable sinner (rather than the saint that you are!)

Brings **positive scriptures** to your remembrance (*Jn. 14:25*). He speaks of the unchanging nature of God, of his steadfast love toward us. He confirms that God stays faithful to his covenant (*1 Jn. 1:9*) even when we prove faithless for a time (*2 Tim. 2:13; 1 Jn. 3:20*). The Spirit reassures us that there is no law that is effective against us who rely on Christ's work. (*Col. 2:14*)	Brings **negative scriptures** to your mind. Shakespeare said, "The devil knows how to quote Scripture to his purpose!" Satan threatens judgment saying, "Grace is denied because you didn't fulfill the conditions!" Satan uses the Law against you, to press you to justify yourself and rely on your own righteousness (*Rom. 10:3,4; Gal. 2:16*). You tend to fixate on Scriptures that speak of judgment.
Draws you into fellowship. The Spirit sends others to minister to you in love. Thus you learn to accept others' words of encouragement and to appreciate one another and their ministry to you.	**Isolates you.** Satan sows suggestions that cause you to withdraw from other Christians and think they reject you. In your isolation, you then feel lonely, judged, hurt, unworthy, misunderstood, angry and rejected by others. Can make you susceptible to wrong doctrine.
Facts of the Word of God. The Holy Spirit states facts, truths about you and God. Feelings must bow and follow faith in these facts! The Holy Spirit gives you correct doctrine; the truth that sets you free.	**Feelings**. The devil tells you that how you feel is the way things really are (i.e. feelings are truth). Feelings of guilt, despair, hopelessness, feelings of doubt of God's love for you, feelings of frustration at God's unfairness, self-pity, feelings of fear.
Disciplines us in love.	Seeks to **destroy** us and our faith.
Reassures you of God's forgiveness and the fact that it is Christ who saved you and that you are secure in him.	**Accuses** you of having committed the unpardonable sin; seeks to trap you into doubting how completely sincere you are/were in trusting Christ.

Go ahead and jot down in these blanks the ways you struggle most with the enemy's accusing, condemning thoughts. Feel free to write down any others that the Lord is bringing to your mind as well. You'll be referring back to these items shortly.

_____

_____

_____

_____

_____

_____

When my (Rich's) friend became sick and tired of being harassed by corrupt traffic cops in Mexico City, he took action. He could have just accepted things as they were but he didn't. He also didn't try and get out of this predicament by himself or by his own logic, persuasiveness or power. That probably would have bought him even more trouble. What he did was appeal to a higher authority, a man who held sway over the police officers. Showing his own business card would have accomplished nothing. Flashing the business card of his Christian friend in high places was all that was needed.

One day after I spoke on this subject, someone handed me a hand-made "business card." It was titled the "I mean business card" and basically said "I belong to the Lord Jesus Christ and he says I am a forgiven, holy, totally cleansed, accepted child of God and saint." Period. End of discussion.

That's God's antidote to the cruel barrage of condemning thoughts the enemy serves up to our minds.

Know who you are in Christ. Stand firm on that truth. With every blow the powers of darkness deliver, counter it with the knockout punch of God's Word. Don't ever give up. Don't ever give in.

"Therefore, put on the full armor of God, so that when the day of evil comes, you may be able to stand your ground, and after you have done everything, to stand"

Ephesians 6:13 (NIV)

And stand you will.

Identity Reminder:

I am God's child.

Jn. 1:12

WRAPPING UP

Truth Point

What, then, shall we say in response to this? If God is for us, who can be against us? He who did not spare his own Son, but gave him up for us all – how will he not also, along with him, graciously give us all things? Who will bring any charges against those whom God has chosen? It is God who justifies. Who is he that condemns?

Romans 8:31-39 (NIV)

Application

Look back now at the items you wrote down after the chart in this day's devotional. Formulate short authoritative statements based on what you wrote, and put them in the format below of "I renounce…" (to renounce means to reject, disown and disavow allegiance to…) and "I announce…" The "announce" part is is a proclamation of truth and any time you can use Scripture as part of your annunciation, it will be even more effective. We've given you an example to get you started. This can be a powerful time of driving a stake of truth into the ground of your life!

I renounce the lie that I must perform well and keep from sinning in order for God to truly love and accept me.	I announce the truth that it is because of God that I am in Christ who has become my righteousness, holiness and redemption. (*1 Corinthians 1:30*)

Dear heavenly Father, train my hands for war. Teach me how to do battle against the accusations of the evil one – to believe none of them and to stand firm in the truth. Silence the voice of the accuser and cause the voice of the Spirit of truth and liberty to ring loud and clear in my heart and mind. Thank you, Father, that in Christ all guilt, condemnation, accusation and shame are gone. I am your child, Father, welcomed into your family as a joint heir with Christ. I am your bride, Jesus, the delight of your heart, clothed in bright white garments of purity. Thank you, Lord, for such freedom! I claim right now that indeed *"there is therefore now no condemnation for those who are in Christ Jesus" (Romans 8:1)*. It's in Jesus, my Defender's name I pray, amen.

- **In Christ I am accepted by God!**
- **In Christ I am a holy child of God!**
- **In Christ I am completely forgiven of all sin – past, present and future!**
- **I declare God's word to be the truth, regardless of what my thoughts, feelings, circumstances, the enemy or even other people might say!**

Identity Reminder:

I am Christ's friend.

Jn. 15:15

Tested Yet Triumphant

Truth Sets Us Free!

The Lord is so powerful, so strong to set captives free, even when they are caught in the trap of cult deception. The following story is a great example of how truth sets us free:

I want to share with you what I've learned about how big God is. One freedom appointment [taking someone through the *Steps to Freedom in Christ*] I had the privilege to be a part of was with a woman who had received her first introduction to God through the Jehovah's Witnesses. At the time she was caught in many types of addictions and in so much bondage that she cried out to the God she had heard of as a kid, saying, "God, if you are real, send someone to tell me about you".

The next day some Jehovah's Witnesses knocked on her door. When she told us this during our freedom appointment, the first thing I thought was, "What angel of darkness was involved here? What kind of battle are we in for?"

By the time we met, God had already put a question in her heart about the Witnesses' "bible". She realized that it did not always match up with the Bible she was familiar with, and she was eager to learn more. After reading and sharing with her who Jesus really is, she readily prayed the prayer on the first page of the "*Steps*" booklet to accept Jesus as her Lord and Savior.

We then had to explain why "Jehovah's Witnesses" was listed in *Step One* as a counterfeit belief. God had already prepared us with knowledge of what that cult believes through a tract that some of them had left with me the summer before. In the tract it told of Jesus being the Son of God, but it never mentioned Him as being God nor of one's need to accept Him as Lord and Savior. It only told of how to try and live for Jehovah God.

It was hard for this woman to renounce the Jehovah's Witnesses as a counterfeit because the two other women she had met with for the past two years had shown her so much love and acceptance. But finally she renounced her involvement with the Jehovah's Witnesses. God then used the *Steps to Freedom* in a powerful way to reveal the twisted gospel that she had come to believe. Each time she had a question about the differences between our beliefs and hers, either God gave an answer through us with Scripture or through the Bible verses in the "*Steps*".

Because of time constraints, we had to meet with her about four times over a six-week period. We found this to be God's timing, too, because she needed to be mentored by us over a period of time. She would take in each "*Step*" and seek to apply it to her life and then come back with more questions. We learned that we did not need to worry about or fear her questions. We would pray and trust that

God had it all under control and that He would supply the answers. And He did… every time!

Jesus broke bondages in her life and helped her leave a lot of baggage at the cross as she walked through the *Steps to Freedom in Christ.* She even said she felt physically lighter when she was done. Praise God!

The toughest part for us was when she told us she had shown her Witness friends *Step One.* They were hurt and confused because their organization was on the counterfeit list. At that moment God filled our hearts with so much love for them, because they were like sheep following the wrong shepherd. God gave us words that helped us explain to her why the Jehovah's Witnesses are considered a cult, without condemning the two women she loved.

When you think about the literally billions of people on this planet who are trapped in religious systems of Hinduism, Buddhism, Islam, Mormonism, the Watchtower Bible & Tract Society (Jehovah's Witnesses) and countless other false religions and cults, it is staggering. What a joy to read of one precious woman rescued and brought safely out of the domain of darkness into Christ's kingdom of light!

In the past two days we have talked about the devil's strategies of *temptation* and *accusation,* the "double whammy" as we called it. Today we want to expose the devil's foundational tactic, which is *deception.* Deception is at the heart of every non-Christian religious system and traps more people than any other strategy. This tactic of deception flows straight from Satan's evil character, as Jesus revealed while rebuking the hardened Jewish leaders:

You belong to your father, the devil, and you want to carry out your father's desire. He was a murderer from the beginning, not holding to the truth, for there is no truth in him. When he lies, he speaks his native language, for he is a liar and the father of lies.

John 8:44 (NIV)

There is no place on planet earth where the devil's lies have not penetrated, as Revelation makes clear:

And the great dragon was thrown down, the serpent of old who is called the devil and Satan, who deceives the whole world; he was thrown down to the earth, and his angels were thrown down with him.

Revelation 12:9 (NASB)

It would be impossible in this lesson to survey the whole gamut of the devil's devices of deception. Let's take a quick look, however, at some of his more common ploys of lying and deceiving*. To be forewarned is to be forearmed!

Deception Strategy*	Deception Strategy Described*
Temptation	Disguising something bad to make it look good.
Accusation	Maligning God's highly-valued, forgiven saints to make them think they are worthless, guilty sinners.
Discouragement	Persuading people that things are going badly and will not or cannot change.
Depression	Robbing individuals of hope by projecting a negative, distorted image of God or self.
Fear	Making people think they are vulnerable and unprotected, at risk of imminent harm.
Anxiety	Inciting worry and obsessive thinking by stealing faith in God's proactive presence.
Tormenting thoughts	Convincing believers that nagging, haunting thoughts stem from the believer's own mind or even from God.
Legalism	Luring people into a religious system that seeks to attain or maintain God's love and acceptance based on spiritual performance rather than by grace.
Addictions	Trapping people in behavior that continually draws them back and out of which there seems no escape.
Cults	Adding to, subtracting from or changing the eternal truth of Scripture – especially about God, Jesus and salvation – so that a new, false religion of works is formed.

* This table should not be taken to mean that the only cause of the areas described (such as fear, depression, etc.) is the work of the powers of darkness. There are usually physiological, developmental, social, temperamental, etc. factors involved as well. But a complete biblical worldview needs to incorporate the reality of the evil supernatural in order to fully understand the nature of human difficulties.

What is the key to dismantling any strategy of deception from the enemy? *To expose the lies that fuel the strategy and choose the truth instead!* Truth, especially the truth of the word of God, provides the knockout blow, but there are other pieces of our armor as well. In fact, the entire array of our defensive and offensive weaponry is called the *armor of God*. Let's take a quick look at **Ephesians 6** and make sure we understand what that armor is.

The Armor of God

The imagery of the armor of God is taken from the equipment used by Roman soldiers, the most efficient fighting machines of their day. Here's the armor of God as described by Paul in Ephesians:

Therefore put on the full armor of God, so that when the day of evil comes, you may be able to stand your ground, and after you have done everything, to stand. Stand firm then, with the belt of truth buckled around your waist, with the breastplate of righteousness in place, and with your feet fitted with the readiness that comes from the gospel of peace. In addition to all this, take up the shield of faith, with which you can extinguish all the flaming arrows of the evil one. Take up the helmet of salvation and the sword of the Spirit, which is the word of God.

Ephesians 6:13-17 (NIV)

Another table will give us a thumbnail sketch of what this armor is, how to put it on and which enemy attack it shields us from.

Piece of Armor	How to Put It On	What It Defends Us Against
The belt of truth	Read, study and meditate on the truths of Scripture – especially knowing God and knowing who you are in Christ.	The lies and deceptions of the enemy, especially as it applies to who God is and who we are in Christ.
The breastplate of righteousness	Know that you are already forgiven (*Eph. 1:7; Col. 1:13,14; Col 2:13,14*) in Christ and that you are already the righteousness of God in Christ (*2 Cor. 5:21*). Make the decision today to walk with God and turn from sin. (*Rom. 13:12-14*)	The temptations of the evil one Guilt and shame.
The sandals of the gospel of peace	Know that you are right now at peace with God (*Rom. 5:1*); experience God's peace that guards your heart and mind as you pray with thanksgiving (*Phil. 4:6, 7*). Be a peacemaker, taking the gospel of peace to a needy world! (*Matt. 5:9; Rom. 10:14,15*)	Anxiety and Fear.

The shield of faith	Stand firm on the truth of God's word in the face of the enemy's attacks.	Discouragement. Demoralization. Intimidation tactics such as persecution, betrayal, unjust criticism, gossip, slander, crime, illness, rejection, financial hardships, natural disasters.
The helmet of salvation	Protect your mind with the truth of God's proactive presence and protection as revealed in the Scriptures.	Fear of God's judgment. Fear of losing your mind. Depression. Harassing thoughts.
The sword of the Spirit (which is the word of God)	Speak the word of God boldly and authoritatively in response to the lies, temptations and accusations of the enemy (see how Jesus warded off the devil's attacks in *Matthew 4*).	This is our main offensive weapon against the enemy. After defending ourselves through knowing the truth (putting on the belt), then scatter the enemy by declaring the truth!

The Bible makes it clear that we are to put on the *full* armor of God if we want to be able to stand firm against the schemes (mental strategies and attacks) of the evil one. Every piece must be in place to ensure victory. In the blanks below, express honestly to God which piece(s) of the armor you especially need his help in putting on.

_____

_____

_____

_____

_____

Identity Reminder:

I have been justified.

Rom 5:1

It is encouraging to us to know that our victory over the deceptive strategies of the enemy is *not* dependent upon our intelligence, giftedness, personality or physical strength. Our victory is dependent upon standing firm in who we are in Christ, who Christ is in us and the truth of the word of God.

No matter how fierce or long the battle, *perseverance* in Christ will always win out in the end!

We also want to encourage you to find others to stand with you in prayer and encouragement and truth-speaking when you are under attack. The passage we read earlier from ***Ephesians 6*** was written to a body of believers to stand firm *together*. Remember, we are not snipers, we are an army! We are not spiritual Lone Rangers, we are a family, the Church, the body of Christ! In fact, Paul appeals to the believers in Ephesus to pray for him in his hour of need (see ***Ephesians 6:18-20***). If the apostle Paul needed prayer and asked for it, there is certainly no shame in our doing the same! In fact, it would be foolish for us to think we could make it on our own.

Truth Point

But you, brothers, are not in darkness so that this day should surprise you like a thief. You are all sons of the light and sons of the day. We do not belong to the night or to the darkness. So then, let us not be like others, who are asleep, but let us be alert and self-controlled. For those who sleep, sleep at night, and those who get drunk, get drunk at night. But since we belong to the day, let us be self-controlled, putting on faith and love as a breastplate, and the hope of salvation as a helmet. For God did not appoint us to suffer wrath but to receive salvation through our Lord Jesus Christ.

1 Thess. 5:4-9 (NIV)

Application

Looking back over the table of ways in which the enemy attacks followers of Christ, prayerfully think through your family and friends. Who is going through a tough time right now? What are they struggling with? Use the blanks below to list their names, what they are battling and what would be the appropriate piece(s) of armor they need now so that they can stand firm against the enemy's schemes.

_____

_____

_____

_____

_____

_____

_____

_____

_____

PRAYER

Dear heavenly Father, I thank you that you did not leave me here on earth to be defenseless. I reject any lie that makes me feel like I am. I claim instead the truth of God's word that says that when I put on the full armor of God I will be able to stand and resist all the flaming missiles of the evil one! Lord, I need help especially in putting on *(list the piece(s) of armor you need most right now)*. Turn this area of spiritual weakness into strength in you! In addition, I come before you to intercede for my family and friends. *(List the names of people written previously and which piece(s) of armor they especially need right now.)* Father, thank you that you have heard my prayers for both myself and other loved ones. You are a gracious God and I trust you to bring about the full power of Christ's victory over sin, death and Satan in these lives, including my own. In Jesus' name I pray, amen.

DECLARATIONS

- **I will put on the full armor of God!**
- **I declare that God's full armor will protect me from all the devil's schemes!**
- **I confess my need for other believers to stand with me!**
- **I will eagerly run to stand with them and pray for them in their hour of need as well!**

> **NOTE: If you are participating in the full** *40 Days of Freedom* **campaign at your church, by now you should have heard about the opportunity to go through the** *Steps to Freedom in Christ.* **We urge you to take that opportunity, as it will help you apply all the truths you have been learning during these last five weeks. You may find it to be one of the most refreshing experiences of God, his cleansing grace and his liberating truth you've ever had!**
>
> **If you are going through this** *Journey to Freedom* **on your own, we encourage you to pick up a copy of the** *Steps to Freedom in Christ,* **either through your local Christian bookstore or through Freedom in Christ Ministries. This is a very good time in the** *Journey to Freedom* **to go through that booklet. It is available online at www.ficm.org or by calling toll free 1-866-462-4747.**

Finishing Free

Finishing Free

Running to Win!

My (Christi's) husband's father, Bill is one of the most determined individuals that I have ever known. Shortly after he suffered the loss of his wife to Alzheimer's disease, he took up jogging. He runs at least 8-10 miles everyday without fail.

Bill is as tough as nails; nothing stops him. When he goes out for a morning jog he is likely to go out in the woods, or should I say up in the mountains, and take off running on a rocky dirt path, *uphill.* Michael and I went with him once on a path like this and we literally could not believe the things we saw that day. It is nothing for him to hit his foot so hard that he loses a toenail, but does this stop him? *Not hardly!* He has fallen and gouged his face and shoulder etc, but he just gets up and acts like nothing ever happened and keeps going. To beat it all, he reprimands us if we show any concern for him when he gets hurt.

He is like an Energizer bunny. Rain, snow or blistering heat, nothing is going to keep him from his daily 8-10 mile jog. Did I fail to mention the fact that he is *72 years old?!* His strength and vitality are amazing!

Last summer we took him on a 17 mile trail, and we followed him on our bikes. Before we could reach the end of the trail I thought my tail was going to have a permanent bike seat imprint on it, but Bill hardly even stopped to take a drink. Get this — it was actually difficult for us to keep up with him.

Bill is full of endurance and fresh aspirations. He is not content with his current level of stamina and resilience, but hopes to be able to run 26 miles before he is ready to retire from the sport. To be quite honest, I cannot see him hanging it up. *Only time will tell.*

Well, here we are nearing the finish line in our 40 day *Journey to Freedom*, with only five days left. How are *your* stamina and resilience holding up?

We pray that you are *filled with hope* and eager to continue on in freedom long after our 40-day journey is completed. We hope your ambitions and desires are set on:

- ☐ Continuing to gain a clear picture of who the God of freedom really is.

- ☐ Continuing to gain a renewed mind regarding your true identity in Christ.

- ☐ Continuing to gain victory over the past, present and future through forgiveness.

- ☐ Continuing to gain a contrite heart through surrender to God's Lordship.

- ☐ Continuing to gain victory over our daily battles through the power and truth of Christ.

If you have been journeying with us for the past five weeks, maybe you will agree that this has been a rather intense and challenging five weeks. We trust, along the way, that the Lord has afforded you plenty of opportunities to live out the truths that you have been learning. Check *(above)* the areas in which you have noticed some change.

Because we are all so different in our approach to new challenges, there are a variety of emotions that you could be feeling right now. Your feelings could range anywhere from excitement about the freedom you have gained to overwhelming guilt and shame because you are still struggling with some key issues in your life. Or maybe, these last five weeks have been so chalked full of new material to you, that maybe your head is still spinning and you are not quite sure which way is up. If you need time to process all this material, that is perfectly okay. Take as much time as you need.

Whatever emotional state you find yourself in today, we want you to know this: your Father God does not want you feeling discouraged, *for any reason!*

So don't get tired of doing what is good. Don't get discouraged and give up, for we will reap a harvest of blessing at the appropriate time.

Galatians 6:9 (NLT)

Let's check in with our emotions to make sure that the enemy is not trying to get his foot in the door through discouraging thoughts or feelings. Circle any of these feelings that you might be experiencing regarding your journey to freedom at this point:

Fearful	Alone	Anxious
Overwhelmed	Defeated	Disappointed with self
Eager to impress God	Like a failure	Frustrated
Immobilized	Inadequate	Pressured or guilty
Rejected	Superior to others	Weary or aloof

Satan would love for you to feel *any or all* of these emotions right now. But we have confidence that God can keep you from falling for Satan's lies! *Emotions* can deceive us and lead us astray, especially when they are being guided by Satan's lies. So let's expose the lies or half-truths that are behind some of the emotions you might be experiencing right now. Believing poisonous lies will always result in emotional responses that can prove damaging to our hope and faith.

Our Emotion	**The Lie**	**Our Reaction**
Fear, defeat	*I can't...*	Immobilization
Loneliness, rejection	*I'm alone...*	Isolation
Anxiousness	*What if...*	Retreat
Overeagerness to please	*I fear rejection*	Spiritually performing
Failure, guilt, inadequacy	*I'm not good enough*	Giving up
Overwhelmed, weariness	*This is too much*	Procrastination
Superiority to others	*I can do this by myself*	Self-rule, independence

This is a lifelong *"marathon"* that we are in, so obviously becoming mature is going to take some time, *God's time*. Finding our way to freedom and then learning to walk in it is anything but a short distance race! So let's trust the Lord to help us settle in for the long haul and become deeply committed to continuing into deeper levels of freedom and maturity in Christ.

You might be wondering, "What is the difference between freedom, and maturity?" Great question! It is one thing to understand freedom and begin to experience it, but it is another thing to live in it to the point of maturation. Notice we did not say perfection because this will not happen until we get to heaven. But as we continue our journey into increasing levels of freedom, eventually we will end up in a place of spiritual maturity and our lives will bear much fruit and we will *finish this marathon free*.

Below we have listed some of the basic differences between "freedom" and "maturity."

Freedom	Maturity
Enables a believer to grow spiritually	Is a lifelong process of spiritual growth
Is living by the presence and power of the Holy Spirit	Is becoming more and more like Jesus Christ, by his grace and the fullness of the Spirit over time
Comes through brokenness	Comes through endurance in suffering
Involves breaking of fleshly strongholds	Involves learning to live by faith in God
Releases the fruit of the Spirit to begin to grow	Produces a deep, ripened fruit of the Holy Spirit
Enables intimacy with God	Is deep intimacy with God
Requires a new understanding of who we are "in Christ"	Comes through a full understanding and living out the truths of who we are in Christ and who Christ is in us over time
Opens the door for a deeper knowledge and love for God	Is characterized by a rich knowledge of and seasoned love for God
Releases passion and power for ministry	Results in much fruit that remains
Produces clearer thinking and renewed zeal for God's word and prayer	Produces a proven dependence upon God resulting in wisdom and discernment

So with all of this in mind, let's take a break to surrender all of our thoughts and emotions to the Lord and trust him to place within us a long term endurance mentality. We can also trust him to fill us with all of the faith we need to *finish free*.

Father God, I'm sorry for believing any and all discouraging lies from Satan, like *(name the lies that you have believed)*. I willfully and wholeheartedly admit to you that I can do nothing without Christ who is my strength. Father God, with you all things are possible in my life. Thank you for the assurance that you are faithful and just and are committed to finishing this work that you have started in my life. I have tasted of your freedom and it is my desire to move on into deeper levels of freedom and on into maturity. I trust you to place within me a "marathon endurance mentality" and give me the consistency and stamina that I need to stay focused and faithfully remain true to you. I trust you to strengthen me to run this marathon with excellence. In Jesus name I pray, amen.

Knowing that Satan is a defeated foe, you can *rest* in Christ and persist in allowing him to fill you with hope, peace, passion, and quiet strength. *He is* breaking the chains, *he is* all-powerful, *he is* with you, *he is* love, *he is* life and you are becoming free.

If the Son sets you free, you will be free indeed.

John 8:36 (NIV)

So how long will these freedoms last? As long as we continue walking in the truth! Remember this?

"And you will know the truth, and the truth will set you free."

John 8:32 (NLT)

Throughout your entire life, each day as you choose to demolish lies, take thoughts captive and allow God to renew your minds to his truth, *freedom will be yours.* If you fear that you are doomed to lose this wonderful sense of freedom that you have gained in your life, get rid of that lie and call it what it is... *a lie.*

No weapon turned against you will succeed. And everyone who tells lies in court will be brought to justice. These benefits are enjoyed by the servants of the Lord; their vindication will come from me. I, the Lord, have spoken!

Isaiah 54:17 (NLT)

The book of Revelation explains how to maintain freedom and defeat the accusations and lying schemes of the enemy, especially as the day of Christ's return draws near.

And there was war in heaven. Michael and his angels fought against the dragon, and the dragon and his angels fought back. But he was not strong enough, and they lost their place in heaven. The great dragon was hurled down--that ancient serpent called the devil, or Satan, who leads the whole world astray. He was hurled to the earth, and his angels with him. Then I heard a loud voice in heaven say: "Now have come the salvation and the power and the kingdom of our God, and the authority of his Christ. For the accuser of our

brothers, who accuses them before our God day and night, has been hurled down. <u>They overcame him by the blood of the Lamb and by the word of their testimony; they did not love their lives so much as to shrink from death.</u>"

Revelation 12:7-11 (NIV)

God's word says that our victory comes through...

1. standing in the truth that your freedom, acceptance and peace with God were fully purchased by the powerful blood of Jesus,

2. by keeping the word of your testimony fresh on your lips, and

3. by surrendering your life fully into Jesus' hands, even to the point of death

The first one is a "done deal" in Christ. You *are* forgiven. Keep claiming that truth no matter what. The third one has likely yet to be tested, though in some nations it is already a daily reality. But the second one applies to your life *right now.* So now let's seal the freedom that the Lord has given you, *and the freedom that is yet to come,* by testifying of the Lord's goodness. Take a few minutes to write down what God has done in your life a*nd* what you are still expecting him to do by faith.

_____

_____

_____

_____

_____

_____

_____

_____

_____

Would you be willing to share this testimony with the people God brings to you? I (Christi) share testimonies of God's goodness as often as I can. Each time I share it, God puts another coat of sealer over it and it becomes that much more protected in my heart. Then the truth digs its way another level deeper into my belief system. Furthermore, Satan, our defeated foe, gets another bruise! So sharing your story is a powerful way to cement the truth in your own life, encourage someone else and strike a blow to the enemy!

Are you still waiting on the Lord to do a certain work in your life? Don't give up; thank him now for what he has promised to do, *by faith*. Remember:

Patient endurance is what you need now, so you will continue to do God's will. Then you will receive all that he has promised.

Hebrews 10:36 (NLT)

While you are patiently waiting, why not also allow the Lord to strengthen you, since he has all of the strength that you will ever need! You can receive his strength by meditating on the fact that *he is* your strength and by truly trusting him to provide all you need.

I love you, Lord; you are my strength.

Psalm 18:1 (NLT)

No matter where we are in our walk with the Lord, at this point in our journey, we are all still in the process of learning. If you are still wrestling with issues, it's okay. Rest in God's peace! He will complete this work in you. And if you take a fall, remember falling is an inevitable part of running. When you fall down don't sit there and sulk, whine or complain. Instead, get up, brush the dirt off, and get back to running ASAP! Also, like John Maxwell says, "pick something up while you are down there!" In other words you can ask yourself, "What can I learn from this mistake?"

Paul, one of our great forerunners, learned many things from the falls he took in life. One of the things he learned was to *turn loose* of his grip on life, with one exception, and that exception was to know Christ. Paul wrote:

...We count all things but loss for the excellency of the knowledge of Christ Jesus my Lord: for whom

we have suffered the loss of all things, and do count them but dung, that we may win Christ.

Philippians 3:8 (KJV)

What Paul was really saying here, if you'll pardon our rough 21st century application of this Scripture, is this: All the things that that I have considered important in life outside of knowing and serving Jesus Christ (including our status in life, the car, the house, the clothes, the hobbies, your financial portfolio, the job title, etc.) are about as important as dog dirt! Paul had learned to take all these things (the waste) to the garbage dump and leave it there so that he could wholeheartedly embrace Jesus and win the race of life!

If we are running to win then nothing else matters... but winning! In this case, winning entails knowing who Jesus is and becoming more like him. This is basically all that matters in the light of eternity. For this reason, we plan to spend the next three days introducing some **VIP's** that will assist you as you run this race and one day *finish* this marathon of life *free!*

There is coming a day when there will be a huge celebration, and you (as God's chosen child who has run the race well), will hear these famous words:

"Well done, my good and faithful servant. You have been faithful in handling this small amount, so now I will give you many more responsibilities. Let's celebrate together!"

Matthew 25:23 (NLT)

Many have gone on ahead of us who have faithfully carried the baton and passed it on. Generations have served God faithfully and have strived throughout their lives to be nothing more than a reflection of God's glory.

May we ask you today, who passed the baton to you? Who is it in your life that carried the baton faithfully and ran with the passion of God and faithful endurance so that you might be handed the legacy of the cross? List the names of those who have been salt and light in your life: (these are any people who have had a strong, positive impact on your spiritual life, even from a previous generation; feel free to even list great heroes of the faith recorded in the Bible).

_____

_____

_____

_____

Take a few minutes to thank God for giving you these team members to run ahead of you. Thank him for giving them the passion and endurance to finish free and to pass on to you the inheritance of the cross.

May we ask you one other question? This one is no less important than the previous one: To whom are you passing the baton? Who is watching your life trying to learn what it means to be a faithful, passionate Christian? List the names of those to whom you are responsible to be salt and light in your life:

_____

_____

_____

_____

What kind of legacy are you leaving behind? Is it a passion for Christ? No matter how you answered these questions you can rest assured that there are hands stretched out toward you, just waiting for you to pass them the baton so that they can, in turn, carry it on to those ahead of them. How you run your leg of the race will have a great impact on their final outcome. So take a few minutes and ask God to help you run this race with single-mindedness, focus, determination, and passion. Ask that you, like Paul, would consider all loss except the excellency of the knowledge of Christ Jesus our Lord. Let's determine in our hearts to strain to reach the end of the race and receive the prize for which God, through Christ Jesus, is calling us up to heaven. *(Philippians 3:14 NLT)*

Thankfully we have the advantage in this marathon. We already know the *final outcome*. We win! Isn't it awesome to run this race knowing that we are going to win? *This is what it means to be free!* We are free to run this race with the confirmed vision of what is to come.

- We are going home with the gold!

- We will see God's flag (banner) go up!

- We will hear the anthems of the Lord's praise raise for all to hear!

- We will dance, shout and sing in joyous celebration!

- We will hear the words, "Well done, my good and faithful servant!"

Let us hold this vision close in our hearts, as it will give us the energy to keep on running.

Truth Point

I have fought a good fight, I have finished the race, and I have remained faithful.

2 Timothy 4:7 (NLT)

Application

Plan to share your story of freedom with someone today.

Father God, Thank you in advance for helping me faithfully endure until the end. You have done so much for me already during this journey to freedom; I have so much to thank you for. I trust you to give me the courage to share with others what you have done so that they might be encouraged and I might be strengthened. I also want to thank you for giving me forerunners who have kept the faith before my eyes and have encouraged me by their faithful endurance. I trust you to make me just as full of faith as they were and to let my light shine bright so that others may find the legacy of Christ and the cross in me. I long for the day when your banner will raise for the last time and when the trumpets will blast and all of heaven and earth will sing your anthem together in one accord! Until then grant me your grace to continue on, racing to win! In Jesus Name, amen.

Identity Reminder:

I am bought with a price; I belong to God.

1 Cor. 6:19-20

- **My journey to freedom is a lifelong race and will take a lifetime of practice.**

- **I will overcome by the blood of the Lamb and the word of my testimony and because I love Jesus even more than my own life.**

- **I praise God for those who have passed on the legacy of Christ to me.**

- **I am committed to passing on the legacy of Christ and the cross to those behind me.**

Finishing Free

VIP #1: Validations from a Great Coach!

Taking care of my (Christi's) animals would definitely appear on my top ten list of favorite things to do. If we weren't in the ministry having so many *people* to take care of, I'd probably own a *zoo!* I like to tease my husband, Michael, and tell him that if he dies before me and I get insurance money, I'm going to buy a monkey to replace his companionship! Whenever I tell him this, it really enriches our relationship and heightens his sense of value.

Among my favorite pets are dogs (Shih Tzus) and birds (Quakers & parakeets). A little over a year ago we purchased a little Shih Tzu puppy and named him Chester. He has grown to be quite the little *wild man* in our household. We have had great difficulty in teaching him both boundaries and manners. He loves my birds, only his idea of love is different than mine because he would love to *eat* them!

Shortly after we got Chester we also got a baby parakeet we call Gracie, except that we are almost convinced that "she" is a boy.

One day when Gracie was just a baby, somehow "she" escaped from her cage. I was in the far end of our house on the computer, lost in the world of writing. I hadn't heard the commotion, but that's not abnormal. When I get focused, the whole house could fall down around me and I might not realize it.

So as I sat there typing, suddenly Gracie fluttered helplessly into the room. Chester was hot on her tail… or what was left of it!. As a matter of fact, she could hardly stand up as all of her tail feathers were

missing! So I jumped out of my seat to rescue her, and at this point, did not even know if she would be able to stand up on her perch or not. She looked pathetic! This broke my heart, but we put her in her cage and took care of her. Thankfully, Gracie pulled through that traumatic experience, and amazingly is still not afraid of Chester. So we have come to call her (or him) Amazing Gracie.

Birds are very fragile. During our years of pet bird ownership, we have had two fatal bird accidents. One day I was on the floor playing with our daughter, Sharia. She was very young at the time and she used to enjoy sitting on my feet and letting me throw her across the room. Unfortunately, our pet bird, Kookaburra, had come out of her cage to join in the fun. I guess you can figure out what happened next. I threw Sharia across the room and she landed smack dab on top of Kookaburra.

The other unfortunate bird death occurred right after I had been given a *tiny* little bird to take care of. I failed to feed it enough food and it died of starvation. This really hit me hard, because I would have *never* allowed that to happen had I known she was such a big eater.

When we adopt pets and bring them home to become a part of our family, they become totally dependent on us to take care of their needs for survival. In the same way that God, making us in his own image, placed Adam in charge of naming and taking care of all of his animals (see *Genesis 1:26-28*), God himself has taken on the responsibility of naming who *we* are and taking care of *us,* as his children. He is the *only perfect* caretaker who is deeply and flawlessly committed to meeting our needs for survival. Though we may not like to think about it, our lives are very fragile as well.

Can you hear the genuinely compassionate heart of Father God as he described just how far he was willing to go... or should we say, has already gone, in meeting our needs for life?

> *"I am the good shepherd; I know my sheep and my sheep know me-- just as the Father knows me and I know the Father--and I lay down my life for the sheep."*
>
> *John 10:14,15 (NLT)*

When it comes to taking care of us; God knows what we need. He is *primarily* interested in providing for our deepest need, which is *salvation* or eternal life with him. In addition, he is interested in providing our second greatest need, which is becoming like his Son the Lord Jesus. God is acutely aware of everything that is going on in our lives at all times. Nothing surprises him. Jesus, in the book of Matthew, assures us of God's awareness of what is going on in the world around us:

> *Not even a sparrow, worth only half a penny, can fall to the ground without your Father knowing it.*
>
> *Matthew 10:29 (NLT)*

It is boggling for our finite minds to try to comprehend the vastness of who God is. We can't really comprehend his ability to be everywhere, all the time, knowing every event that is taking place, in every person's life, at the same time — and on top of that, he knows every intent of each heart, at all times as well. We can't figure everything out, especially God himself. Instead he instructs us to be like children in our faith, innocently trusting him as a child trusts his or her parent.

WALKING ON

So God's job is to be the perfect caretaker.... *and he is!*

Our job is to **trust.** Sound simple enough?

What does "trust" look like? Here's a glimpse...

- Don't try to figure everything out or act like you already know.

- Have innocent childlike faith.

- Have confidence in God as your caretaker.

- Rest in God's presence, knowing you are in God's hands!

This might sound pretty simple, but believe us, it is *not* easy. Learning to walk in freedom – trusting God at every turn through the good, the bad and the ugly, for the long haul – is not easy at all! At times it can be down right *agonizing,* because in reality, trusting God to make us like Jesus means trusting him to help us die... to all the things we cling to so strongly for life (apart from God and his promises.) And death is not easy for anyone. Even Christ in his humanity struggled to surrender to death. We teach these principles and concepts confidently by the grace of God, but in all honesty, in *our personal* daily lives learning to live a consistent life of freedom in Christ is no less hard for us than it is for you!

Once again, consider with us, by way of review, the main components that are involved in walking in freedom:

Week 1: Remember to keep God (who we can't physically see) first and foremost in our lives, making him the center of our attention and heart of our focus.

Week 2: Walk around in the world with the confidence of who we are in Christ all the time – even when the world tries to broadcast to us a very different message.

Week 3: Be a continually forgiving person by persistently letting go of the past and repeatedly forgiving all existing and forthcoming sins of others no matter how painful they are.

Week 4: Remember to exist in a spiritually prostrate position before God in complete surrender and submission to his divine authority.

Week 5: Wake up everyday with the awareness that we are in an invisible battle; continue to summon the God-energy needed to be able to suit up and fight.

Week 6: Remember that we are in a marathon and that we must not get discouraged and give up. Instead we must dig deep into God's enabling resources, press in to intimacy with him and press on by faith with stamina and perseverance until we reach our final destiny.

In light of these spiritual challenges, you have (hopefully) given up trying to attain these goals on your own. In yesterday's devotion, we promised to introduce you to some **VIP's** that will help you *finish* this marathon of life *free!* These VIP's have been strategically placed in your life to help you *win the race of life* and *finish free.* So today, we gladly introduce you to:

VIP #1: Validations from Coach God!

We learn and grow most effectively through the concept of positive reinforcement. This is mainly because we have a strong need for *validation.* The Father even validated Jesus. An example is recorded in Matthew:

> **And a voice from heaven said, "This is my beloved Son, and I am fully pleased with him".**
>
> *Matthew 3:17(NLT)*

By validation we mean confirmation of the truth about who we really are, especially in relationship with the Lord. This involves *acceptance, support, encouragement* and *loving correction.* Opposites of validation are *personal attacks* or *rejection.* The quickest way to shut down or stunt a person's growth at any age or level of maturity is through personal rejection.

I (Christi) was raised in a fairly legalistic spiritual environment. Some of the teachers that I sat under spent too much time telling us what we *should and shouldn't do* as Christians, rather than teaching us how to have an intimate *relationship* with our wonderful God. As a child, I remember being afraid I would do something to mess up or ruin my relationship with God. I adapted the belief that what I did (mainly how dutifully I read my Bible and prayed) determined God's love and acceptance of me. Because of my fouled up belief system, in times of prayer I would often experience nagging, accusing and condemning thoughts from what I thought was God but know now was the accuser. Satan was trying to make a loser out of me and wreck my relationship with God.

God is *not* like that! We should never settle for our relationship with him becoming simply a dry and dusty *duty!*

Now you can rest assured that when I figured out that it was actually Satan's voice that I was "hearing" (getting in between the lines of conversation between me and God) my desire to hang out with God changed immensely! Wouldn't you rather hang out with people that love and encourage you as opposed to those who emotionally beat you over the head? Now that I know the truth about God, the highlight of my day is listening to what he has to say to me about who I am and who he is!

One huge key to living free is learning how to tune in to God's validations of both who you are and who he is! Considering the fact that hearing these validations is crucial to our spiritual health, vitality and freedom, how might we cultivate a more deeply alive, real, growing intimacy with him?

First, we need to realize that there are a couple different ways of communicating with God; we can connect with him both while working and while resting.

By a "working connection," we mean inviting God to become more involved in your routines and activities as you're out and about in your daily life.

This includes your vocational life (work, school, etc.) as well as when you are actively engaged with people or activities. Brother Lawrence's book, *Practicing the Presence of God* is a treasure for describing this kind of life. It is a moment-by-moment seeking to be in communion and harmony with his person and purposes, no matter what you are doing. A good question to ask God frequently in trying to stay more attuned to him while "busy" is, "Father, what would you have me think about, feel or do right now?"

God is both watching us and validating us (remember, validations might also entail loving corrections) continuously. If we are *not hearing* God's validations throughout each day, then we need to check to see if we are *listening*. It is easy to become so absorbed in the activities of the day that we forget God is present. Taking periodic prayer breaks (thanking God, asking him for wisdom, thinking briefly of a Scripture, etc.), even if only for a few seconds, can keep your fellowship with him fresh and refreshing during even the busiest times. Give it a try! God will then enable you to filter what goes into your mind and what comes into your life to keep your attitudes and actions in alignment with his truth. Learning to stay close to God during the active parts of our day in "working connection" with him is a wonderful habit to get into and very beneficial to your spiritual, emotional and physical health.

Now by a "resting connection," we mean one-on-one intimacy with God, finding that secret place where you meet with God (preferably without interruption) to really seek and experience his presence and find his will for your life. It is helpful to have a designated time and location each day for this private intimate meeting with God.

I (Christi) like to view this time with God like pulling up to a gas station and getting filled up, filled up with the power to move ahead in God's will for the day.

This "resting" intimate relationship with God involves two-way conversation. We are not talking about hearing the *audible* voice of God - though with God anything is possible. We are talking about God connecting with us in our spirit (the place where he communicates with us) especially through his word, the Bible. It is in this secret place of private intimacy with him that some of his most precious validations of us take place – validations that touch, heal, encourage, refresh, challenge and correct us. Then we respond back to him in prayer, worship and repentance based on what he has communicated to us. This two-way conversation can only happen when we are willing to listen to and obey God. If I am adamant about doing all the talking, I might as well hang up the hopes of having this type of intimacy with God.

If we are going to live free it is imperative that we connect with God in this way. To illustrate this, say you pull your car up to the gas station with an empty tank and proceed to tell the gas station attendant how much your car really needs gas, then list all the places you have to go and simply drive off! How far do you think you will go? Not far, because you never put any gas in the tank! Connecting with God is much more than pulling up and telling him how much we need him and listing all the things that we need him to do. We have to let him actually put the gas in our tank and through his word encourage and empower us for living through the filling with the Holy Spirit.

Many followers of Christ call this "resting connection" with God a "quiet time."

A beneficial quiet time will likely include:

- Pouring out your concerns to God.
- Recognizing that God has all of the answers.
- Receiving God's instructions for living.
- Allowing God to empower you to live out what he has instructed.

Notice we *didn't* say, "A beneficial quiet time should include 30 minutes of Bible reading, 5 minutes of confession of sin, 10 minutes of thanksgiving and worship and 15 minutes of praying for needs" or something like that! Like a dance, let the Lord lead you in how to spend your time. Going in with a plan (e.g. "I'd like to start/continue reading through the gospel of Matthew") is fine. Just be sensitive to the Lord. He may desire that you camp on a certain verse or he may lead you to others.

Much of my (Christi's) personal time with God consists of God reminding me who he is and who I am in him. This fills up my tank *real fast!* There is nothing else quite like receiving *validations* of truth in our spirit from our great coach Father God who loves us immensely.

And I pray that Christ will be more and more at home in your hearts as you trust in him. May your roots go down deep into the soil of God's marvelous love. And may you have the power to understand, as all God's people should, how wide, how long, how high, and how deep his love really is.

Ephesians 3:17-18 (NLT)

We pray that you are energized just thinking about being in God's presence and receiving your daily validations. If you miss your time with God, don't allow the enemy to condemn you. Instead, receive God's grace and anticipate the next time that you will be able to bask in God's presence. Since my eyes have been opened to what a real relationship with God is supposed to be, I find myself joining in with the psalmist David regarding his hunger and thirst to meet with God! He couldn't even sleep for thinking about the goodness of God! May the Lord ignite our spirits and burn this kind of passion into our mind, will and emotions.

O God, you are my God; I earnestly search for you. My soul thirsts for you; my whole body longs for you in this parched and weary land where there is no water. I have seen you in your sanctuary and gazed upon your power and glory. Your unfailing love is better to me than life itself; how I praise you! I will honor you as long as I live, lifting up my hands to you in prayer. You satisfy me more than the richest of foods. I will praise you with songs of joy. I lie awake thinking of you, meditating on you through the night. I think how much you have helped me; I sing for joy in the shadow of your protecting wings. I follow close behind you; your strong right hand holds me securely.

Psalm 63:1-8 (NLT)

Are you hungry for a deeper more meaningful relationship with God? Why not increase your intimacy with God by telling him how you feel about him and his goodness in the space provided below. Go ahead and try your hand at making your journaling intimate by revealing your heart like David did. Don't worry if you don't *feel like it,* the feelings will come. Maybe David did not *feel* like writing this either, given that he was in the desert and threatened by deadly enemies (*vv. 9-11*).

_____

_____

_____

_____

_____

_____

_____

_____

_____

_____

_____

WRAPPING UP

Too many times we get it all backwards. We get caught up in searching for validations from finite, fallible people rather than from the infinite, infallible God. Often we desperately search for affirmation from people, hoping they'll tell us…

- We're okay, or acceptable.
- We are enjoyable to be around.
- We can do it.
- We are important.
- We are safe.
- We are loved.
- We can win.

Clearly, we are commanded in Scripture to encourage one another and this is our topic for tomorrow. Primarily, however, we need to know deep down what God says is true about us and we need his Spirit to bear witness with our spirit that we are children of God (***Romans 8:16***). It is one thing to be affirmed by people like us. It is another thing altogether to be affirmed by the Most High God himself!

Here are just a few validations from the treasure of God's word:

You are acceptable!

God alone made it possible for you to be in Christ Jesus. For our benefit God made Christ to be wisdom itself. He is the one who made us acceptable to God. He made us pure and holy, and he gave himself to purchase our freedom.

1 Corinthians 1:30 (NLT)

You are enjoyable to be around!

The LORD your God is in your midst, a victorious warrior. He will exult over you with joy, He will be quiet in His love, He will rejoice over you with shouts of joy.

Zephaniah 3:17 (NASB)

You can do it!

Whatever I have, wherever I am, I can make it through anything in the One who makes me who I am.

Philippians 4:13 (MSG)

You are important!

Yes, there are many parts, but only one body. The eye can never say to the hand, "I don't need you." The head can't say to the feet, "I don't need you." In fact, some of the parts that seem weakest and least important are really the most necessary. And the parts we regard as less honorable are those we clothe with the greatest care. So we carefully protect from the eyes of others those parts that should not be seen, while other parts do not require this special care. So God has put the body together in such a way that extra honor and care are given to those parts that have less dignity. This makes for harmony among the members, so that all the members care for each other equally.

1 Corinthians 12:20-25 (NLT)

You are safe!

Even when you are chased by those who seek your life, you are safe in the care of the Lord your God, secure in his treasure pouch! But the lives of your enemies will disappear like stones shot from a sling!

1 Samuel 25:29 (NLT)

You are forever loved!

Do you think anyone is going to be able to drive a wedge between us and Christ's love for us? There is no way! Not trouble, not hard times, not hatred, not hunger, not homelessness, not bullying threats, not backstabbing, not even the worst sins listed in Scripture.

Romans 8:35 (MSG)

You are a confirmed winner!

So, what do you think? With God on our side like this, how can we lose?

Romans 8:31 (MSG)

Truth Point

As the deer pants for streams of water, so my soul pants for you, O God. My soul thirsts for God, for the living God. When can I go and meet with God?

Psalm 42:1, 2 (NIV)

Application

Looking over the Scripture verses in this *Wrapping Up* section, pick out one and write it down on an index card. Look at it periodically during the day, thinking about it and seeking to commit it to memory. By the end of a day or two you will have it memorized... a validation from God treasured in your heart!

Father God, how wonderful it is to draw near to you and to live in intimate relationship with you each day. What pure joy captures my soul when you confirm that I am accepted by you in Christ and that you have made me to be your child, even a saint. Thank you that I can do all things because your strength is within me, that I am necessary to the body of Christ, that I am safely held in the palm of your hand; that nothing can separate me from your love and that I am on the winning team. Father you are an awesome coach and caretaker. As I think of the birds and lilies even they are meticulously taken care of by you! I trust you today to both deepen and enrich my intimacy with you while I am active and when I pull aside to rest in your presence. In Jesus' name I pray, amen.

- **Father God is the *only perfect* caretaker who is flawless in his care taking.**
- **Father God knows what our true needs are and is faithful to meet them.**
- **I am hungry for a deeper more meaningful relationship with God.**
- **I need to hear God's validations daily.**

Finishing Free

VIP #2: Influential Team Members!

Dick and Rick Hoyt are a father-and-son team from Massachusetts who together often compete in marathon races. If they're not in a marathon they are in a triathlon — that daunting, almost superhuman combination of 26.2 miles of running, 112 miles of bicycling, and 2.4 miles of swimming. Together they have climbed mountains and once trekked 3,735 miles across America.

It's a remarkable record of exertion — all the more so when you consider that Rick can't walk or talk. For the past twenty-five years or more Dick, who is 65, has pushed and pulled his son across the country and over hundreds of finish lines. When Dick runs, Rick is in a wheelchair that Dick is pushing. When Dick cycles, Rick is in the seat-pod from his wheelchair, attached to the front of the bike. When Dick swims, Rick is in a small but heavy, firmly stabilized boat being pulled by Dick.

At Rick's birth in 1962 the umbilical cord coiled around his neck and cut off oxygen to his brain. Dick and his wife, Judy, were told there was no hope for their child's normal development. The couple brought their son home determined to raise him as "normally" as possible.

After 4 years of marathons, Team Hoyt attempted their first triathlon — and for this Dick had to learn to swim. "I sank like a stone at first" Dick recalled with a laugh "and I hadn't been on a bike since I was six years old." With a newly-built bike (adapted to carry Rick in front) and a boat tied to Dick's waist as he swam, the Hoyts came in second-to-last in the competition held on Father's Day 1985.

They have been competing ever since, at home and increasingly abroad. Generally they manage to improve their finishing times. "Rick is the one who inspires and motivates me, the way he just loves sports and competing," Dick said. The business of inspiring evidently works as a two-way street. Rick typed out this testimony:

"Dad is one of my role models. Once he sets out to do something, Dad sticks to it whatever it is, until it is done. For example once we decided to really get into triathlons, Dad worked out up to five hours a day, five times a week, even when he was working."

The Hoyts' mutual inspiration for each other seems to embrace others too — many spectators and fellow competitors have adopted Team Hoyt as a powerful example of determination.

"The message of Team Hoyt is that everybody should be included in everyday life."

Dick is clearly a *powerful influence* in his son's life. What do you think makes Dick such an influential team player in Rick's life?

_____

_____

_____

_____

We believe his powerful influence stems from his inner determination to sacrificially *give and connect* with Rick. No doubt there has been a great amount of "*blood, sweat, and tears*" spent helping Rick aspire to his dreams, but the bottom line has to be *love.*

Who has been a powerful influence in your life? Have these influencers helped pull you toward your aspirations, or pushed you away from them? Before we go any further, let us take the opportunity to introduce you to some other **VIP's** that will help you learn to walk in freedom and become mature in Christ!

VIP #2: Influential team members (Jesus and other brothers and sisters in Christ)

Jesus is, *hands down,* the greatest influential team member in our lives. He entered into our world to identify with us and understand us. He spent time imparting life to us practically, emotionally and spiritually. Then he willingly laid down everything he had and rose from the dead to provide for our connection with him forever. In doing so, he revealed the depth of his love for us. We cannot deny one ounce of his passionate love.

How has the life and example of Jesus Christ powerfully influenced who you are today? Think about how he is affecting you practically, emotionally and spiritually. To help you get started, here are a few examples of what we mean. Jesus affected you *practically* by creating you, giving you life, providing for your needs, etc. He affects us *emotionally* by loving us, accepting us, giving us joy, etc. He affects us *spiritually* by dying on the cross, rising from the dead, forgiving us, giving us eternal life and many other ways. Take some time and think through your answers and then record them in the table below. Use this exercise as a time to give thanks to God for his indescribable gift to us, the Lord Jesus!

Practically	Emotionally	Spiritually

Who else is influencing your life? No matter how alone you might think you are, there are other people in your life who play a significant role in shaping who you are and who you are becoming.

Not only do we tend to be influenced by the lives and opinions of others, but also we tend to be influenced by the media and culture in which we live. Over all, we are a people that are highly susceptible to *influence.*

In West Virginia there was a terrible coal mining accident and 12 miners were trapped. The families gathered together in a small church near the accident to pray their loved ones would be rescued. You might remember the incident. After over 40 hours of the grueling mission, someone overheard that the rescuers had found all the miners alive. That person called one of the family members to share the news and in no time everyone at the church, including the media were jumping, yelling, screaming and going crazy celebrating the news that their loved ones were alive. Sadly, the person who had influenced these people to begin rejoicing had been misguided. The truth was that only one miner was alive. Many dear hurting people were powerfully influenced in the wrong direction, which in turn caused much deeper pain in their lives.

Are the "meaningful others" in your life influencing you in the wrong direction and causing more pain in your life? If so, maybe you need to consider phasing those influences out of their places of authority in your life. Why not step out of your comfort zone to meet some new strong godly influencers? As God leads, begin opening your heart to them. That can seem a bit scary, especially if you've been hurt before. But we encourage you to take a step of faith and allow God to bring people into your lives who will love you with his love. This should encourage you:

There is no room in love for fear. Well-formed love banishes fear... 1 John 4:18 (MSG)

We hope the greatest influencers in your life are not negative, leading you away from growing in your faith and freedom. We hope most influencers are very positive! Take a few minutes to evaluate the truth regarding the influencers in your life. Begin by recalling the names of the people that play a strong role in influencing your actions. List their names in the first column marked **Team member** in the chart below. Now consider for a moment, are these people positively influencing your life practically, emotionally and spiritually? Or are they negatively influencing you? Hopefully, they are positive influencers and hopefully they have become a great source of help to you as you reach toward your aspirations of finding freedom in Christ and developing maturity in Christ.

To help you out in this exercise, below this chart are some ideas of ways people might positively influence us towards freedom *practically, spiritually and emotionally.* If the people you listed are negative influencers you can determine where they are taking you in these three areas.

Team member	Practically	Emotionally	Spiritually

Practically	Emotionally	Spiritually
study God's Word together	builds me up in Christ	inspires me
pray together	accepts me	prays for me
minister together	appreciates me	urges me to stay in fellowship
spends time with me	encourages me	forgives me
worship together	sees me through God's eyes	guards my heart
grow spiritually together	is patient with me	gives me wise counsel
provide financially	affirms my gifts	convinces me to use my gifts
serve in practical ways	confirms my significance	speaks blessing over my life

According to **Acts 20:35**, it is more blessed *to give* than *to receive*. Coach God has also instructed us that we need to learn to freely give out of the abundance that we have received from him *(remember those validations?)* So let's turn the tables for a minute. Who are *you* powerfully influencing *practically, emotionally and spiritually?* Go ahead and list the names first, then determine where you are helping them grow in these three areas. Be honest with yourself.

Team member	Tangibly	Emotionally	Spiritually

Most likely both of these exercises were challenging for you. Why do you think they were so challenging? Here, in the 21st century, we have great difficulty creating time for God and time for each other, *especially quality time!* By quality time we mean time spent meeting the needs of others in practical, meaningful ways. According to Scripture this difficulty that we are having might be because:

> **As the end approaches, people are going to be self-absorbed, money-hungry, self-promoting, stuck-up, profane, contemptuous of parents, crude, coarse...**
>
> *2 Timothy 3:2 (MSG)*

Also, we submit to you that *unhealthy busyness* is a huge tool of the enemy! Satan is fully aware of the power and potential of *quality time spent sacrificially giving and meeting one another's needs!* Many of us, however, are falling prey to the temptation of being driven to attain selfish ambitions and self-centered goals. As a result we are often so weary and drained that we don't think we have the time or energy to pursue healthy, godly relationships. But that is what God created us for and it brings the deepest satisfaction in life!

In the box below is a list of some of the barriers that keep us from becoming involved in each other's lives *practically, emotionally, and spiritually.* This list is tough, and may require some real soul-searching. What is hindering you from getting more deeply involved in the lives of others?

too much work already	too many activities	selfishness
weariness	lacking compassion	lacking forgiveness
fearing rejection	fearing exposure	fearing loss
lacking trust of others	lacking trust of God	lacking trust of self

We believe that the greatest deterrents to deep meaningful relationships (especially within our homes) are *selfishness and unforgiveness*. I (Christi) would like to have a nickel for every couple that has sat in my counseling office frustrated over their relationship with their spouse. Or, we might as well go ahead and add in all those who came in distraught over their relationships with their children, extended family members, friends, other church members, coworkers or authority figures... the list seems endless.

Being trained in temperament therapy, it usually doesn't take long to determine the *"differences in temperament"* of those involved in the conflict. Most people believe it is their *differences in temperament* that *causes* the conflicts. I have discovered that no matter how different people are, if you boil conflicts down you will discover right in the center of the conflict, two people are trying really hard to get the other person to see and do things the way that *they* see and do things. James discovered the *root cause of conflicts* long ago through the inspiration of the Holy Spirit.

Where do you think all these appalling wars and quarrels come from? Do you think they just happen? Think again. They come about because you want your own way, and fight for it deep inside yourselves.

James 4:1 (MSG)

Sadly, most of our conflicts derive from *selfishness*, which is sin. Is it at all surprising to discover that the reason we are sinfully selfish is because we have unmet needs, unmet *practical, emotional, and spiritual needs?* What a cycle of defeat!

1. We fail to get our primary needs met by God.

2. As a result we end up with empty tanks, having little to give to others.

3. We then look primarily to people to meet our needs and fill up our tanks.

4. They are not capable because their tanks are empty as well so we get angry.

The problem? Empty, selfish lives lead to a lack of deep meaningful relationships. The solution? *God's plan*, it comes in two parts and looks like this:

Part A: We abundantly receive validations from God so the void in our heart is filled to overflowing.

Part B: We give to others out of the abundance that we have received from God.

Did you hear anything in that plan that consisted of *taking*? We didn't either.

Don't push your way to the front; don't sweet-talk your way to the top. Put yourself aside, and help others get ahead. Don't be obsessed with getting your own advantage. Forget yourselves long enough to lend a helping hand.

Philippians 2:3-4 (MSG)

Now don't get us wrong. We are not saying that it is wrong to graciously receive from others when they give to you out of the abundance of their heart. To refuse would be to rob both them and you of a great blessing! But there is a big difference between *taking* and *receiving* and it is destructive to a relationship to try and get your needs met by *"taking"* or demanding of others.

When you grab all you can get, that's what happens: the more you get, the less you are.

Proverbs 1:19 (MSG)

The bottom line is if we are trapped in the cycle of *taking*, then we will likely end up having a negative or critical attitude towards one or more of our valuable team members, for they will rarely live up to our unrealistic expectations. So let's refuse all selfishness and echo the spirit of the Psalmist:

Turn my heart toward your statutes, and not toward selfish gain.

Psalm 119:36 (NIV)

Just think how our relationships would change if we all abundantly *received* from God and freely *gave* to others out of this abundance… nobody "taking" and nobody proudly refusing to receive! We would be more deeply connected to one another – our powerful, influential team members, *and God would be glorified because the world would see Jesus!*

> **Your love for one another will prove to the world that you are my disciples.**
>
> *John 13:35 (NLT)*

Our Coach God has surrounded us with influential team members, the greatest being Christ Jesus, and the second being other believers in Christ. God says that we are stronger when we are united. His desire is for us to be close with one another and to develop such relationships that we are able to speak into each other's lives, sharpening each other.

> **Two people can accomplish more than twice as much as one; they get a better return for their labor.**
>
> *Ecclesiastics 4:9 (NLT)*

> **As iron sharpens iron, a friend sharpens a friend.**
>
> *Proverbs 27:7 (NLT)*

We can increase intimacy in our relationships and broaden our window of influence by meeting each other's practical needs, emotional needs, and spiritual needs. Likewise, we decrease intimacy and narrow our window of influence by selfishly taking from others, fighting to get our own way and demanding that others meet our needs. We can clearly see that our primary and most critical need in life is to be filled to overflowing with the the abundance of God's rich provisions, so we can truly love and serve others.

Jesus, our first and foremost powerful influencer, has set a wonderful example for us. If we were to sum up the power of his influence, this is what we would find:

Identification + understanding + quality time + sacrificial love to the point of death + rising from the dead = impartation of life!

Jesus identified with us by putting on skin and entering into our world.

He fully understands us because he faced all that we face on a daily basis.

He spent 33 years of quality time with us, loving us, teaching us, delivering us and healing us.

He proved his love by sacrificially laying down his life for us so that we could be free from sin.

He rose from the dead to give us his life.

Jesus took time to get to know us, to share in our joys, sufferings and sorrows. He also imparted the gospel into our lives mainly through imparting his life into our lives.

Are you willing to impart your life into the lives of others?

> **Dear friends, since God loved us that much, we surely ought to love each other. No one has ever seen God. But if we love each other, God lives in us, and his love has been brought to full expression through us.**
>
> *1 John 4:11-12 (NLT)*

Truth Point

> *Having thus a fond affection for you, we were well-pleased to impart to you not only the gospel of God but also our own lives, because you had become very dear to us.*
>
> *1 Thessalonians 2:8 (NASB)*

Application

With whom will you spend quality time meeting practical, emotional, spiritual needs? Ask the Lord to show you his will and fill you with his love.

Who?	When?	Contact Info:
_____	_____	_____
_____	_____	_____
_____	_____	_____
_____	_____	_____
_____	_____	_____

Father God, the ground at the foot of the cross is level. You love every one of your children the same and you created each of us in your own likeness. Though we are all created unique, with different needs and gifts, we all have several things in common. *We all* need you. *We all* battle against temptation. *We all* struggle to maintain a true belief system concerning our identity in Christ. *We all* find it difficult to forgive those who hurt us. *We all* battle with the flesh. *We are all* in a daily war against Satan. And *we all* need to confess to you the ways we have allowed excuses and walls to keep us from being powerful influential team members. *So together,* we trust you to help us learn to do life together as you so will. In the name of Jesus I pray, amen.

- **I need to abundantly receive from God so that I might become a free giver.**

- **I need to put away selfish activity and be trained to give the gift of love.**

- **I will utilize God's power to become a powerful influential team member.**

- **I will allow others to be powerful influential team members in my life.**

NOTE: Perhaps through the *40 Days of Freedom* campaign, you have begun to participate in a small fellowship group. If so, you have no doubt come to see some of the benefits this involvement has brought to your life. Don't let this great connection with other believers end when the campaign is over. Take the initiative to speak with your group leader or contact your church office to find out how to stay connected!

Finishing Free
VIP #3: Penetration of the Great Plan!

Before my (Christi's) first mission trip Michael had tried to get me to go with him overseas several times. My problem was that I couldn't bring myself to leave the country without our daughter, Sharia. He really wanted me to go with him, so he began pressing me and finally said, "Let's just take Sharia with us." After he dismantled all my excuses, I finally gave in and agreed to go, mainly to please him.

Leaving day for Argentina rapidly arrived, and I was ready, or as ready as I could be considering that I didn't really want to go. I had packed all of Sharia's and my favorite clothes in a garment bag that we would carry on the plane.

Getting to Argentina was wearying; including layovers, it took us 24 hours to get there. Nearing the end of those 24 hours, somehow my garment bag (with all of our favorite clothes) came up *missing*. I was tired and irritated... *and now this*. Although I withheld expressing my frustration in front of the students on the trip with us, my inner attitude was in need of some serious adjustment. As usual, God "had my back." He would make sure that before long, my attitude would get the precise adjustment it needed.

We finally arrived in Santa Fe, Argentina and met with the resident missionary. We loaded our things onto a bus that would take us on to the city and our accommodations. As the bus pulled out, I sat there sulking, staring out the window. I was hot, tired and frustrated over the fact that I had nothing to wear to worship services (we had to wear skirts, and mine were in the missing garment bag). As I stared out the window, what I began to see grabbed my attention. The houses were *shacks, and scarcely that!* The people were in such need; the little children were barely clothed... and most likely, physically hungry. Then I began to wonder, "How many of these people have not had a sufficient opportunity to hear about Jesus, and meet him as their Savior and Friend?"

With all the spiritual heat God was supplying, it didn't take long for my heart to reach melting point. Tears started to trickle down my cheeks and I began repenting for having been so uptight about a few little pieces of fabric!

God has a way of supplying reality checks when we need them, and I needed one that day! Our trip to Argentina ended up making a lasting impact on my life. The people of Argentina easily made their way into my Holy Spirit-transformed heart. Leaving the Argentines was painstakingly difficult; it took me half the trip home to begin to regroup emotionally. I pray I will never fail to remember the truth regarding what is important *(souls)* and what is not *(everything else)*.

Michael and I have seen the movie, *End of the Spear*. This movie is based on a true story from in 1956. Five missionaries to Ecuador were attempting to share the gospel with a people group called the Waodoni, who had never before been reached with the gospel. The Waodoni were known as the *most violent* society ever documented in history. Not only did the Waodoni reject the missionaries, but they also speared each one of them to death! Remarkably, the missionaries knew ahead of time that their lives were at great risk, but they chose to reach out to the Waodoni regardless of the outcome. When asked if they would use their guns to defend themselves if the Waodoni people tried to hurt them, Nate Saint told his son Steve, *"We can't shoot the Waodoni people. They are not ready to go to heaven yet, but we are."* After their husbands were brutally murdered, some of the wives and children of these great men of faith went back to the Waodoni determined to show them God's grace and love. Through the power of forgiveness, this tribe came to a saving knowledge of Jesus Christ.

What would cause these missionaries to be so willing to lay down their lives?

We believe it is because their hearts had been deeply *penetrated* by *God's Great Plan*.

What is God's Great Plan? The Great Plan is the sum of God's word, the whole message of God's truth, the gospel of Jesus Christ revealed and proclaimed to a lost world.

Take a moment for a heart check. On a scale of 1-10, to what level do you think that the Great Plan has penetrated your heart? *(10 being willing to lay down your life for the sake of others coming to know Christ, 1 being "not at all")*

1   2   3   4   5   6   7   8   9   10

The good news is that no matter what level your heart has been penetrated by the Great Plan, God is a Master at embedding this plan even deeper into our hearts. He knows exactly what level of freedom you are currently experiencing and what it will take to bring you to a deeper level.

Regardless of your age or spiritual maturity we hope that you never buy into the lie that you have reached the point of complete saturation of the word of God or his Great Plan. Complete saturation will not happen for you, or us, until we see him as he is. So until then, we continue on, seeking to know him more and allowing the Holy Spirit to move us into deeper levels of understanding, surrender and dedication. With that in mind, let's meet…

VIP #3: Penetration of the Great Plan (through the illumination of the Holy Spirit)

The Holy Spirit… you can't see him, but he's always there. You can, however, see the effects of where he is and where he has been. He brings light to every dark place. He brings sight to blind eyes and causes finite minds to understand things that are not understandable by mere human reason. He opens up the way and points us to Christ. He builds us up and grounds us in the faith; in walking with him we will become mature saints in Christ.

Who in your life would you consider to be a strong, faithful, mature saint of God?

_____

_____

_____

When we think of strong, faithful, mature saints of God who are rock solid in their faith and trust in God, they can be pictured as *strong trees planted by the riverbank.*

> **Blessed are those who trust in the Lord and have made the Lord their hope and confidence. They are like trees planted along a riverbank, with roots that reach deep into the water. Such trees are not bothered by the heat or worried by long months of drought. Their leaves stay green, and they go right on producing delicious fruit.**
>
> *Jeremiah 17:7-8 (NLT)*

No doubt this is the kind of faith our Ecuadorian missionary friends had. Now you might be saying, "*Whoa,* I would love to have the kind of profound saintly faith that those missionary heroes had... *but I could never be that strong!*" Don't be so quick to count yourself out! The mountainous faith that each missionary hero displayed first took root in his heart as just one little *seed of faith.*

One seed of God's living word was planted deep in their hearts, and one day that seed took root and began producing a root system that could not be easily shaken. By the watering of the Holy Spirit and the light of the Word their trees grew tall and began producing a great harvest of fruit.

Realize that these guys did not have a corner on God, nor were they more loved or more eagerly chosen by God than you are. They simply allowed the seeds of God's truth to take root in their hearts and grow through the watering of the Spirit and the light of the Word. Their faith seed started out as the same size as ours.

> **The Kingdom of Heaven is like a mustard seed planted in a field. It is the smallest of all seeds, but it becomes the largest of garden plants and grows into a tree where birds can come and find shelter in its branches.**
>
> *Matthew 13:31-32 (NLT)*

The question is not, "Who has been given the better seed?" for we have all been given the same seed. Rather, the question is, "Will we allow our seed to take root and grow into a tall fruit-bearing tree through the water of the Spirit and the light of the Word?"

Think about the seeds of freedom that have been planted in your heart over the last 38 days. What is going to happen to those seeds? It is your choice what happens to them!

Let's take a look at our options. They are recorded in *Matthew 13:3-8 (MSG)*:

> **"What do you make of this? A farmer planted seed. As he scattered the seed,**

1. **Some of it fell on the road, and birds ate it.**

2. **Some fell in the gravel; it sprouted quickly but didn't put down roots, so when the sun came up it withered just as quickly.**

3. **Some fell in the weeds; as it came up, it was strangled by the weeds.**

4. **Some fell on good earth, and produced a harvest beyond his wildest dreams."**

Now let's look at Jesus' explanation of that parable (story), which is provided in *Matthew 13:18-23 (MSG).*

Circle what you want to happen to the seeds of truth sown in your life.

> **"Study this story of the farmer planting seed."**

1. When anyone hears news of the kingdom and *doesn't take it in, it just remains on the surface,* and so the Evil One comes along and plucks it right out of that person's heart. This is the seed the farmer scatters on the road.

(You hear the truth but do not receive the truth into your mind will and emotions and thereby do not allow it to transform your life. Soon it is gone.)

2. The seed cast in the gravel—this is the person who hears *and instantly responds with enthusiasm.*

But there is no soil of character, and so when the emotions wear off and some difficulty arrives, there is nothing to show for it.

(You are excited about the truth you've heard and the idea of being set free, but your emotions alone are your guide. Because you do not make the choice to live according to the truth, when hard times come you give up and bail on God, going back to life as it was before.)

3. The seed cast in the weeds is the person who hears the kingdom news, but *weeds of worry and illusions about getting more* and wanting everything under the sun strangle what was heard, and nothing comes of it.

(You are doing great now, but distractions like desiring more money and stuff are lurking right around the corner. They ambush you, interrupting your connection with the truth and your growth in freedom.)

4. The seed cast on good earth is the person who *hears* and *takes in the News*, and then *produces a harvest beyond his wildest dreams.*

(You have heard God's word and have received his truth into your spirit, mind, will and emotions. God's truth is becoming your guide as you learn to walk by faith. Because truth is your guide you are becoming more and more confident and able to recognize and dismantle lies. You are finding that your new confidence in Christ is enabling you to do things that are outside of your normal human abilities. God is supernaturally empowering you to labor in his vineyard and begin to reap a harvest.)

Is your seed malnourished and about to wither, or is it well-watered and destined to flourish, growing into a strong deeply-rooted tree? One thing I (Christi) have noticed about the strong trees that God has placed in my life is that they are full of God's Word and seem to overflow with it. They are also full to overflowing with the Holy Spirit. When their pot gets knocked around, what comes spilling out is... *righteousness.*

In *End of the Spear* when Nate Saint had been stabbed and was lying on the ground dying, he looked up at his attacker and said, (in the Waodoni language) *"I am your friend, your <u>sincere</u> friend."* Wow! This kind of character is what the watering of the Spirit and the washing and enlightening of God's Word will cause us to have. Fresh renewing truth from Scripture and a fresh filling of the Holy Spirit will empower us to reveal Christ to others. This is the ultimate purpose of the Great Plan!

Go out and train everyone you meet, far and near, in this way of life, marking them by baptism in the threefold name: Father, Son and Holy Spirit.

Matthew 28:19 (MSG)

We don't know about you, but that lights up our world! What a reason to live! What a reason to dive into God's Word and to invite the Holy Spirit to fill us and illuminate Scripture so that we will move into deeper levels of understanding, deeper levels of surrender and faith, deeper levels of reaching out to those around us with the love of God!

Let your roots grow down into him [and his word] and draw up nourishment from him, so you will grow in faith, strong and vigorous in the truth you were taught.

Colossians 2:7 (MSG)

Identity Reminder:

I am a member of Christ's Body.

1 Cor. 12:27

WINDING DOWN

Jesus says to those who are hungry for God and his Word:

You shall be satisfied right now:

God blesses you who are hungry now, for you will be satisfied.

Luke 6:21 (NLT)

You shall be satisfied throughout eternity:

Jesus replied, "I am the bread of life. No one who comes to me will ever be hungry again. Those who believe in me will never thirst.

John 6:35 (NLT)

The Holy Spirit says to those who are thirsty for God:

Enjoy God's presence!

May his reign be as refreshing as the springtime rains—like the showers that water the earth.

Psalm 72:6 (NLT)

Enjoy your salvation!

With joy you will drink deeply from the fountain of salvation!

Isaiah 12:3 (NLT)

Enjoy the Spirit!

For I will give you abundant water to quench your thirst and to moisten your parched fields. And I will pour out my Spirit and my blessings on your children.

Isaiah 44:3 (NLT)

Enjoy God's blessing!

The Lord will guide you continually, watering your life when you are dry and keeping you healthy, too. You will be like a well-watered garden, like an ever-flowing spring.

Isaiah 58:11 (NLT)

The Living Word says to those who desire to reap a harvest of souls for his Kingdom:

God will Protect you:

The Lord is my light and my salvation—so why should I be afraid?

The Lord protects me from danger—so why should I tremble?

Psalm 27:1 (NLT)

God will Direct you:

Your word is a lamp for my feet and a light for my path.

Psalm 119:105 (NLT)

God will Shine through you and Empower you :

You are the light of the world—like a city on a mountain, glowing in the night for all to see.

Matthew 5:14 (NLT)

Are you hungry for God's Word and thirsty for his Spirit? Do you desire to be an enormous healthy tree in God's kingdom? Do you want to reap a harvest of seeing others planted and grow up in Christ? If so then you will need to be connected to the one true Vine. Jesus says:

I am the Vine, you are the branches. When you're joined with me and I with you, the relation intimate and organic, the harvest is sure to be abundant. Separated, you can't produce a thing.

John 15:5 (MSG)

Over the last three days we have given you tools to help you maintain your lifelong journey to freedom well after our 40-day journey is complete. We pray that the seeds of freedom that have been planted in your life will be well nourished, and become strong, deeply rooted in Christ and not easily shaken. So let's take a few minutes to review the VIP's that will help us *finish free.*

VIP #1: **Validations from Coach God!**

VIP #2: **Influential team members (Jesus and other brothers and sisters in Christ).**

VIP #3: **Penetration of the Great Plan (through the illumination of the Holy Spirit).**

We need all of these VIP's in our lives if we are going accomplish, through God, his will for our lives.

Truth Point

And I pray that Christ will be more and more at home in your hearts as you trust in him. May your roots go down deep into the soil of God's marvelous love.

Ephesians 3:17 (NLT)

Application

Spend this time seeking God for a fresh infilling of the Holy Spirit and for a deeper penetration of his Great Plan in your life. Ask him to give you a heart to pray for his kingdom work around the world! Seek opportunities to give to his missionaries and ministers! Be available as the Lord leads to go and join in God's Great Plan to bring the gospel to the lost and dying without Christ, both here and abroad!

Father God, in humble adoration, I stand before your throne. In brokenness I seek to know you as Lord. You are the only One who can make me whole. Thank you for raising me up, holy and righteous, to sit with you in Christ. Father God, let your Holy Spirit come and breathe a fresh filling into me. Let your power come and change me. You are all I need. I choose this day and every day to surrender my entire life and all of my body to you, no matter what you may ask me to sacrifice. I trust you to show me your Great Plan and the role that you have chosen for me. I choose to present myself fully to be used by you. You have been my strong tower, my rock and my fortress, so I will trust you no matter what life brings. In times of tribulation, I will call out your name for you are my help and my salvation! Through the filling of the Holy Spirit in my life, make me your bold and confident witness. In the powerful name of Jesus I pray, amen.

- **The seed of God's living word has been planted in my life.**

- **I will allow the water of the Spirit to nourish these seeds.**

- **I trust God to cause roots to grow deeper.**

- **By faith I will pray, give, speak and go as the Lord leads and empowers me to take an active part in his Great Plan.**

- **By the grace of God I will reap a great harvest and will not be easily shaken.**

Finishing Free

Free to Finish Strong

Congratulations! You've made it to the end of our *Journey to Freedom!!*

We've covered a lot of ground over the past six weeks. We started out by looking at our amazing God of freedom and how to begin and strengthen a relationship with him. We then took a week to examine who in the world we really are… *in Christ.* The next couple weeks were pretty tough as we discussed how to face and be free from our pain and how God breaks and molds us into the image of Christ. We spent Week Five out on the battlefield, spying behind enemy lines to understand spiritual warfare. In this final, short week we have tried to give you some tracks to keep running on in freedom.

As you can see, just like in Day 20, we are changing our format today. In this case it's simply because we want to have one more heart-to-heart talk with you before we're done.

We've called this last week *Finishing Free.* Part of the reason for that title is that we pray and hope the Lord has brought a significant measure of freedom to your life, and that you are completing this *Journey to Freedom* excited about the liberation that is yours in Christ. But more than that, we want you to finish *your life* free. No matter how many minutes, hours, days, weeks, months or years you have left on this side of eternity, we want you to run the race of faith well and finish strong, to *finish free.* Hebrews captures the heart of this goal:

Therefore, since we have so great a cloud of witnesses surrounding us, let us also lay aside every encumbrance, and the sin which so easily entangles us, and let us run with endurance the race that is set before us, fixing our eyes on Jesus, the author and perfecter of faith, who for the joy set before Him endured the cross, despising the shame, and has sat down at the right hand of the throne of God. For consider Him who has endured such hostility by sinners against Himself, so that you may not grow weary and lose heart.

Hebrews 12:1-3 (NASB)

This Scripture is about *endurance,* one of the most important keys to finishing strong and free in our Christian lives. We are guessing that *endure* is not likely one of your favorite vocabulary words. We would much rather talk about *enjoy* than *endure,* but three times in those three verses a form of the word *endure* is used.

God puts a high premium on endurance and perseverance… keeping on running no matter how hard it gets.

My brothers and sisters, consider it nothing but joy when you fall into all sorts of trials, because you know that the testing of your faith produces endurance. And let endurance have its perfect effect, so that you will be perfect and complete, not deficient in anything.

James 1:2-4 (NET)

Maybe you're thinking right now, "Hmm, I've never really liked those verses and I've never really cared for James. He always seemed a bit hard core to me." Well, these were words inspired by the Holy Spirit and James didn't happen to be alone in expressing these thoughts. Check out the words of the apostle Paul:

Therefore, since we have been declared righteous by faith, we have peace with God through our Lord Jesus Christ, through whom we have also obtained access by faith into this grace in which we stand, and we rejoice in the hope of God's glory. Not only this, but we also rejoice in sufferings, knowing that suffering produces endurance, and endurance, character, and character, hope. And hope does not disappoint, because the love of God has been poured out in our hearts through the Holy Spirit who was given to us.

Romans 5:1-5 (NET)

The writer of Hebrews, the apostle James and the apostle Paul are all in agreement. Endurance is a good and necessary thing. Jesus endured and we will need to also, because the race is long and sometimes hard.

The only way we can keep going is to keep our eyes fixed on Jesus. What does that mean? Here are some ideas. Ask God to strengthen you to do them:

1. Regularly bring to your mind Christ's great suffering and sacrifice for you. That will keep your heart warm toward him and your love alive.

2. Keep picturing Christ at the finish line of life, waiting to receive you into his glory and rest. Becoming like him is the goal. He waits at the finish line to transform you completely into his likeness.

3. Keep thinking about Christ and his word. Fix your eyes on the truths of Scripture and when you need a refresher course in Jesus – his power and love – read one of the four gospel accounts.

4. Remember that Jesus is not only your goal in life; he is running with you and in you to give you the strength you need each day. Keep your eyes focused on the truth that "Christ is your life" (*Colossians 3:3*).

5. Cultivate a life of worshiping Jesus. You can't fix your eyes on him for long without breaking out in thanksgiving, praise and worship!

6. No matter how hard things get in life, remember Jesus never quit. He paid the ultimate sacrifice and therefore, he knows how to sustain you in the midst of pain.

"For since he himself was tempted in that which he has suffered, he is able to come to the aid of those who are tempted."

Hebrews 2:18 (NASB)

It can be a real challenge to keep our eyes fixed on Jesus, however. What are the dangers that await us and potentially keep us from fixing our eyes on Jesus? What are the things that seek to prevent us from finishing strong and free? From *Hebrews 12:1-3* we see those dangers are…

*   Encumbrances or unhealthy burdens on our lives.

*   Sins that trap us and trip us up.

*   Growing weary and discouraged at the difficulty and length of the race of life.

Take a moment and ask the Lord these questions: *Are there unhealthy burdens in my life that are weighing down my heart and slowing down my walk with you? Are there sins that still have themselves wrapped around my legs and life? Am I growing tired of seeking and serving the Lord, tired of living this Christian life?*

By the way, many times a "yes" answer to the third question reveals a "yes" answer to at least one of the first two! Why do we say that? Because Jesus told us:

Come to Me, all who are weary and heavy-laden, and I will give you rest. Take My yoke upon you, and learn from Me, for I am gentle and humble in heart; and you shall find rest for your souls. For My yoke is easy, and My load is light.

Matthew 11:28-30 (NASB)

When we are weary from life's loads and Jesus' talk about finding rest for our souls sounds like a foreign language, we've likely taken on too much. When we find the going with Jesus is too much to handle, chances are we are being slowed down and weighed down with baggage we're (unnecessarily) carrying or we are being tripped up by bondage to sin. We've spent a good deal of time facing the sins in our lives in this *Journey to Freedom*. If you know there are still sin issues in your life that you haven't yet dealt with, we strongly encourage you to read over Week Two and then take an unhurried time through Weeks Three and Four.

But what about burdens? We haven't talked too much about them and, by and large, our churches don't either. Maybe it's because we feel like we're meddling in people's lives too much if we do. But hey, has that stopped us before? So let's plunge in. What are some of the unhealthy burdens we tend to carry? Here are just a few...

- **Financial debt**

  God tells us to owe no man anything except to love one another (***Romans 13:8***), yet consumer debt is eating us alive in this nation, Christians included. If you are in debt and do not have an intentional, aggressive plan to pay back what you owe, we urge you to consult a Christian financial ministry for help... today! Chances are you already know how crushing a burden this can be to carry. If your debt load is large, you can't get out of it instantly. But you can start the process today, and you'll be amazed at how good that makes you feel!

- **Unhealthy diet and lifestyle leading to obesity, sickness and energy loss**

  Overweight people are literally carrying an unhealthy extra load of fat. We know that our society puts far too much emphasis on being sleek and lean and "in shape." We are not talking about an obsession with our personal appearance. We are talking about being healthy. What we are talking about is cutting back on the fats, sugars and processed foods and starting to eat more healthy and fresh foods. If you are not on any kind of exercise program, consult your doctor and then get on one that he or she recommends... even 20 minutes of walking a day can make a

huge difference in your energy level and outlook on life!

- **Overwork and drivenness to succeed and accumulate wealth and possessions**

  "Keeping up with the Joneses" has become a national pastime. But it can be deadly to family relationships and intimacy with Jesus... not to mention deadly to your health... when we are driven to achieve "the American dream." With your eyes fixed on Jesus you will be led by the Spirit into discovering "God's dreams for your life." Otherwise you might be shocked to find the "American dream" turning into the "American nightmare."

- **Trying to keep all the people around you happy or all the circumstances around you under control**

  Talk about a crushing burden — just try living this one out for a while! On second thought, don't! Even God doesn't control people like that. Ask the Lord to purge you from all people-pleasing tendencies and ask him to make you a God-pleaser. The apostle Paul wrote, ***"For am I now seeking the favor of men or of God? Or am I striving to please men? If I were still trying to please men, I would not be a bond-servant of Christ" (Galatians 1:10 NASB).*** If you are trying to control all the circumstances and people swirling around your life, good luck! It can't be done and the more you try, the more you will drive people away. Plus, you will eventually become more and more frustrated, exasperated and finally despondent. Why not let God be God? ***Cast your anxieties onto him because he cares for you. (1 Peter 5:7)***

- **Legalism**

  This was likely the topic Jesus was addressing in ***Matthew 11:28-30*** (See previous page). Our religious systems and churches can foster the mentality that God loves us more when we "keep our noses clean" and work really hard for the church. Of course God wants us to walk in holiness and he hates our sin, but his love for us does not fluctuate like some kind of Dow Jones Average of Spirituality. We are accepted and loved by his grace alone, and that never changes. Are you seeking to gain the approval of God or of other people by your spiritual performance? Isn't it time to throw off that yoke and take on Jesus' yoke of acceptance? You'll find rest for your soul!

We trust you feel better and *freer* already!

You see, the sooner we all *really* grasp that life is a race to be run with our eyes fixed on Jesus (not ourselves!) the sooner we will begin to run well. The race isn't easy; it requires *endurance*. But entangling sins and encumbering burdens will *dis*courage us rather than *en*courage us, and will drain us of the energy we need to endure.

Sure, there will be times of great joy and delight in our running the race, journeying to freedom. The wind will be at our backs, the sun shining warmly on our faces, our muscles loose and strong. Other times it will seem like the entire universe is set against us and we can barely get out of bed, let alone race.

The hope of seeing God – a smiling God – face to face one day can buoy us up when our legs feel like lead. We trust this poem will encourage you in your race:

The Race

(adapted slightly from Dee Groberg)

"Quit! Give up, you're beaten," they shout and plead,

"There's just too much against you now; this time you can't succeed."

And as I start to hang my head in front of failure's face,

My downward fall is broken by the memory of a race.

And hope refills my weakened will as I recall that scene,

For just the thought of that short race rejuvenates my being.

A children's race, young boys, young men; now I remember well.

Excitement, sure, but also fear; it wasn't hard to tell.

They all lined up so full of hope; each thought to win that race

Or tie for first, or if not that, at least take second place.

And fathers watched from off the side, each cheering for his son,

And each boy hoped to show his dad that he would be the one.

The whistle blew and off they went, young hearts and hopes of fire

To win, to be the hero there, was each young boy's desire.

And one boy in particular, his dad was in the crowd,

Was running near the lead and thought, "My dad will be so proud."

But as he speeded down the field across a shallow dip,

The little boy who thought to win, lost his step and slipped.

Trying hard to catch himself, his hands flew out to brace

And mid the laughter of the crowd, he fell flat on his face.

So down he fell and with him hope; he couldn't win it now.

Embarrassed, sad, he only wished to disappear somehow.

But as he fell his dad stood up and showed his anxious face,

Which to the boy so clearly said, "Get up and win that race!"

He quickly rose, no damage done, behind a bit that's all,

And ran with all his mind and might to make up for his fall.

So anxious to restore himself to catch up and to win,

His mind went faster than his legs, he slipped and fell again.

He wished that he had quit before with only one disgrace.

"I'm hopeless as a runner now, I shouldn't try to race."

But, in the laughing crowd he searched and found his father's face,

That steady look that said again, "Get up and win that race."

So, up he jumped to try again, ten yards behind the last.

"If I'm to gain those yards," he thought, "I've got to run real fast!"

Exceeding everything he had, he regained eight or ten,

But trying so hard to catch the lead, he slipped and fell... again.

Defeat!! He lay there silently, a tear dropped from his eye.

There's no sense running anymore, three strikes I'm out – Why try?

The will to rise has disappeared, all hope had fled away,

So far behind, so error prone, loser all the way.

"I've lost, so what's the use?" he thought, "I'll live with my disgrace."

But then he thought about his dad, who soon he'd have to face.

"Get up," an echo sounded low, "Get up and take your place.

You were not meant for failure here, get up and win the race."

With borrowed will, "Get up," he said, "You haven't lost at all,

For winning's nothing more than this – to rise each time you fall."

So up he rose to win once more, and with a new commit,

He resolved that win or lose, at least he wouldn't quit.

So far behind the others now, the most he'd ever been.

Still he gave it all he had and ran as though to win.

Three times he'd fallen stumbling, three times he'd rose again

Too far behind to hope to win, he still ran to the end.

They cheered the winning runner as he crossed, first place,

Head high and proud and happy; no falling, no disgrace.

But, when the fallen youngster crossed the line, last place,

The crowd gave him the greater cheer for finishing the race.

And even though he came in last, with head bowed low, unproud;

You would have thought he won the race, to listen to the crowd.

And to his dad he sadly said, "I didn't do so well."

"To me you won," his father said, "You rose each time you fell."

And now when things seem dark and hard and difficult to face,

The memory of that little boy helps me in my own race.

For all of life is like that race, with ups and downs and all,

And all you have to do to win is rise each time you fall.

"Quit! Give up, you're beaten" they still shout in my face

But another voice within me says, "Get up and win the race."

Brothers and sisters, keep your eyes fixed on Jesus. Fall passionately in love with Him. Get to know Him deeply. There is no higher pursuit and no more urgent need in the Church.

Times are going to get tougher. The Bible promises a time of testing beyond any we have ever experienced on this planet.

"…but the people who know their God will display strength and take action."

Daniel 11:32 (NASB)

"And those who have insight will shine brightly like the brightness of the expanse of heaven, and those who lead the many to righteousness, like the stars forever and ever."

Daniel 12:3 (NASB)

Let's pray.

Dear heavenly Father, we've been looking at freedom through your eyes for nearly six weeks, but we know we are just getting warmed up. You have much more to teach us, much more in us to change. We thank you for the wonderful truth and freedom that is already beginning to shine in us. Shine the Light brighter and brighter in and through us, Lord, until the full day of your coming back again! Grant us the strength, stamina and steadfastness to keep running the race toward your smiling face until we fall into your loving arms and enter your rest. In your name, Jesus, amen.

Epilogue: Free to Worship

Living free and finishing free will always involve a life of *worship.* The word "worship" is a shortened form of the old word *worthship,* and it means to declare the value or worth of someone or something. All of us are constantly worshiping, whether we realize it or not. By our words, actions, attitudes, etc. we are proclaiming to the world around us what is truly valuable to us... *even if what is valuable to us is worthless to God!*

A life of true spiritual freedom in Christ is characterized by deep, sincere worship of God. It is what we were made for. It is what God the Father is seeking in his people. Jesus said:

> **But an hour is coming, and now is when the true worshipers shall worship the Father in spirit and truth; for such people the Father seeks to be His worshipers. God is spirit, and those who worship Him must worship in spirit and truth.**
>
> *John 4:23, 24 (NASB)*

Jesus had been talking with a woman from Samaria. She had been very concerned about the *where* of worship. Jesus was concerned about the *how.*

What does it mean to worship God *in spirit?* To worship him in spirit requires a spirit to Spirit connection. We must first be spiritually alive in Christ (see **Ephesians 2:4-6**). Then it requires that our worship come out of our inner being, our new and alive spirit. In other words, we must worship with our hearts.

Singing the greatest hymns of the faith without your heart being in it is not true worship in spirit. Singing words that simply make you feel good but are not coming from a heart that truly loves the Lord and is in awe of him is not true worship in spirit. Worship in spirit means that from deep down in your heart and spirit – even when life has brought great pain to you – you are expressing God's great worth.

What does it mean to worship God *in truth?* To worship him in truth means to declare who he really is according to the Scriptures. Those of other religions often worship far more fervently than we do, but their worship is not according to truth. They are not worshiping the true and living God and therefore their worship is not acceptable to God. In addition, any of our "Christian" hymns or songs that incorrectly describe God would be unacceptable worship to him.

God takes worship seriously and the heart that is truly free does, too. The writer of Hebrews exhorts us:

> *Through Him* [Jesus] **then, let us continually offer up a sacrifice of praise to God, that is, the fruit of lips that give thanks to His name.**
>
> *Hebrews 13:15 (NASB)*

There are many avenues by which we can worship God continually in spirit and truth. Here are just a few from Scripture:

- Singing with joy   *(Psalm 95:1)*
- Shouting joyfully   *(Psalm 95:1)*
- Giving thanks   *(Psalm 95:2)*
- Bowing down   *(Psalm 95:6)*
- Kneeling   *(Psalm 95:6)*
- Telling others of his greatness

     (Psalm 96:3)

- Thinking about his greatness

   (Psalm 145:5)

- Telling others of his goodness

   (Psalm 145:7)

- Using musical instruments

   (Psalm 150:3-5)

- Dancing and leaping   *(2 Samuel 6:16)*

- Giving offerings   *(2 Samuel 6:17)*

Worship brings delight to God and blesses him. He enjoys it when we praise him! Why? Certainly not because he is a selfish god who needs affirmation to feel good about himself!

Then why does God enjoy our worship? *Simply because it is right.* God is worthy of all praise and worship, and it is the right thing for those who are righteous to do (see *Psalm 33:1*)!

But what is the most important act of worship? What brings God the greatest joy of all? Powerfully using spiritual gifts? Preaching his word? Performing great acts of faith? Giving away all your money and possessions? Being willing to die for your faith? No, actually not. In fact, every one of those acts could be worthless to God if not done from a heart of love. (See *1 Corinthians 13:1-3*)

The greatest act of worship is to surrender one's life to God because of his great love and mercy toward us.

I urge you, therefore, brethren, by the mercies of God, to present your bodies a living and holy sacrifice, acceptable to God, which is your spiritual service of worship.

   Romans 12:1 (NASB)

More than our work, more than our money, more than our songs, God wants *us*. To present ourselves completely to him for him to make us like Jesus is our most important act of worship. To surrender to God in that way and to trust in his great mercy then opens the door to make every righteous act of our lives an act of worship!

We tend to think of worship as what we do on Sunday morning, but we can give glory to God at work or school on Monday morning, while driving home Friday evening, or working around the house or yard Saturday afternoon… and everytime in between! This is a true biblical principle of life.

Whether then, you eat or drink or whatever you do, do all to the glory of God.

   1 Corinthians 10:31 (NASB)

And so *that's how* we can *"continually offer up a sacrifice of praise to God"* as *Hebrews 13:15* says to do… by giving thanks to God and honoring him in all that we do. Through Christ, we can be *free to worship God* 24/7. That is what freedom is for.

So there you have it. Our *Journey to Freedom* is a journey to be free to worship. Those who have entered this lifestyle know the joy of it. For when we are worshiping God in spirit and truth, we are most fully alive, most fully human and most fully accomplishing the purpose for which God put us in this world.

And it is the primary purpose for which we will live in eternity… to fully, freely, continually worship God in spirit and truth. We conclude with this Scriptural glimpse into the future… a worship service in heaven that will be the mightiest, most triumphant victory celebration ever. We can't wait to join you there.

And the four living creatures [mighty angels of God]*, each one of them having six wings, are full of eyes all around and within; and day and night they do not cease to say, "Holy, Holy, Holy, is the LORD God, the Almighty, who was and who is and who is to come." And when the living creatures give glory and honor and thanks to Him who sits on the throne, to Him who lives forever and ever, the twenty-four elders will fall down before Him who sits on the throne, and will worship Him who lives forever and ever, and will cast their crowns before the throne, saying, "Worthy are You, our Lord and our God, to receive glory and honor and power; for You created all things, and because of Your will they existed and were created…*

…And when He [Jesus] *had taken the book, the four living creatures and the twenty-four elders fell*

*down before the Lamb, having each one a harp,
and golden bowls full of incense, which are the
prayers of the saints. And they sang a new song,
saying, "Worthy are You to take the book, and to
break its seals, for You were slain, and purchased
for God with Your blood men from every tribe
and tongue and people and nation. And You
have made them to be a kingdom and priests to
our God; and they will reign upon the earth."*

*And I looked, and I heard the voice of many
angels around the throne and the living
creatures and the elders, and the number of
them was myriads of myriads, and thousands of
thousands, saying with a loud voice, "Worthy
is the Lamb that was slain to receive power and
riches and wisdom and might and honor and
glory and blessing."*

*And every created thing which is in heaven and
on the earth and under the earth and on the
sea, and all things in them, I heard saying, "To
Him who sits on the throne, and to the Lamb,
be blessing and honor and glory and dominion
forever and ever."*

*And the four living creatures kept saying,
"Amen." And the elders fell down and
worshiped.*

Revelation 4, 5 (NASB)

[bracketed comments ours]

Amen.

Let us worship.

About Freedom in Christ Ministries

Freedom in Christ Ministries (FICM) is a 501(c) 3 nonprofit corporation committed to seeing God's children, His Church, free and joyfully living the life Christ made possible through His life, death and resurrection. FICM brings a message and ministry of hope and liberation to individuals, couples, families, churches and Christian organizations.

History of Freedom in Christ Ministries

While Dr. Neil T. Anderson was teaching students at Talbot School of Theology, he began counseling students with personal and spiritual conflicts. He discovered that those students had two things in common: they did not understand their identity in Christ and they were not experiencing that "Abba! Father!" connection with God. In response to that need, Dr. Anderson wrote the best-sellers *Victory Over the Darkness* and *The Bondage Breaker.* He also started teaching at conferences around the country and the world and **Freedom in Christ Ministries** was born in 1989. Since then, more than three million people have been reached with the message of freedom through our FICM staff and Ministry Associates (volunteers), FICM conferences, and FICM resources being used in more than sixty countries.

Facts

Many of God's people (the Church) are living as captives - deceived, oppressed and complacent - because they do not understand their true identity and the power and authority that are theirs "in Christ."

According to research reported by the George Barna Group in 2006, "only 23% of those attending church named their faith in God as their top priority in life". This reveals a startling need for the mission and ministry of FICM.

Vision of Freedom in Christ Ministries

To see church and ministry leaders and their people joyfully alive and free in Christ in communities all across the nation and around the world.

Mission of Freedom in Christ Ministries

To provide a biblically-based implementation process and the resources by which church and ministry leaders and their people discover:

- Who they are in Christ.

- Who Christ is in them.

- How to live out the truth of those two powerful realities every day!

This empowers those ministries to become healthy, healing places resulting in a more powerful impact on their communities all across this nation.

Contact Information

Freedom in Christ Ministries
9051 Execuitve Park Dr. Suite 503
Knoxville TN 37923
Phone: 865.342.4000
Fax: 865.342.4001
Toll free line for materials ordering only:
866.462.4747
www.ficm.org
Email: info@ficm.org

Other Books by Rich Miller

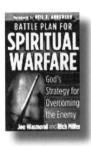

B012 - Battle Plan for Spiritual Warfare
Authors: Joe Wasmond and Rich Miller
Vividly illustrated principles of spiritual warfare will provide basic training for you to prevail over the enemy. This book is designed to equip men ... but women will want to read it too!

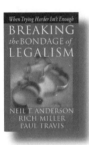

B016 - Breaking the Bondage of Legalism
Authors: Neil T. Anderson, Rich Miller, and Paul Travis
Scriptural insights from the authors will help you understand the bondage that results from legalism, shame, guilt, pride and a critical or controlling spirit. You'll learn about the path of hope and liberation, knowing who you are in Christ, and come to a true understanding of grace, the life you can now live in Him and be able to experience a joyful intimacy with God your Father and Jesus your Friend.

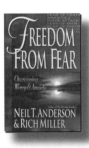

B028 - Freedom From Fear
Authors: Neil T. Anderson and Rich Miller
Anxiety disorders are the number-one mental health problem in America. God's Word speaks directly to these challenges. Worry and fear don't have to control you any longer! Neil and Rich identify how mental strongholds of fear and anxiety develop, then reveal powerful biblical strategies for defeating them.

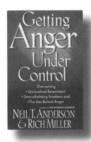

B034 - Getting Anger Under Control
Authors: Neil T. Anderson and Rich Miller
This book helps readers evaluate their own anger level, take appropriate steps to alleviate angers destructiveness, and depend on Jesus' power and wisdom to regulate emotions.

B112 - Leading Teens to Freedom in Christ
Authors: Neil T. Anderson and Rich Miller
Leading Teens to Freedom in Christ provides you with a biblical blueprint for counseling young people ages 13-21. With this guide, you can help them climb out of the "less" mess and find lasting freedom in Christ.

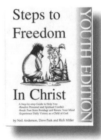

G104 - The Steps to Freedom in Christ Youth Edition
Authors: Neil T. Anderson and Rich Miller
This version of *The Steps to Freedom in Christ*, written especially for teenagers, helps them break away from old strongholds and live in victory.

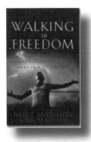

B027 - Walking in Freedom Devotional
Authors: Neil T. Anderson and Rich Miller
Filled with hope and encouragement, this inspiring 21-day devotional will help you stand firm in your freedom in Christ and build a holy shield against the enemy's attacks. [Includes the original *Steps to Freedom in Christ*.]

Check out these books and other life-transforming resources on our website, **www.ficm.org** *or call toll free* **1.866.462.4747** *to place your order.*